THE SPORTING STATESMAN

NOVAK DJOKOVIC

AND THE RISE OF SERBIA

Chris Bowers is a freelance writer and broadcaster who has covered the global tennis scene for more than 20 years. He is best known as a commentator for the European sports television channel Eurosport but also appears on the American sports channel ESPN and various radio stations around the world. He has written several books on tennis, notably the first English-language biography of Roger Federer, and also *The Book of Tennis*, the International Tennis Federation's centenary commemorative book *A Century of Contribution*, and four Davis Cup yearbooks. He is also active in environmental and political fields, and in 2011 wrote the biography of Nick Clegg, the leader of the British Liberal Democrats and deputy prime minister. He is the son of a refugee and lives with his daughter in East Sussex, England.

THE SPORTING STATESMAN

NOVAK DJOKOVIC

AND THE RISE OF SERBIA

CHRIS BOWERS

JOHN BLAKE

Published by John Blake Publishing Ltd,
3 Bramber Court, 2 Bramber Road,
London W14 9PB, England

www.johnblakepublishing.co.uk

www.facebook.com/Johnblakepub facebook
twitter.com/johnblakepub twitter

First published in hardback in 2014

ISBN: 978-1-78219-770-6

British Library Cataloguing-in-Publication Data:
a catalogue record for this book is available from the British Library.

Design by www.envydesign.co.uk

Printed in Great Britain by CPI Group (UK) Ltd

3 5 7 9 10 8 6 4 2

Papers used by John Blake Publishing are natural, recyclable products made
from wood grown in sustainable forests. The manufacturing processes
conform to the environmental regulations of the country of origin.

Every attempt has been made to contact the relevant copyright-holders,
but some were unobtainable. We would be grateful if the
appropriate people could contact us.

For my daughter Tamara, who must have felt she was sharing her dad with some Serbian sportsman for a good 15 months of her life.

CONTENTS

INTRODUCTION AND ACKNOWLEDGEMENTS

Vukovar, Srebrenica, Mostar, Banja Luka. Smallish towns in what was once Yugoslavia, which became nightly recurring names on international television news bulletins in the 1990s. Equally recurring names were those of Slobodan Milosevic, Franjo Tudjman, Alja Izetbegovic, Radovan Karadzic, Ratko Mladic – the leading protagonists from that same conflict, the four wars that characterised the break-up of Yugoslavia. The reconstruction of Europe after the Second World War based on economic interdependence was supposed to prevent future wars in Europe. But 46 years after the end of the war and 34 years after the founding of what is today the European Union, neighbour turned against neighbour in the most appalling bloodbath, which a United Nations tribunal said included genocide. All on European soil.

It's tempting to see wars as neat packages of time – like the world stopped between 1914 and 1918, and stopped again from 1939 to 1945. It's never like that. Life goes on, despite the fears and privations of war. People learn to survive, they educate their kids, and some of those kids can still learn to dance, or play a musical instrument or a sport the way they would have done during peacetime.

As such, it should surprise no one that out of the wreckage of war-torn Yugoslavia should come some gifted athletes. But that six world-class tennis players should come from Serbia, a country of just 7.1 million inhabitants, 88,000 square kilometres and no real tennis tradition, is something remarkable. And we are talking about six. Novak Djokovic, Ana Ivanovic, Jelena Jankovic and Nenad Zimonjic were all world-ranked No. 1 in the space of a few years: the first three in singles, Zimonjic in men's doubles. Add to that Janko Tipsarevic, who reached eighth and spent two years in the top 10, and Viktor Troicki, who was once ranked 12th, and it is a remarkable generation, almost on a par with the Swedes, who defied their miniscule population to produce a phenomenal crop of tennis players that dominated team tennis and many of the major titles from the mid-1970s to the late 1990s.

Of these six Serbs, Djokovic is by far the most successful. Ivanovic's achievement of winning the 1998 French Open and reaching the top of the women's rankings should not be under-estimated but she held the top spot for only a few weeks and has never looked even close to winning a second major since. She is a charming and stunningly good-looking ambassador for her country but her results limit how effective she can be. Jankovic is one of only three women players to have topped the rankings without having won a Grand Slam singles title – her achievement speaks for her phenomenal consistency in 2008–9, but she too has looked a long way from taking herself off that list in the intervening years.

By contrast, Djokovic has notched up six Grand Slam titles and needs only the French Open to complete a career Grand Slam. More importantly, he has shown he is the equal of Roger Federer and Rafael Nadal in having the charisma and gravitas to represent his sport, and has set an example by his dignified and gracious behaviour. And that is of massive importance to his country. His career is moderately well documented and his natural charisma is enhanced by one or two of his sideshows – his impersonations of fellow professionals, his habit of calling the trainer during matches (now largely extinct) and his voluble father. But no one has yet set it against the background of his country's emergence from the horrors of the 1990s bloodshed. This book is an attempt to do that.

It would be tempting – though not entirely true – to say the seed for this book was sown in September 2010.

I was in Belgrade for the first time, covering the Davis Cup semi-final between Serbia and the Czech Republic. I arrived on the Wednesday evening, and when I hooked up with the people I was working with, found that they'd arranged to eat at Novak's, one of the two restaurants in Belgrade owned by Novak Djokovic. How appropriate – my first ever meal in Belgrade at the restaurant of the man who was putting Serbia on the map! And just one block from the Beogradska Arena, the 17,000-seater indoor stadium that had become the spiritual home of Serbian tennis.

The following morning I had to interview Djokovic for television, and while we were waiting for the cameraman to get set up, I told him that I'd eaten at his restaurant the night before. He asked me what I thought of it. I hesitated, trying to think of the politest way to say that the food was very good (it was) but it was rather a long time coming (I've since learned that you do wait a long time for your food in Serbian restaurants and Novak's isn't particularly slow). But I never got to say that because Djokovic interjected with 'Don't tell me – it was too smoky, wasn't it?' I had to admit it was, to which he added, 'Yes, we're getting there but it's slow and we've a long way to go.'

What struck me about his response was that it encapsulated the dual role Djokovic plays. He's totally comfortable outside Serbia, fully integrated into the western European and North American culture where smoking in public places is now unacceptable (normally banned), where all good restaurants offer healthy options and where patriotism is welcomed but nationalism is viewed with suspicion, especially when it gets vociferous. Yet he's also totally comfortable in his own country, even though he acts with a slightly different register – he's a bit more jingoistic, happy to join in with Serbian songs and cultural rituals, even a bit of blatant nationalism. That, at least, is my impression. He himself denies it, saying he always acts the same: 'I always try to be respectful and kind to everyone no matter what country they come from, or where I am on the map. That applies to my compatriots, too.' That may indeed be his intention, though I stand by my sense that there are subtle changes he makes when he's in his homeland.

That brief exchange wasn't the genesis of this book but it played an important role when John Blake Publishing came to me in 2012 and asked if I would write a biography of Djokovic. My first step was to approach Djokovic's agent and see if an authorised biography or ghosted autobiography might be on the cards. I was told that neither was an option, as Djokovic wants to write his own book when his playing career ends. That left me with the option of an independent biography of Djokovic, or nothing. As I had written Roger Federer's biography on that basis and updated it several times, I had no particular desire to write another straight tennis biography, so I told Blake I wasn't up for the Djokovic book.

Blake's staff came back saying they were particularly keen to have a book about Djokovic, so would I reconsider? I thought about it and kept being struck by my realisation about how Djokovic spans these two cultures: the Serbian and the international. I've also been struck by how little the western world understands about Serbia, so I went back to Blake and offered them a book that was a mixture of Djokovic's own story and Serbia's story. They jumped at the suggestion and this is that book.

For a book like this to work, the author needs a bit of good fortune and I had two distinct strokes of luck.

The first came when I got an email from Chris Bowers. If this sounds like a bad case of talking to myself, it isn't. I have a namesake who used to work at the BBC at the same time as I did and he contacted me confessing to a 20-year guilty conscience about having accepted a dinner date from a female admirer who, it transpired, had heard my voice on the radio, not his. I found that touching – and, no doubt, a little flattering – but more significant was his email address. I recognised that he worked for the British foreign ministry and, through him, I was able to re-establish contact with a colleague of his and an old tennis-playing friend of mine, Mike Davenport. And Mike just happened to be the newly minted British ambassador to Belgrade, who subsequently proved of immense help to me in researching this book. I therefore gladly accept Chris's confession.

The second came when the most important interview for this book not only materialised but provided me with one of the most uplifting moments of my journalistic career.

I had identified early in my preparation that the most important person I needed to talk to was Jelena Gencic, the woman who taught Novak to play tennis. In March 2013 I went to Belgrade on a bit of a flyer – I had a trip planned for the following month but wanted to make sure I actually had some interviews arranged, so decided it would be best to make an exploratory advance trip. It was on that exploratory trip that Gencic was not only available but gave me two and a half hours of her time in her favourite watering hole, the Café Ozon in the Dedinje suburb of Belgrade. The question about *Desert Island Discs* (see page 41) came fairly early, and when she listed 'Mahler's Adagio', I interrupted her and said, 'Do you mean the Adagietto from Mahler's Fifth Symphony?' Her eyes lit up. 'Ah, you know it,' she said and from then on the connection between us was a wonderful one. As I left the café, I felt moved to hug her, even though I'd known her for barely two hours.

The following day I was mulling over what she'd told me and was beginning to see the chapter 'Nole and Jeca' that appears in this book. It all seemed too good to be true. Gencic had reminded me of my own grandmother, a great story teller but something of a *Märchentante*, a German word for a teller of stories that often improve with the telling. So I asked my contact who had introduced me to Gencic whether I could trust what Jelena had told me. She seemed puzzled at my question. I explained that it seemed almost like a fairy tale – the cultured woman from the affluent Yugoslav intelligentsia finding she had a total meeting of minds with this boy from a moderately simple family, and taught him a lot more than just forehands and backhands – and I wanted to be sure it wasn't all a massive tale told to impress the journalist from abroad. My contact, who knew Gencic fairly well, assured me that she was not the kind of woman to embellish stories, at least not more than in a very minor way, and she always stuck to what she believed was the truth.

When I went back to Belgrade the following month, Jelena and her sister welcomed me to their home. I wish I had enjoyed the Turkish coffee they gave me – I confess I found it utterly disgusting but I very much appreciated the hospitality. I admired her trophies, asked her a few more questions and checked a few details from my interview a few weeks earlier. As I left, she promised to check anything else I wasn't sure about if I'd just email it to her. I never saw her again.

Jelena Gencic died on 1 June 2013. Unbeknown to me, she had been fighting breast cancer for some time, but it wasn't that that killed her. Most people close to her knew she had breast cancer and she had largely beaten it. But few knew that she also had liver cancer, and that finished her. I saw her five weeks before she died. She was spending 7–10 hours a day on the tennis court, not running around but doing lots of coaching. She looked like she could have planned her 90th birthday party but at 76 her life came to an abrupt end.

I was told about her death by text message. I was at Roland Garros and the message came with the strict instruction that I was to say nothing to anyone close to Djokovic until he had gone on court for his third-round match against Grigor Dimitrov. That was wise advice, for when Djokovic came off court, he was given the news, burst into tears and promptly cancelled all media obligations because he was so upset. After his fourth-round win, he was happy to talk about her and his 10-minute English press conference was almost exclusively about Gencic. I remember that Saturday night for the strange emotion of grieving for someone I'd met just twice and hardly knew but who I felt I knew very well. I was also the last journalist to do a formal interview with her, so was consumed by the uncomfortable mix of relief and elation of having got her to talk before she left us, and terrible sadness that she should die with so much vitality apparently still left in her.

As such, in the months since her death I have mulled over whether I have become too emotional in the section about her. And whether I have afforded her an importance in the Djokovic story that goes beyond what she warrants. I don't think I have. Djokovic himself talks about destiny, and while he's likely to have made it to the top in tennis even without Gencic's input, I remain convinced that he would not be the person he is today without her influence and his route to the top would not have been as painless. After all, he does have a number of health issues that he has had to overcome through a lot of trial and error – would he have been open to the holistic approach of an Igor Cetojevic (see pages 174–6) if he had not been exposed to Gencic's open-mindedness at an early age? And would he, without Gencic, have developed the sense of statesmanship that allows him to straddle the two worlds of his fiercely patriotic Serbia and a global community that has grown to like him but still mistrusts the country he hails from? It would be wrong to overplay Gencic's role in Djokovic's tennis development – she never travelled with him and he did have four years in his early adulthood when he wasn't even in contact with her – but I am convinced she deserves a chapter of her own.

A classic question people ask when they see a biography is whether it is 'authorised' or not. I dislike the term 'authorised', as it implies something official, with the content controlled by the subject. I have no desire to write a book about Novak Djokovic that is controlled by him – he is intelligent enough to write his own book if he wishes, in which he can say what he likes (as he is highly likely to do at some stage). That will have validity as his take on his career with the inside story on certain events, but it will only be his side of the story. This book has many people's input on his life and career (so far).

This, therefore, is an *independent* biography, both of Djokovic and of Serbia. It is my take on him and his country. People can disagree with what I say and some of it is opinion rather than peer-reviewed research. In terms of his own approach to it, because he wants to write his own book when he retires, he wasn't keen for his closest family to talk to me – something I have respected. Those who are part of his team are bound by a confidentiality agreement but many people who are close to him have been willing to talk to me, for which I sincerely thank them. And Djokovic himself has helped me by answering a number of questions I put to him about his role as a sporting statesman.

It's important to make this clear because Djokovic is a superstar.

'Do you realise just how much the country stops when he plays?' asked Guy De Launey, the BBC's Belgrade correspondent, when I met him to get his views for some of the chapters on Serbia. And Djokovic's friend Dusan Vemic says, 'If Novak is playing some big matches during the Grand Slam season, the streets are empty. Everyone is at home cheering for him.' He has therefore attained the status of something approaching a secular saint in Serbia, much of it deserved, but it is still important to look at him dispassionately. This is why I have been critical of him at certain points in this book – not out of malice but simply because he is a human being made of flesh and blood, and in our celebrity-dominated era, it's important to be able to see that even the people we most admire are packages of good and not-so-good attributes.

A word about accents. A number of accents are used in central and eastern European orthography, many of them reflecting the transfer of Slav names from the Cyrillic to the Roman alphabet. I had to make a decision whether to use accents or not and, realistically, it was all or nothing. My instinct as someone who has learned three languages beyond my mother tongue was to put the accents in, but in the end, I opted not to. The main reason for this is that the name 'Djokovic' is a westernisation of how his name is written at home. The Roman alphabet version is 'Đoković', with the j added in typefaces where the line through the D is not available (like the way an e is added in German when the *Umlaut* is not available, so 'Schüttler' becomes 'Schuettler', 'Görges' becomes 'Goerges', etc.). Given that Novak is known across the English-speaking world as 'Djokovic', it would have gone against the grain to call him 'Đoković' throughout this book and the logical extension was to exclude all accents. I beg forgiveness from fellow-linguists who feel that judgement was wrong.

And while we're on the name, let me try and lay to rest the

indefatigable question of how you pronounce the first vowel in 'Djokovic'. The Americans have pushed the line that it should be pronounced as in the word 'joke', while the rest of the world has tended to say 'jock'. The idea of 'joke' comes from a belief that the best thing you can do is to copy the way the person says his own name. Indeed, this continued even into the 2013 Australian Open when Jim Courier used a question in a post-match on-court interview to try and get Djokovic to give him the definitive pronunciation of the troublesome vowel.

The sentiment of asking the person concerned how he (or she) pronounces their name is a nice one but it misses a very simple relevant fact: how they pronounce other words with the same vowel. If you listen to the way Djokovic says words like 'on' and 'over', it's clear his (and other Serbs') pronunciation of his surname is the same vowel as 'on', not 'over'. That means the pronunciation based on 'jock' is the correct one and ought to come as a relief to the entire English-speaking world, as the strictly accurate pronunciation is more like 'or' (so 'Djorkovic') than 'jock' or 'joke'. Where the Americans can claim some justification is that the vowel sound in 'Novak' is pretty much the same as in 'Djokovic', so really the English-speaking world should be saying 'Novak' as in 'of' and 'Djokovic' as in 'jock'. But no doubt the debate will rage as long as he's playing, so radio and television pronunciation units can continue to justify their existence.

Finally, I couldn't have produced this book without the help of lots of people. I list them here in alphabetical order with more thanks than I can convey and a fear that I have left one or two out: Edoardo Artaldi, Simon Cambers, Igor Cetojevic, Estelle Couderc, Michael Davenport, Guy De Launey, Jelena Gencic, Mitzi Ingram-Evans, Goran Ivanisevic, Ana Ivanovic, Momir Jelovac, Cathy Jenkins, Jonathan Jobson, Ladislav Kis, Angela Lavinski, David

Law, Ivan Ljubicic, Stevan Lukic, Janice McKinlay, Neda Miletic, Helen McCarthy, Joanna Mather, Peter Miles, Stuart Miller, Zoran Milosavljevic, Ana Mitric, Vladimir Novak, Bogdan Obradovic, Nebojsa Parausic of MN Press Photo, Belgrade, Dejan Petrovic, Riccardo Piatti, Nikki Pilic, Monica Seles, Greg Sharko, Cedomir Soskic, Toplica Spasojevic, Vojin Velickovic, Gavin Versi, Nebojsa Viskovic and Jonathan Wilson. And a massive nod to Toby Buchan, my editor at John Blake Publishing, with whom I feel I have had a very productive meeting of minds.

CHRIS BOWERS, March 2014

CHAPTER ONE

AN ETHNIC MIX

The philosopher and travel writer Hermann Keyserling once wrote, 'I am not a Dane, not a German, not a Swede, not a Russian nor an Estonian, so what am I? – a little of all these.' Thus, in an era where transport allows for inter-nation marriages as a matter of course, no one should be too surprised to find that Serbia's leading global flag-carrier, Novak Djokovic, should be a real ethnic mix. At least he was born in Serbia – unlike India's spiritual leader Mahatma Gandhi, who was born in South Africa, or America's most patriotic Davis Cup player John McEnroe, who was born in Germany. But from his ethnic heritage you could argue he was half-Montenegrin and half-Croat.

Does this matter? Hardly at all. As Djokovic's close friend Ivan Ljubicic says, 'You can be patriotic without being nationalistic.' And Ljubicic should know – born in the Bosnian town of Banja Luka to a Bosnian Muslim mother and a Croatian Catholic father, he barely passed through Croatia en route to the relative safety of Italy during the Yugoslav wars of the 1990s, yet became Croatia's national hero when he steered the still-young republic to the Davis Cup title in 2005 with a record-breaking 11 straight wins in live matches. In the Balkans there are thousands of people who are the products of inter-nation marriages. In fact, having links to Serbia, Montenegro, Kosovo and Croatia probably broadens Djokovic's Balkan fan base.

Tracing the Djokovic family tree back, the records are sketchy but the first obvious ancestor is Djoko Damjanovic, who appears to have established the Djokovic surname around 1730. The suffix '-vic' means 'son of', like '-son' in England, 'Mc/Mac' in Scotland, "O' in Ireland, etc. So Djoko Damjanovic's children had the surname Djokovic, after which the same surname was passed through male descendants. Damjanovic set up home in Jasenovo Polje, a village whose name means 'ash fields' near the Montenegrin town of Niksic. In 1928 the head of the family, Nedeljko Djokovic, moved east from Montenegro to a village called Vocnjak in Metohija, part of the province of Kosovo, which at that time was part of the Yugoslav republic of Serbia. In 1951 Nedeljko's son Vladimir, Novak's grandfather, moved to Mitrovica, the main ethnic Serbian town in Kosovo. In 1961 his son Srdjan was born and in 1964 he had a second son, Goran.

There had been one Novak Djokovic in the family. He grew up in Jasenovo Polje before emigrating to Chicago in 1905 but returned to fight for his country. Apparently, when filling in his immigration form as his ship docked in the USA, under 'Nationality (country of which citizen or subject)' he wrote 'Montenegro' and under 'Race of people' 'Montenegrin'. Montenegro at that time was already recognised as a sovereign state, having come to a form of independence in 1878 under the same settlement that saw Serbia become independent from the Ottoman Empire.

In 1986 Srdjan married Dijana Zagar. She was born in Belgrade in January 1964, the daughter of two military personnel. Her father

Zdenka was a high-ranking officer in the Yugoslav National Army and a pharmacist, who became purchasing manager for a military hospital. Her mother Elizabete was a major in the army and a chief medical officer in the military hospital (Dijana's sister is a pharmacist as well). They were originally from Vinkovici, a town in the eastern part of Croatia near the Serbian border, and they moved to Belgrade before Dijana's birth when Zdenka was transferred by the army to the military hospital in what was then the Yugoslav capital. Not surprisingly, Djokovic has lots of relatives in and around Vinkovici.

Very little is known about either family. The few interviews that Srdjan gives are generally about his son or Serbian tennis politics, while Dijana gives virtually no interviews. The Serbian tennis writer Vojin Velickovic says, 'Because Srdjan is so volatile, we never asked him too much because we didn't want to go too far, and I don't need that kind of information for my tennis reports.' Some reports say Srdjan was at one stage a footballer on the books of Mitrovica's main club FC Trepca, while the fact that he and Dijana gave skiing lessons leads to the assumption that they were gifted skiers. 'Maybe Srdjan was a football player,' Velickovic says, 'but no one remembers. If he did play, it would be at a very low level. We assume he was a good skier but that's also a grey area.'

Dijana's family is known to have a fair bit of volleyball talent but she didn't play much. Velickovic adds, 'A friend of hers told me she was a very gifted gymnast. Obviously Novak is very flexible, so when I spoke to him once, I told him that I'd heard he'd inherited his genes from his mother, not his father, because he was so flexible. And he joked, "Yes, I'm a champion because of my mother, not my father." But she never wanted to give an interview to the media, maybe because she doesn't want to be in the spotlight.'

One person who got some insight into the Djokovic family home was Djokovic's first coach, Jelena Gencic. She got to know the family when Novak was five, which was about the time his paternal grandmother died. She recalled, 'Srdjan's father Vladimir, known as Grandfather Vlada, was a very good man. He was a man of great warmth who made you feel nice. His wife died the year I started working with Novak, so I didn't know her but everyone says she was an excellent woman, such a humanitarian, so unbelievable – maybe Novak has his humanity from her? It was a very patriarchal family. The grandfather was the patriarch. We couldn't start eating until the patriarch had sat down and started to eat. And we couldn't get up until he had given his approval. So Novak had a very good family education. The family wasn't primitive but only ever had just enough.'

On 22 May 1987 Srdjan and Dijana celebrated the birth of their first son, Novak, in Belgrade. It was just four days after Srdjan's 26th birthday. At that stage they were restaurateurs in Belgrade. Two years later, with the political and economic situation in Yugoslavia starting to look very precarious, they and Srdjan's brother Goran opened up a second restaurant, a pizzeria which also sold pancakes, and a boutique in Kopaonik, a mountain resort on the boundary where Kosovo started, about 50km (as the crow flies) from Mitrovica. They didn't spend all year there – only the peak skiing season in winter and the hiking season in summer. In winter they had the punishing regime of giving skiing lessons by day and working in the restaurant at night. The rest of the time they lived in Belgrade.

In August 1991 Marko Djokovic was born, and a third son, Djordje, was born in July 1995. Once Novak began going to school, it meant that during the skiing and hiking seasons he often had to stay in the Belgrade flat of the newly widowed Grandfather Vlada, sometimes for several weeks at a stretch. He was later to seek refuge from the 1999 Nato bombing of Belgrade in the basement store of that flat. When Vlada died in April 2012 during the Monte Carlo Masters, the media remarked that Djokovic didn't seem quite the same and in fact did very well to reach the final where he lost to Rafael Nadal. The death of a grandparent affects everyone differently but this was no ordinary grandparent – Vlada was a parental substitute who was a massive figure in Djokovic's life.

This dual existence of the urban landscape of Belgrade and the rural, mountainous landscape of Kopaonik not only shaped Djokovic but gave him a heightened sense of his own country. Asked for this book where he feels the soul of Serbia is, he replied, 'It's very difficult to answer that question. My country has a very rich history, centuries long. Each stone, mountain, city, village has some powerful story to it, that I am very proud of. That's why we Serbs have very strong sense of belongingness, because of our history. Everybody has heard of Belgrade, but my country has so many beautiful cities and villages that people should come and see. So many legends they can hear about my people, kings and queens... I honestly think that the soul of my country lies within villages in the south. Kosovo is a cradle of Serbian history. It has over 2,000 monasteries and churches that symbolise our culture and the beginnings of the Serbian Orthodox religion. Belgrade is a modern metropolis, it can give you everything, but the true Serbia is in the south. I remember myself as a kid spending a lot of time on Kopaonik and admiring every time the view of Serbia I had from this beautiful and powerful mountain.'

Like any boy of five, young Novak enjoyed kicking a football and was taught to ski from a very early age. There was no history of tennis in the family – Srdjan and Dijana could probably have told you very little about it when one day their elder son caught sight of tennis on the television. It ignited a spark in him that led him, a few weeks later, to approach the woman who would set him on the road to being the best in the world.

CHAPTER TWO

WHO ARE THE SERBS?

To all but the keenest historians or current-affairs aficionados, the term 'Serbia' probably doesn't mean a great deal – in fact, to many, the first image the term conjures up is probably that of Novak Djokovic, even to those who don't call themselves tennis fans. Some who have vague recollections of their history lessons at school may remember that Serbia had something to do with the outbreak of the First World War, and those watching the news in the 1990s will have heard the name Serbia on many occasions, often in connection with the word 'atrocities'. But even those who were regular news followers in the 1960s, 1970s and 1980s can be forgiven for not knowing where or what Serbia was.

The reason for this is that, while the Serbs have existed in the south-eastern corner of Europe known as the Balkans since the sixth century, for most of that time they have not been a country in their own right. In fact, Serbia on its own has only been a sovereign state three times: from 1166 to 1459, from 1878 to 1918 and from 2006 to the present. The Serbs, therefore, are by no means a new people but they are a new country, hence the scope for a dominant world sportsman to become a statesman and standard-bearer for his country. (Technically, the term 'Serb' denotes an ethnic Serb, while a 'Serbian' is a citizen of Serbia, so the difference can be important.)

The Serbs are one of the Slav peoples. Because the Slavs are the fourth biggest ethno-linguistic grouping in the world, it's hard to give a precise definition of Slavs but they are an Indo-European race who are generally divided into three groups: the eastern Slavs populating today's Russia, Ukraine and Belarus, plus parts of central Asia and Siberia; the central Slavs populating countries and areas such as Poland, the Czech Republic, Slovakia and Silesia; and the southern Slavs, of which the Serbs are the biggest group, along with the Croats, Montenegrins, Bulgarians and Macedonians (but not Slovenes or Albanians). The southern Slavs are largely Christian, though with various differences. For example, the Serbs are largely Orthodox Christian, while the Croats are Roman Catholic.

For much of the 14th century Serbia was the most powerful state in the Balkans, but it was defeated in the battle of Kosovo Field in 1389, marking the end of its pre-eminence. After the battle of Smederovo in 1459, the independent kingdom of Serbia was subsumed into the Ottoman Empire, the Turkish empire ruled from the ancient city of Constantinople (now Istanbul). The 1389 defeat in Kosovo became a scar on Serbian national consciousness, which lingered into the 20th century, as the province of Kosovo became of psychological importance to Serbia, even though by the late 20th century it was populated largely by ethnic Albanians. It has some relevance to the Djokovic story: Djokovic's father and grandfather were from Kosovo, the ski resort of Kopaonik where Novak first learned to play tennis is right on the border between the undisputed

Serbian territory and Kosovo, and Djokovic had to shelter from the 1999 Nato bombing raids on Belgrade that resulted from the ethnic Serb-Albanian conflict in Kosovo.

Until 1918 most of the southern Slav peoples were under the control of larger empires, generally either the Ottoman Empire or the Austro-Hungarian Empire. But long before the First World War those empires were decaying. The Ottomans' heyday had been in the 16th and 17th centuries; by 1850 the empire was becoming harder to hold together, while Austria-Hungary was ruled by the Habsburg royal family of Vienna, who were increasingly fighting domestic battles closer to home as nationalist fervour grew in states that are today's Czech Republic, Slovakia and Hungary.

Some suggestions had been mooted in the middle of the 19th century that the southern Slavs might join forces in a united country but the largest of them also had their eye on becoming nation states of their own. Serbia and Montenegro were the first of them to break free from Ottoman control, becoming countries in their own right in 1878 following the Russo-Turkish war. Russia's foreign policy at that time was geared towards trying to get access to the Mediterranean Sea and, to this end, it developed friendly relations with Serbia, a fellow Slav nation. Out of that grew Serbia's military and diplomatic alliance with Russia, which played a part in the outbreak of the First World War. The traditional interpretation has been that, when a Serb radical, Gavrilo Princip, shot dead the heir to the Austro-Hungarian throne, Archduke Franz Ferdinand, in Sarajevo in June 1914, it triggered the diplomatic tit-for-tat and mobilisation of forces that led to the outbreak of war five weeks later: Austria declared war on Serbia to avenge the killing, Russia was compelled to come to Serbia's aid, Germany came to Austria's aid and the whole thing became the world's first global conflict. Recently it has been suggested that this is too simple – that Germany was dead-set on going to war and was looking for an excuse to declare war on Serbia. Whatever the ultimate motivation, by the summer of 1914 Europe was like a tinder-dry forest just waiting for a spark to set the whole continent alight, and the Sarajevo assassination was the spark that started what became known as 'the Great War'.

With the Ottoman and Austro-Hungarian empires effectively crushed during the war, 1918 was the obvious time for new nations to emerge in south-eastern Europe. But the legacy of being ruled by a large empire, allied to fears that Italy might try to sweep up a lot of territory along the Adriatic coast, led to the formation of a country made up initially of several southern Slav peoples. It was called the Kingdom of Serbs, Croats and Slovenes but it also included Montenegro, Bosnia-Herzegovina, Croatia-Slavonia, a semi-autonomous region of Hungary, and Dalmatia (Monica Seles, Yugoslavia's most successful tennis player, was ethnically a Hungarian who came from Novi Sad in the Serbian province of Vojvodina). The new kingdom was proclaimed in December 1918 and ruled by the Serbian royal family, initially under King Peter I. For many Serbs, the kingdom was a continuation of the Serbian sovereignty that had existed since 1878, and certainly it amounted to a form of self-determination compared with being under Turkish or Austrian rule. But it's perhaps easier for the Serbs to feel this way, as they were the dominant nation in the new kingdom, whereas Croats, Slovenes and other nations find it harder to see this as full independence, at least compared to the independence and sovereignty they have enjoyed since the early 1990s.

Religiously, the Serbs are Orthodox Christian while the Croats are Roman Catholic, but the Serb language is very close to Croatian (almost as close as British English and American English are to each other), and Macedonian and Slovenian are also related to Serbian and Croatian. Given that there had been lots of migration and intermarriage among the southern Slav peoples, the new kingdom ought to have worked. After all, in 1871 22 German-speaking kingdoms, principalities and duchies had come together to form a new country called Germany, and while it had led itself – and the world – into a disastrous war, it had worked as a country and was still intact. The ethnic, linguistic and cultural differences between the Serbs and Croats are not as pronounced as those between the Prussians and Bavarians, so the new southern Slav country had every chance of succeeding.

Or so went the theory. In practice, the nationalism that had been growing for the previous 70 years continued, only now it was directed against the new kingdom based in Belgrade, rather than against the archaic rulers in Constantinople or Vienna. The first result was a strengthening of state powers in 1929, making the kingdom effectively a dictatorship. The outward sign of that was a change of name – as the kingdom was an alliance of southern Slav peoples, it adopted the name Yugoslavia, from the Slav words 'jugo' (of the south) and 'slavija' (Slavs).

Yugoslavia survived the assassination of its tennis-loving king, Alexander I, in 1934 – he was shot dead by a Macedonian working with Croatian separatists – but it didn't survive the outbreak of the Second World War. In 1941 it was taken over by the Axis powers (Germany and Italy), who set up a particularly nasty Croatian-led fascist government, the Ustase. The Ustase set about liquidating Jews and gipsies, and relegating Serbs to somewhere well below the status of second-class citizens.

It was, in effect, ethnic cleansing, a term that only came into widespread use in the 1990s. When people talk about the Yugoslav civil war, they generally refer to the battles of the 1990s that led to the break-up of Yugoslavia and the establishment of new sovereign states, but the period 1941–45 saw an equally brutal civil war which left unresolved many of the resentments that flared up again in the 1990s. The Ustase's brutality (even some members of the Nazi high command in Berlin felt their acolytes in Zagreb were going too far) led to resistance from the Cetniks, a pro-monarchist Serbian movement, and from the Partisans, a communist movement led by a former Russian revolutionary, Josip Broz Tito. So while the Second World War raged to the north, the Ustase, Cetniks and Partisans fought out the bloody civil war for the remains of Yugoslavia.

In short, Tito and his Partisans won that civil war and set up a new Yugoslav republic taking in six federated states: Serbia, Croatia, Slovenia, Bosnia-Herzegovina, Montenegro and Macedonia. The Yugoslav capital was the Serbian capital, Belgrade. Tito's pitch was a communist one (in the sense of a state-controlled economy working in the interests of the working class), with the slogan 'brotherhood and unity'. He also had immense personal charisma, plus a transnational profile based on having a Croatian father, a Slovenian mother, and operating from Serbia's principal city. Having gained material support from the Allied powers (Great Britain, the USA and the USSR), he was seen by many of his compatriots as the man who had liberated Yugoslavia, so he was a popular leader after 1945.

Tito ruled Yugoslavia for the next 35 years. Originally a supporter of Stalin's communist state in Russia, he broke from Moscow in 1948, pursuing his own form of communism independently of the USSR's influence. During the Cold War, Tito and Yugoslavia gained a respected global position as one of the leading players in the Non-Aligned Movement, a loose association of largish countries who refused to ally themselves with either the USA or the USSR. He also oversaw an economic boom in the 1950s and 1960s, and allowed Yugoslav citizens to travel abroad for work and pleasure, something other countries in the Soviet bloc did not permit.

The West loved Yugoslavia. As western nations battled with the threat posed by the Soviet Empire run from Moscow, they enjoyed having a communist state in eastern Europe that was not under Moscow's thumb. But as Tito aged, so the fears grew about whether it was only he who could hold together the six disparate states, and many asked what would happen when he died. Some were unworried, saying the governing structure of Yugoslavia would survive the demise of one man, or another leader would emerge, while others feared the worst. Both were proved right, after a fashion.

Tito died in 1980 and for a while Yugoslavia carried on as normal. But the nationalist passions that Tito had held under control (at times by raw oppression – his regime has been described by some as 'an iron fist in a velvet glove') gained in confidence and, as the concept of communism fell into disrepute across eastern Europe in the late 1980s, the nationalism of the six Yugoslav states grew and grew.

Those who had hoped a dominant figure might emerge to assume Tito's role thought they might have found their man when Slobodan Milosevic became the president of Serbia. He was certainly a very charismatic and ambitious leader, who wanted to preside over the whole of Yugoslavia. But Tito was a war hero who had the mixed Croat-Slovene parentage and was at home in Belgrade, whereas Milosevic was Serb through and through. And while his oratory might have roused the Serbs, it was anathema to the other peoples of Yugoslavia, so he was never going to become a leader in the Tito mould.

Once he realised that Serbia was never going to take over the whole of Yugoslavia, Milosevic embarked on a policy that effectively laid the foundations for the wars that broke up the federation. He was relatively happy for peoples that formed different nations to secede from Yugoslavia, as long as they didn't take any predominantly Serb areas with them. So, for example, he was content for Slovenia to go, as there were very few Serbs there, and he was also willing for Croatia to have independence, as long as it didn't take the mainly Serb region of Krajina with it. Yet Serbs, Croats, Bosnians, Montengrins, Macedonians, Albanians and others had migrated and intermarried within the southern Slav states for decades (including Novak Djokovic's Kosovan Serb/ Montenegrin father and Croatian mother), so such a clean division into ethnically defined states was always going to create massive problems.

When Milosevic met with the emerging Croatian leader Franjo Tudjman, a veteran of the bloody civil war of 1941–45, to agree the ethnic divide of Bosnia in March 1990, so Bosnian Serbs and Bosnian Croats could be part of the emerging Serbia and Croatia, they were effectively setting out the conditions for war. That war broke out the following year with appalling consequences.

CHAPTER THREE

NOLE
AND JECA

There used to be a saying: Behind every successful man is a powerful woman. The dictum has somewhat fallen victim to changing social circumstances – marriage break-up, same-sex relationships, and support teams rather than old-fashioned family structures. But it can still prove to be true. There is certainly a woman behind Novak Djokovic's success but not quite in the way one would expect. That woman is Jelena Gencic.

Some day an imaginative film-maker might like to make a film about the relationship between Djokovic and Gencic. It might be called 'Nole and Jeca' after the names the two used to call each other ('Nole' is a classic nickname for 'Novak', pronounced 'No-lay'; 'Jeca', pronounced 'Yet-sa', is a common short form for Jelena among a certain age group). It would be a quiet, understated film, in which the eyes of the boy playing Novak would be crucially important and the use of classical music would play a central part, perhaps with the Adagietto from Mahler's fifth symphony reprising the haunting role it played in Luchino Visconti's 1971 epic *Death in Venice*. The scope is certainly there because the relationship between the two is a remarkable one, partly because it defies all conventional attempts to categorise it. And while Djokovic would probably have become a great tennis player without Gencic, it's likely he wouldn't have become the person he is without her.

As well as Djokovic, Gencic worked with Monica Seles and played a minor but significant part in the formative years of Goran Ivanisevic. For that, she is entitled to be regarded as one of the leading tennis coaches of her era. She not only rejected that notion, she didn't even like calling herself a tennis coach. In an era where it's virtually impossible to do anything professionally unless you have a formal qualification, she coached until a week before her death having never taken a test or exam that led to a tennis-coaching qualification. Her university degree was in art history, she had a secondary qualification in psychology, and her career was as a television producer, editor and director.

Jelena Gencic was born in October 1936 to a Serb father and Austrian mother. The family was moderately prominent in Yugoslavia. Her grandfather Lazar Gencic studied medicine in Vienna and went on to become surgeon general and set up a military hospital. He was a great believer in a healthy mind residing in a healthy body and insisted on outdoor exercise for his children and grandchildren every day, whatever the weather. Her great-uncle was interior minister in the first Yugoslav government after the First World War. Her father Jovan wanted to be a pianist – it didn't work out but he became a respected lawyer. And she had an aunt, Ana Marinkovic, who was a prominent artist (1882–1973). As a child she followed her father's example and learned the piano to a high level, but her passions were two sports: tennis and handball. She played for the Yugoslav national handball team and won 32 national tennis titles.

At that time, tennis was an amateur sport and Yugoslavia was a country with a collectivist (state-controlled) economy. Gencic had everything paid for but was expected to give something back, in the form of helping youngsters. She therefore began informal coaching well before her tournament-playing days ended in 1976.

The restrictions of Tito's Yugoslavia in the 1950s and 1960s meant that only the best two players were allowed to travel abroad. There were no entourages the way there are today, and Gencic would frequently have to play a match at Wimbledon or Forest Hills (the former home of the US Open) the day after an arduous journey. It was one early-round defeat that started her on the road to helping the likes of Seles and Djokovic. 'Because I knew that when I stopped playing tournaments I wanted to help young people play tennis,' she said, 'especially those who didn't have a coach, and I knew I wanted to explain and show them how to play, I used a defeat in the second round at Forest Hills to go out and buy some books. America has very good articles and books about tennis, so I bought nothing but tennis books, that's the only thing I bought, in particular Vic Braden, and I built up my library.'

By the time tennis went 'open' (professional) in 1968, Gencic was 31 and, realistically, past the age when she could earn her living as a player. Besides, by then her career in television was well in train. But inevitably she was asked to get involved in the administration of tennis. As she had played for Partizan Belgrade (the leading clubs in many European cities are multi-sports clubs, so Belgrade's teams Partizan and Red Star are widely known as football teams but have all sorts of other sporting teams too, including tennis), the board of the tennis club asked her to join them with a view to preparing her to be president of the club and possibly the Yugoslav Tennis Association. So she worked her way up the lay administrator ladder, all the time doing her day job in television. It was a dual existence she clearly revelled in.

There was a potential overlap between her two worlds but it never actually happened – she never worked in sport in her television career. She worked almost exclusively on cultural programmes, mainly history of art in Serbia and the world, but she also made programmes on classical music and theatre. Every five years she changed her emphasis as she had a lot of interests. But she never worked in sport because Yugoslav television grouped political reporting and sport together; sport and politics came under one heading, while culture and the arts were separate.

Things began to change in the early 1980s when Gencic, by then in her forties, saw a little girl who looked smaller than her eight years. She was an ethnic Hungarian from Novi Sad, a city in the north of Serbia whose population was made up of around 20 per cent ethnic Hungarians. Her name was Monica Seles. 'She was so little, so tiny,' Gencic recalled, 'but I saw something in her eyes. I watch the eyes with every child. If a little boy or little girl comes to me, and if they have the patience to look at me for more than 10 or 15 seconds without their eyes wandering, I say, "This boy or girl has a good concentration, motivation and patience – maybe this boy or girl would be very good at practising." If you try to speak to a six- or seven-year-old, they're looking all around. I was watching Monica. She was eight and her father Karolij asked me to come to Novi Sad. I ended up working with her for more than three years and doing a lot of travelling with her.'

Many accounts say Gencic coached Seles. She was never her formal coach – she was effectively captain of the Yugoslav Tennis Association's juniors and therefore travelled with the country's best youngsters. Seles was not the only one of whom great things were expected: there was another gifted Yugoslav tennis player just a year and a half older than Seles, a Croatian boy called Goran Ivanisevic. Gencic accompanied Seles and Ivanisevic to tournaments like Bruehl in Germany (Steffi Graf's home town) and Blois in France, and

Gencic gave Seles and Ivanisevic coaching tips. But the only formal coaches Seles ever had were her father Karolij and her brother Zoltan, in the sense that they spent hours on court with her (she doesn't even count Nick Bollettieri as her coach, even though she acknowledges the immense value of the assistance he gave her).

The shift in Gencic would probably have happened anyway – with her sporting, emotional and educational make-up, it's hard to see her not having become a tennis coach in some way. But what seeing Seles did for her was to put her various skills together and goad her into helping young tennis players formally. One day, when she was off work sick, she said to herself, 'Jelena, some day you will stop working on television. We don't have a coach, you've been a tennis teacher at university, you've got a second degree in psychology – why don't you become a coach? It's easy to teach everyone forehands, backhands and smashes but not how to win matches, how to be mentally strong. How do you recognise a future champion? I could learn something myself too.' It was more than just learning. Gencic was one of seven children (four girls, three boys) but never had children of her own. Working with Seles was the start of her own extended family, the start of a process that saw her work with a number of talented youngsters.

Seles speaks very highly of Gencic:

I have so much respect for her – not just [because of] what she's done in tennis but what she's done for women and girls in Serbia. Women were not put on the same rank as men, they didn't have the same opportunities – my father was always fighting for us to have good facilities to practise, I started by playing in a parking lot and it was one of the reasons we decided to leave when I was 11 – we often just couldn't get a court. Jelena was a pioneer in women's sports, and Ana Ivanovic and Jelena Jankovic probably owe more to her than they realise. I never saw her after I was 11 years old but I remember her very fondly. She was a very positive influence, always smiling. She was a gentle soul who dedicated her life to tennis in a country where tennis and women had no real place in the sports culture.

The 'gentle soul' found herself tested with the young Ivanisevic, who even at that stage was known as a wild child. 'When we were alone, I never had a problem with him,' she said. 'Goran, Monica and me – we travelled everywhere together and everyone asked me how I handled Ivanisevic. And I replied, "He's an excellent boy." I never told him any ugly words, I'm always positive. Everyone had a problem with him except me. Monica helped me handle Goran too – they were very close. They were like a son and daughter of mine.'

The general gist of that comment may be true, but lest anyone think it was all plain sailing, it wasn't. Gencic was with Seles and Ivanisevic for the European under-14 championships in Heidelberg – the 12-year-old Seles dutifully won (she was only four years away from winning the French Open) but Ivanisevic was disqualified in the semi-finals, having behaved badly and broken at least one racket. 'His nerves were so bad,' Gencic admitted, 'it was very ugly to see.' On another occasion, Gencic, Seles and Ivanisevic shared a room together at the prestigious Orange Bowl tournament, a situation ripe for tensions to rise inside the head of the wild child. One afternoon, while Gencic and Seles were having a nap, Ivanisevic ripped the head off Seles' doll. 'Jelena punished me,' recalls Ivanisevic. 'She said, "Don't do that again," and I had to run laps, all because I took the head off the doll.' Asked why he felt the need to decapitate a doll, Ivaniseivc replies, 'Because it was an ugly doll and it was getting on my nerves. When you're 12, you do these stupid things.' Seles has no recollection of this incident.

*

In 1992 the president of Genex, the state tourism operator in Yugoslavia, asked Gencic if she would be the director of a tennis camp it wanted to run at its complex in Kopaonik. Kopaonik is a ski and walking resort in the mountains on the Serbian-Kosovo border. It does well during the winter months but, despite its setting in picturesque countryside, it struggles a little in the summer months. So running summer-holiday tennis courses on the handful of hard courts it had built opposite a small shopping precinct seemed a good idea.

Gencic was interested but had the problem that the summer camp was nine weeks. She hadn't taken any holiday but even to use up her entire holiday allowance wouldn't have covered the nine weeks. But the board of Yugoslav TV decided to give her an extra three weeks, so she was able to say yes. There was no question of a fee – Gencic didn't want one and the camp was effectively run by the state, so while she didn't get any payment, she did get all the equipment she wanted and enough coaches for one per court. That allowed her to work out her programme, tell the coaches what she wanted and keep a watchful brief, monitoring all the courts like a foreman. Because Jelena Gencic was a name that meant something to the parents of athletic youngsters, the camp proved very popular.

After about an hour on the first morning, Gencic became aware of a small boy who wasn't part of the group but who had pressed himself against the fence behind one of the courts and was watching the action intently. At first she ignored him but after a while, with the boy still there, she remarked to one of the coaches that they had a very keen spectator. She then moved to another court and observed that the boy moved court too so he could see what Gencic was monitoring. He stayed there until the end of the session.

As the camp broke for lunch, Gencic walked up to the boy and said, 'Hello, I saw you watching us. Do you know which sport this is?'

The boy replied, 'Yes, this is tennis. I tried to play one month ago in Belgrade.'

'How old are you?' she asked.

'Five.'

'OK, would you like to play with us?' asked Gencic.

'I've been waiting for you to ask me to join you,' he said.

Gencic took a step back at this boldness by the tiny boy. 'All right,' she said, 'you can join us this afternoon. What's your name?'

'Novak. Novak Djokovic.'

'How long are you staying here?'

'I'm here all summer.'

'You live here or what?'

'My mother and father work here; they have a pizzeria just across from the tennis court.'

'Can you come at two o'clock? We're having lunch now for two hours and at two we will continue working. Do you have a racket?'

'Yes, I do.'

'Do you have shoes and everything?'

'Yes, I do.'

'All right, see you at two.'

Before leaving for her lunch, Gencic called over her coaches and told them, 'Please watch this boy. In particular, watch his eyes. He came alone, without parents, without anyone – that's very interesting.'

Gencic's apartment in Kopaonik was also close to the courts, in a high-rise building, so she could see the courts from her window. At 1.30pm she looked down and saw the boy waiting with his kit bag. So she made sure she was there before 2pm. 'I'm sorry,' she lied to him, 'I've forgotten your name.'

'My name is Novak,' he said. 'You should not forget my name.'

'I'm sorry, son, I'll never forget your name again.'

She looked at his kit bag and said, 'OK, come in, let's talk about tennis. What do you have in your bag?'

'Everything I need,' the boy replied, showing her one racket, one bottle of water, two sweatbands, a towel, a banana and three clean T-shirts.

'How do you know what you need?'

'I've seen it on TV.'

'Who have you seen on TV?'

'Sampras, Agassi, Edberg.' It was the second week of Wimbledon, so there was a lot of tennis on television at that time.

'Who packed your bag?' Gencic asked. 'Your mother?'

The boy frowned with anger. 'I packed it! I'm playing tennis here, not my mother.'

'Oh, Novak, that's the second mistake I've made – please forgive me.'

Only in December 2012, more than 20 years later, did Djokovic admit to Gencic that he'd lied and his mother had indeed packed the bag, not him, although he had told her what she needed to pack from his television research. But somehow it doesn't seem to matter – he was making a statement and Gencic got the message. 'He was five years old and so strong,' she said. 'He was convinced I should not forget his name – I hadn't forgotten, I was testing him, I've always tested him – and his ability to keep his eyes focused on me when we were talking made me think right away that this was a very unusual boy.'

Gencic insisted that she saw enough in that first afternoon to know that she had a potential world-beater on her hands. At the time, Monica Seles was world No. 1 in women's tennis and here was a boy who she said she felt could be the same in men's tennis.

I tested him the way I test all my beginners, and he could do everything. At first I showed him how to hit strokes, but I soon realised that he had great motor skills, massive concentration, an ability to listen and watch. I called other coaches over and said, 'Watch this boy.' Within a few minutes I offered to hit with him – he was so happy. I had three or four coaches I'd been working with for about 20 years and I called one of them over and said, 'I don't want to say this but I'll do it anyway – I predict that Novak won't be in that group for long, he'll be in the older group.' I didn't want to say he was excellent because he had to show that he is. I didn't want to put pressure on him – he had to fight for it mentally.

At the end of the day, Gencic asked the boy to introduce her to his parents. It wasn't a long trip as the pizzeria was just across the road. And so ensued the conversation that was to set Djokovic on the road to being the world's best tennis player. Gencic explained:

He was standing behind his mother with his head nestling into her side. I told his parents what I'd seen in Novak and said, 'You have a golden child. In the eight years since I stopped working with Monica Seles, I've never found as great a talent as your child. By the time he's 17, he'll be in the top five in the world.' They were shocked. They looked at each other and looked at me. They didn't know who I was, they only knew that I was a coach at this camp. Suddenly it became clear how much emotion there was between Novak and me. When I said he'd be in the top five when he's 17, slowly, one step after another, Novak came up to me and put his head in my back. I knew that our emotions were on the same wavelength.

Such was Gencic's recollection of the events of that late June day in 1992. Is it really true? It's a great tale but has the story perhaps improved with the telling? Possibly it has – after all, Gencic was a consummate film-maker who knew how to bring artistic and cultural stories to life through her television work, so it's possible a few details have been embellished. But Djokovic himself has corroborated a lot of it in interviews, and others who were around at the time say it all stacks up.

A central feature of Gencic is that she was interested only in tennis and personal development. She was not into money – she received countless offers to run private tennis camps but always turned them down. She was a woman of left-of-centre political views and was clearly at home in a state-controlled economy where, if a service was offered, it was offered to everyone regardless of income or other means. She said, 'I was a tennis player, so I didn't want to receive anything, I wanted only to help.' She also had a deferential attitude to those she coached: 'I never say I'm the best, I only try to get better and help the children get better. The best is the child who is No. 1.' In the course of her interviews for this book, she was given plenty of opportunities to claim clairvoyant skills for other aspects of Djokovic's progression but declined, often with a firm 'no'. So even if the story has improved with the telling, it is likely to be a true story at heart.

However true it is, the sequence of events was weird and rushed enough for Dijana and Srdjan Djokovic to have been forgiven for being a tad mistrustful when this fifty-something coach walked into their restaurant with their first-born and said he could be a world-beater by 17. Gencic had clearly got the bit between her teeth and was purring enthusiastically about little Novak. She even claimed to have said to them, 'This boy is mine, I must make him the best in the world,' which sounds almost dangerous. Shortly afterwards, she said, she came to the conclusion that she needed to give up everything except her TV job – which she needed to earn her living – to make sure Djokovic had the start he needed.

At first the Djokovics didn't say a word. Then they went away and tried to find out who this strange woman was and whether she was as crazy as she seemed. Everyone who knew her told them she had discovered and worked with Monica Seles, which at the time was about the best reference she could have had. So they let Gencic work with their boy.

She did, however, bring them somewhat down to earth the following day. She told them, 'If you want me to work with Novak, I have only one condition – I will do my best for his tennis but don't ask me about money – that's your problem not mine.' Gencic knew that within a couple of years they would need much more money for equipment, tournaments, travel, etc. Initially, it all came free – Gencic didn't charge anything; she used her position as president of Partizan Belgrade, one of only two state-funded tennis clubs in the country, to get him rackets, balls and everything else he needed. But to make it in the fiercely competitive world of professional tennis, he would need to find some money before long.

Gencic and Djokovic started to work on day two of the summer camp. Gencic worked out a programme for him – one that lasted for five years. It needed to take account of the fact that he went to school in Belgrade but spent the summer months and part of the winter in Kopaonik when there was money to be made from the pizzeria and the boutique. He only had three weeks' Christmas holiday but Gencic went to his head teacher and asked for one week more so she could do more work with him.

Gencic's insistence that she would look after the tennis but the family had to find the money shielded the young boy from the family's and country's growing financial challenges, which were becoming more acute anyway – the Serbo-Croat war was raging and an embryonic capitalist system was replacing the collectivist economy that had been Yugoslavia's reality since 1945. The programme she prepared for him was not just a coaching plan but also a tournament plan for years one to five, including how much it was likely to cost year by year and thus how much money the family had to be prepared to find. 'This is the terrible part of the Djokovic family's life,' she said. 'I knew they didn't have anything but neither did I. So I said they had to go to find some sponsors. They did find the money but with some terrible conditions. Srjdan has said publicly that he got loans with high interest rates, and when the day came to pay the money back and he hadn't got any, he sometimes found a knife at his throat. The only way out was to take out a second loan to pay off the first loan, normally at very high rates.'

These days, while Djokovic enjoys a very high standing among his compatriots, the same cannot be said for the rest of his family. His father and uncle have made enemies, both in broad society and specifically in tennis. In early 2011 a coup led by the Djokovic family resulted in the president of the Serbian Tennis Federation, Slobodan Zivojinovic, being ousted shortly after Serbia had won the 2010 Davis Cup and replaced by Vuk Jeremic, the president of the United Nations General Assembly and an ally of Srdjan Djokovic. But Gencic said the wider context has to be understood:

People who criticise his parents don't know or don't want to know the full story of the Djokovic family from the beginning. They see only money now; they think he [Srdjan] is arrogant. The family were very friendly until they needed money for Novak. That was terrible. They knew that Novak would be the best, but how do you find money? They went out every day looking for money. Srdjan did get very angry but then he knocked on every door, including the government's, asking for help – he constantly came up against 'Who is this boy?', 'We don't have money for this little boy.' Now they like to say, 'We made him.' I'm very happy for Srdjan to claim the credit for it because what he did allowed Novak to go to tournaments. The Djokovic family has had a terrible life until now. These days they have the money but I'm not interested how they're living.

I'm only interested in how Novak and [his younger brothers] Marko and Djordje are doing.

The work developing Novak Djokovic into a world-class tennis player progressed slowly but surely. He learned quickly but was a small boy, so Gencic sometimes had to wait for his body to catch up before she could move forward.

Having grown up in the pre-Connors and pre-Evert era, Gencic's natural inclination was to teach the one-handed backhand. So for the first year or so of his tennis career, Djokovic hit his backhand one-handed. Then one day, when he was about six and a half, he walked up to Gencic and asked very politely, 'Please, Jeca, can I try to play the backhand with two hands?' Gencic replied, 'Of course, why not, but first of all I must explain to you how you must hold the racket for a two-handed backhand because you have three options: a left-handed forehand, a one-handed backhand with the second hand, or a genuinely two-handed shot. Try all three and after a week you will tell me which one is the best for you, and whether you want to play with two hands or one hand.' Exactly a week later, Djokovic came up to her unprompted, saying, 'A week has passed and I'd like to explain to you – I'd like to play the backhand with two hands.' She told him that was OK, as long as he stuck to a one-handed backhand slice and worked on it as a tool to get him to the net. He said he felt his backhands were much stronger with two hands than with one, so she said, 'OK, we'll go to work on that.' They then worked very slowly without any pressure from Gencic, but she found him so intelligent and able to learn that he picked up the two-handed backhand very quickly.

One of Djokovic's principal attributes is his footwork, and he was complimented on that from the beginning. Gencic said she recognised from day one that he was a good skier, something she could also claim for herself, so essentially she taught him to adapt the basic flexibility in the ankles and legs that are core features for the skier to his tennis game. That even allowed him to slide on hard courts, something that's a common feature today but was very rare then.

Another feature of Gencic's coaching was that she tried to link it with the heroes her kids were seeing on television. She asked Djokovic what appealed to him when he saw the likes of Pete Sampras, Stefan Edberg and Andre Agassi playing in the biggest tennis arenas. On one occasion Djokovic said he wanted to play Sampras's running down-the-line forehand, so Gencic said she'd teach him. He wanted to serve and volley like Edberg, so she taught him that (and was a little aggrieved that he doesn't do that much of it as a professional). And when he said he wanted to hit Agassi's forehand, Gencic told him to watch where Agassi was standing during rallies. 'Agassi stands inside the baseline,' she said, 'so I taught him to stay on or inside the baseline. This was important because he was very little and didn't have much power, so he had to take the ball early and go forward, with a very fast follow-through. He looked at Agassi, and started to play that way. That was good, because he didn't have much power so he had to finish points much sooner than you think. I told him not to get involved in long rallies – when you get a shorter ball, go for it.'

Djokovic also had very good volleys but was reluctant to make great use of them. He once told her, 'Jeca, you want me to play volleys, but when I go to the net I feel like I'm in a battlefield facing a thousand bombs.'

Another observation Gencic made about the young Novak was that he never once said he was tired. In fact, he was more likely to ask to stay another hour at the end of the programmed practice period. 'They were all playing four hours in the morning,' she said of her camps in Kopaonik, 'then two hours off and then two hours more in the afternoon – so six hours including two hours of fitness work. We did it every day except when it was raining.'

And he never tired mentally. Whenever they finished a practice session, Gencic knew the boy would ask her something about what they were doing. At one stage she said to him, 'Novak, I have two university degrees – I think I now have a third degree because of all your questions I've answered!'

Gencic even claimed she had done her best to make him taller. 'He was very late in growing,' she observed.

> I read physiology books and asked people which exercises they could do to make a boy taller. And I found nine exercises every day, three times a day, and you will be taller than you would have been. They're very easy but you must really work at them; if you don't work, you don't get anywhere. I worked on fitness but only on the tennis court, only on flexibility and agility, speed off the mark. I never worked on power with him, and no long-distance running. When you're through puberty, you can start to work on power and your musculature will be long, which gives them flexibility and you can then work on the strength. But I wasn't coaching him by then.

As the months went by, word spread that this was a boy worth watching. Part of that word was spread by the boy himself. At seven he was invited on to a national television programme where children interview children – appearing with the peak of his cap turned to the back, he turned in a very cocksure performance that included the prediction that he would be No. 1 in the world. The clip is still available on the Internet, and even if you don't understand Serbian you can see the confidence shining through – but it's the seven-year-old's confidence without arrogance; he was just answering a question as honestly as he could. 'When I was seven or eight, I said I was going to be world No. 1,' Djokovic told the American television station CBS in 2012, 'and most of the people laughed at me. Those were very critical times for our country, so it seemed like I had a one per cent chance to do that.' But he believed he could do it and even enacted the scene of his greatest individual triumph that was to come nearly 20 years later – he fashioned a trophy-like vessel out of a cheap plastic vase and, speaking English for one of the first times in his life, raised the vase above his head with the words, 'Hello, I'm Novak Djokovic, I'm Wimbledon champion.'

The precocity of the young Novak was spotted by a man who was later to become a Davis Cup team-mate and one of his coaches, Dusan Vemic. Vemic, 11 years older than Djokovic, was still in the youth squad at the Partizan club in Belgrade when he found his squad coaching sessions taking place on a neighbouring court to one being used by Gencic to coach the seven-year-old Djokovic. 'Even at that stage, he was almost independent in some way,' recalls Vemic. 'You could see he was like those kids brought on to TV shows as little prodigies in different spheres of life – maths, music – they're like little professors. He was one of those kids: very intelligent, very eloquent, great ideas, very clear in his head. He had something about him and the whole situation brought out more from him. The tougher the situation, the better he is. He's proved that over and over as a professional.'

Although he was spending three-quarters of the year in Belgrade, Djokovic thought of Kopaonik as his tennis home. He would play on the three hard courts in summer and, in winter, when those courts were covered with snow, he would profit from the indoor sports facility at the Grand Hotel, which had been built by the state tourism authorities in the 1980s and could be used as an indoor tennis court. Together with the clay courts of the Belgrade facilities, it gave him access to hard, clay and indoor surfaces, so a well-rounded tennis education. But it wasn't all tennis – Gencic wanted all the boys and girls on her camps to socialise together, so it was a massive youthful community with all the friendships and frictions that go with it. Reminiscing with Gencic in his twenties, Djokovic said to her, 'You know, Jeca, Kopaonik is my Mount Olympus.'

Djokovic refers to Gencic as his 'tennis mother', and having coached him from when he was five until he was twelve, she certainly taught him the fundamentals of tennis. But she saw her role as much wider than that.

If the term hadn't been commandeered by a branch of the personal development industry, you could describe Gencic as Djokovic's life coach, in the sense that she coached him in various aspects of life that she knew he would have to deal with. She taught him about table manners; she recognised that the family he came from had just about enough to live on but no more, but that as a top-level tennis player he would sit at tables with more than one knife and one fork, more than one glass, so she told him which glass was for the aperitif, which for the white wine, which for the champagne, etc.

Mindful of the pride involved in a patriarchal family where a woman had come in to coach the eldest son in a discipline the family was unfamiliar with, Gencic insisted she only ever told him about table manners and such like when they were alone. And only once did Djokovic ask me why she was telling him about etiquette. 'Every day I told him, "You will be the best in the world," starting from the second day I knew him. I said we must work, we must believe each other. If you don't understand something, you must ask me. If you feel you haven't put the work in, put it in. I told his parents, "Don't put pressure on your child, he has to be an individual. The motivation has to come from him." But these kinds of things I said privately, so Novak didn't hear what I told his parents and his parents didn't hear everything I told him.'

As well as etiquette, Gencic was very big into music, literature and general education. One day she told him she liked classical music and, when she was tired, she would lie down and listen to some. She suggested he did the same and introduced him to some of the classics. She said,

I always explained who the composer was. I explained if it was baroque, classical, romantic, who Beethoven was, etc. What we listened to depended on his tiredness and level of interest. When he was very tired, we listened to Chopin, Debussy, Grieg – piano music to which we can slowly relax. And very often because we often finished the day near my home, I played pieces on the piano for him. The first time he was listening, I saw in his eyes that he would prefer to listen to heavy metal and such like but I said he had to learn to listen to classical as well. He would listen to rock and heavy metal for half an hour before he went to bed, so he had both. I never said, 'Don't do it.' That's a terrible thing to say to a youngster.

One day, when he was about seven, I was very tired, maybe a bit depressed, and was looking for a piece of music to put on. I like to listen to strong music, full orchestra music, so I played the 1812 Overture – for myself. And I saw him – he was listening, so I turned the volume up a little. Suddenly Novak told me, 'Jeca, I've got goose bumps.' He was listening so strongly. I said, 'OK, Novak, I'll explain something very important. In a match, you'll be in one of two situations. It could be a very good situation where you're closing in on victory, one or two points away from winning, and you'll feel goose bumps. In that situation, be quiet and finish the match, don't get excited, stay calm. But you may be a few points from losing a match, so remember this music and the feeling, remember both, and the adrenalin will start to kick in and you may well win.' I think this lesson has been so important for his mental strength.

Alongside the poets – particularly Serbian and Russian ones – Gencic encouraged Djokovic to learn at least two languages other than his mother tongue. English was an obvious one and he chose German as his second, which came in useful when he began going to Munich at the age of 12.

And she taught Djokovic about Nikola Tesla. To most travellers, Tesla is just the name of Belgrade's international airport but the man himself was a leading, if somewhat eccentric, figure in the history of science. A Serb who emigrated to America, he is credited with being the father of alternating current, the AC in AC/DC (DC stands for direct current), and some credit him with the science underlying the major discoveries associated with Edison, Marconi and others. Gencic knew a lot about Tesla and one day found an article about him in a newspaper that had a good cultural section for children. Djokovic, then about seven and a half, was very interested and asked her a question about Tesla. Gencic replied with, 'What's the first idea of Nikola Tesla? Answer: visualisation. First Tesla saw in his mind a new idea, then he put it down on paper and then tried to realise it.' Only once did Djokovic ask her what 'visualisation' means. He asked, 'Do you think you will see into the future what will happen?' – this at seven. Gencic explained that, for tennis tactics, visualisation is a very important part of practice. So she played Smetana's symphonic poem *Vltava* to him, saying he should listen, and when she stopped the music he had to tell her what he saw, what he felt and anything else about the music – in short, what he visualised. Then Gencic shared with him what she had been feeling. She admits to one mistake with *Vltava* – she told him it was a river but that was because she felt a seven-year-old needed a helping hand, which this particular seven-year-old probably didn't. At times they visualised with a different piece of music every day, which explains why Djokovic has a very good knowledge of classical music and still uses it to calm his mind today.

The Gencic teaching extended to aspects of nature as and when they encountered them. She once offered her summer group in Kopaonik the option of a training session or a four-hour walk in the mountains – they all, including Djokovic, opted for the walk in the mountains. She told them about the fauna and flora, often explaining why she liked something. She taught him what to pick to make up a small bouquet. One day, when he was about nine, he made a really big and beautiful bouquet; an impressed Gencic complimented him and picked a blue flower that she felt would go well in it. He looked and said, 'But Jeca, don't you see? I have this flower in there already.' Indeed he had, she just hadn't noticed, and stood corrected. It transpired it was his mother's birthday that day and it was clearly important to him that he should make his own bouquet for her free from any outside influence.

And, of course, as the niece of a leading artist, the broad education included art. This was a message the young Novace picked up very quickly (in the first few months Gencic called him 'Novace', pronounced 'No-VA-chay'). When he was seven and a half and her birthday was approaching, he insisted to his parents that he wanted to buy her a present – a painting. He spent two hours looking for the right one and eventually found it in a market. It hung in her living room until her death, among the more critically acclaimed Marinkovic works.

To what extent Djokovic would have been the person he is without the influence of Jelena Gencic will never be known. He clearly had the confidence to take in her wide-ranging package of education, and the intellectual capacity to know where she was coming from and why what she was teaching him would help him in the future. Given the determination it takes to get to the top of a ferociously competitive global sport, it's distinctly possible Djokovic would have had a much rockier road to the top without her input. He might have pursued a route similar to Andre Agassi's – Agassi's natural curiosity and good nature eventually triumphed over the rebelliousness of his unchannelled youthful aggression, but it took many years and may well have cost him half a dozen Grand Slam singles titles.

From the beginning, Gencic had an unshakeable belief that Djokovic would be the best in the world, so she saw her role as teaching him to speak very well as much as teaching him a good backhand, encouraging him to speak good English as much as encouraging him to go to the net, and to be very helpful and diplomatic. She maintained he loves everybody – he probably doesn't, but he does a good job of making those with whom he comes into contact feel very loved.

The relationship between a coach and a player is a strange one. Some coaches are anathema to some players but a match made in heaven with others. It takes a certain chemistry, perhaps allied to the right timing. For some players, Gencic might have been a disaster – maybe there is a potential champion who missed the boat because he or she had a Gencic figure, rather than a more traditional nuts-and-bolts coach. But she was so right for Djokovic.

And even in what proved to be the last few months of her life, she never described herself as a professional coach. 'I'm not professional because that means you work for money but I never work for money,' she said. 'I don't want money because I coach children. If their parents have no money, I still want to coach them. For most of my life, the tennis courts were excellent in Yugoslavia and Serbia because the government paid for everything in a tennis school. We could buy balls through the tennis school, rackets and strings, and the state paid for coaching.'

In some ways, she was a loveable eccentric. Even in her mid-70s she spent up to 10 hours a day on court, coaching and supervising other coaches, and there was no shortage of children who wanted to learn. Every day she would break for her unchanging lunch of a baguette and a litre of yoghurt. One year, on her birthday, all her children and their parents gave her a baguette and a litre of yoghurt as an affectionate joke.

Officially, she was Djokovic's first coach: the woman who taught him how to play tennis. From when he was 12, when he had other coaches in Belgrade and visited Nikki Pilic's academy in Germany at regular intervals, she became just a friend and ex-coach. He frequently visited her, but once he was full-time on the tour, he had less and less time to see her. There was a period of about four years in his early adulthood when he didn't see her at all. She said she fully understood, though there was a sense that she was a little upset by the length of time she didn't see him. During that period, Djokovic had the habit of mentioning a work of classical music in some of his interviews for Serbian tele-vision or radio. Sometimes he would say, 'I like to listen to Tchaikovsky,' or another classical composer. Gencic interpreted this as Djokovic telling her through television that he was thinking of her, even if he didn't have time to contact her. Djokovic confirmed in an interview with her that this was how he intended it – whether he was just being nice to an old lady for whom he clearly felt immense affection and gratitude is not certain, but it would be nice to believe such references to the classics genuinely were coded messages sent to her.

Another thing she never said but seemed to hint at was that she was sad never to have travelled with him. The family frequently struggled to find money for tickets, but occasionally there was a budget for Novak to go to a junior tournament with one accompanying adult. So the question was always who would go with him and it was always his father or mother, or Uncle Goran or Bogdan Obradovic – never Gencic, although he would sometimes talk on the phone to her. Only once did Djokovic ever invite her to accompany him to a tournament. That was for the first day of Wimbledon 2012 when he was opening the defence of his title at 1pm on the first day and he invited her to sit with his team in the players' box. She said she replied, 'Novak, if you're only inviting me for one day, I think it's much better if it's the last day, not the first.' So she didn't come and Djokovic never made it to the final – he was beaten by Roger Federer in the semis and, by the following year's Wimbledon, she was dead.

But if she never travelled to Wimbledon, Wimbledon came to her. At the end of the 2011 season, Djokovic arranged to visit her and asked if he could bring along a TV crew. In the end he brought two – one American and one Serbian – so both Serbian and US television captured the moment when Djokovic walked through the gate of her house with his Wimbledon replica. 'This was what we were working for, wasn't it?' he said as they gave each other a heartfelt hug – he in a warm winter overcoat, she in a cricket sweater. 'This is the trophy, this was our dream. We were standing in front of the mirror and lifting up the improvised trophy and dreaming of holding this one one day. I always wanted to do this,' he said as he placed his replica on the table containing all her trophies, 'alongside your trophies – not just any trophy, but the one, *the* one.' It was a wonderful moment, not cheapened in any way by the presence of the cameras.

That wasn't the last time they saw each other but it was a form of closure. And the end came suddenly. She was on court until a week before she rapidly went down with the spread of her secondary liver cancer, and she died on the middle Saturday of the 2013 French Open. Word went out on the Serbian Tennis Federation's website at noon that day, but with Djokovic due to play Grigor Dimitrov late that afternoon in the third round in Paris, Djokovic's coach and team decided to keep the news from him. After beating Dimitrov comfortably, he did a cheerful on-court interview with Fabrice Santoro, signed a few autographs as he left the court, and was then given the news.

Normally a post-match press conference is obligatory but he was exempted all his media obligations that night. Two days later, after winning his next match, he said of the previous 48 hours:

It hasn't been easy but this is life – life gives you things and takes away close people. Jelena was my first coach, she was like my second mother – we were very close throughout all my life. She taught me a lot of things that are part of me, part of my character today. I have the nicest memories of her. This is something that will stay with me for ever and, hope-fully, I will be able to continue and follow up where she stopped with her legacy because she left so much knowledge to me and to the people who were close to her and I feel the responsibility to continue doing that in the future. She worked with kids from about five and six years to 12 and 13 years old, and she dedicated all her life to that generation and to tennis. She never got married, she never had kids, so tennis was all she had in life. Even last week she was giving lessons to kids, so she didn't really care about the nature of the illness – she had breast cancer and she survived that. She's one of the most incredible people I ever knew, so it's quite emotional, yeah.

The Serbian Tennis Federation hastily organised a service of thanksgiving in Belgrade for Gencic's life. It took place two days after her death, on the second Monday of Roland Garros, so there was no way Djokovic could be there. But he sent a letter, which his mother read out at the service. It included the passage,

> I am completely unprepared for our parting. Not being able to see you off makes me endlessly sad. Still, I know that you'd be mad if I gave up or decreased my chance to fulfil this final wish of ours, winning Roland Garros. Thank you for your patience, your enormous love. Thank you for your everyday support, for the advice I remember, for the warm words which always carried an extraordinary message. You know that I've memorised them all and that I always follow your rules.
>
> Our last conversation, two weeks ago, didn't suggest that any-thing was wrong. I'm sad because even then you made an effort to keep me free from any concerns and assured me that everything was all right, that you were in the hospital for a routine check-up – that I shouldn't worry but win.
>
> You were an angel. Both when you coached me and afterward, I felt your support wherever I went. Sincere. Strong. Unconditional. You left an indelible mark on Serbian tennis. Everyone who holds a racket in his or her hands today is indebted to you. I promise that I will speak your name to future generations and that your spirit will live on on our tennis courts.

If this was a fairy tale, Djokovic would have won the French Open seven days later. But it isn't, and he didn't. He was beaten by Rafael Nadal in a four-hour, 38-minute semi-final in which he had his chances but, ultimately, couldn't resist the irrepressible momentum that Nadal had created after seven months off the tour in 2012–13. If Gencic was Djokovic's angel, she was off guardian duty that afternoon. But it's hard not to see Djokovic having three or four more cracks at the French Open title and maybe winning it will mean just as much a little further down the line.

In many ways, the person of Novak Djokovic, more than the tennis player, is Jelena Gencic's legacy. She didn't seem to mind not having had children of her own, saying, 'All boys and girls are my children,' but it was easy to feel she would have made a wonderfully nurturing mother. If Djokovic was the son she never had, he's the kind of son any mother would be proud of. Yet perhaps she needed him too much. She said she'd had two very talented boys a couple of years after she met him but she didn't want to work with them, ostensibly because she didn't have time, what with coaching Djokovic and her TV work, but deep down she didn't want to create competition for him. 'I wanted to keep him to be the best in his own right,' was how she put it. Such devotion, though admirable, can be stifling, and maybe Djokovic needed to get his distance from her, which may explain the four years in which they never saw each other.

There was something inspiring yet sad about Jelena Gencic. Her eyes sparkled with enthusiasm, yet there was also a sadness there. If she had one regret as a professional, it was that there is very little left of her work as a television-programme maker. She ended her TV career in 1999 when the Serbian television centre was destroyed in the Nato bombing; the bombing destroyed the archives, so most of the 1,500 programmes she made, many of them award winners, were obliterated.

If she had ever been marooned on the BBC's fictitious 'desert island' (from the long-running radio series *Desert Island Discs*) with nothing to keep her company except eight pieces of music, she would have wanted a Beethoven symphony (any one would do), the Adagietto from Mahler's fifth symphony, Rachmaninov's C minor piano concerto, some Chopin piano music and some Serbian national and church music, plus a bit of music she had composed for her television work. But knowing her, she would probably have captured a baboon and spent most of her time trying to teach it how to hit a coconut shell over a low horizontal branch.

As Djokovic summed it up, her biggest legacy is simply her own personal ethos and emotional intelligence, which distinguishes her massively from your average tennis coach. 'If I give everything from my soul to a child on a tennis court,' she said in her last interview, 'this boy or girl must receive it – maybe not all of it but much of it. If they don't receive it, that's no motivation for me. I am very proud of Novak. This is a boy who understands me, who learned so much, who wanted to learn so much, who wanted to receive from me. And I received from him too. The biggest thing I've learned is to be patient. Never be sad, explain if you're feeling sad, explain to yourself and speak to each other about it. It's very important.'

Interviewed for this book in early 2014, Djokovic looked back on the role Gencic played for him. 'Jelena had a vision,' he said. 'She saw in me something special from the start. She was always preparing each of us for something greater than the game of tennis. She was preparing us for life. My family taught me to always be respectful and polite to people older than me. She was my coach, somebody who my parents chose to be my guide and mentor. I never questioned her methods and ways to transfer her knowledge to me. I was like a sponge and I was only asking for more and she was happy to give me all she could. As I said, she had a vision in how to shape me into a good person and good player – and that would have applied even if I had only been known within Serbia, nobody made any guarantees that I would be a top athlete of the future, travelling around the world and representing my country. Even though she passed away last year during Roland Garros, she still feels very alive to me. She is part of each of my training sessions, each win, loss... I just don't think that people like her can pass away. She is beyond physical life. I am eternally grateful for having her in my life as a tennis mother.'

CHAPTER FOUR

THE EMERGENCE OF SERBIA FROM THE YUGOSLAV WARS

I t's hard to find a country that does not have some stain on its historical character. Some are easy to highlight, like Germany, a culturally mature country that has produced Goethe, Beethoven and Dürer but was still capable of starting two world wars and inflicting awful suffering on a group of people simply because of their ethnic origin. Russia's part in its war against Japan in 1904–5 was as awful as it was stupid, sending its Baltic fleet around the world in a nine-month manoeuvre to preserve the Tsar's prestige, only for it to be sunk in 45 minutes in the Tsushima Strait; Russia also has Stalin's show trials and purges of the 1930s on its record. Rwanda has the horrendous genocide of 1994, Chile has its Pinochet era, South Africa the apartheid era. The USA has had its fair share of dodgy deals with unsavoury regimes, plus its slowness to afford non-white Americans their rights under the US constitution. And a close examination of British foreign policy over the past 200 years shows up all sorts of things the great empire builders wouldn't want publicised, like the first concentration camps in the Boer War, the Amritsar massacre of 1919 and other low-profile examples of colonial arrogance and despotism.

All this and more should be stated before laying too strongly into Serbia for its actions in the 1990s. But there's no doubt it was an era in Serbian history that the likes of Novak Djokovic do not reflect comfortably on. He has often spoken about how part of his statesmanlike role is to convince the world that Serbs are not all the bloodthirsty louts they were frequently depicted as on the world's television screens in the 1990s, as Yugoslavia broke up in a wave of bloodshed. 'I'm very conscious of that in every moment of both my public and private life,' he says, 'especially when I am abroad. It is something that is built-in with most of us Serbs of my generation and older. We were always told that once we go out of the country, there will be a lot of stereotypes attached to us because we come from Serbia. They will think a lot of nasty and bad things, and we need to be very conscious about our behaviour. We are the ambassadors of our families and our country, and we need to always show the best in us. So I carry this responsibility with big respect and honour, and I hope that I am managing to portray my country in the best possible light.'

The tragedy of the Yugoslav wars is that they should never have been necessary. There is a view among some ethnologists that the Serbian approach to nationhood in 1918 was an inclusive one – that those peoples related to the Serbs through a closeness of language and religion (whether practised religion or just a label of identification with a faith) could easily belong in the same country, be it a 'Greater Serbia' or a 'Yugoslavia'. Not everyone would agree with this view but it is undeniable that there is generally an ease of relations between Serbs, Montenegrins, Croats, Slovenes, Macedonians and others on a personal level, and the fact that the language spoken in Yugoslavia was generally known as 'Serbo-Croat' is a reflection of how close Serbian and Croatian are.

Yet by 1990 antagonisms between the constituent republics of Yugoslavia had reached the point where you were 'either with us or against us'. This was bad enough in the five republics that reflected an ethnically recognisable people: Serbia, Croatia, Montenegro, Slovenia and Macedonia. It was even worse in Bosnia-Herzegovina, a small state that didn't really have ethnic Bosnians. The largest constituent ethnic group of Bosnians were Muslim (known as Bosniaks) but with a good number of Serbs and Croats. It was here that the tragic neighbour-versus-neighbour violence – when friends and neighbours who had recently celebrated festivals together suddenly turned against each other – was at its worst and left a legacy that the new republics are still recovering from today.

The break-up of Yugoslavia happened in the course of four wars concentrated largely around the areas where the different ethnic groups were most mixed. It's important to understand the difference between how the terms 'republic' and 'nation' are used in this part of the world – Croatia is the republic, the Croats are the nation; Serbia the republic, Serbs the nation, etc. This was a battle of nations and what happened was the emergence of nationalism over citizenship, or what is often known as 'state chauvinism'. Instead of a government trying to serve all the citizens in its area of jurisdiction regardless of ethnic or religious origin, the new governments were looking to rule on behalf of the majority 'nation'. That inevitably relegated those who were not of the majority nation to minorities, normally discriminated against and treated as second-class citizens.

Some put the starting point of the wars at Tito's death in 1980 and the chain of events that led to the wars of 1991–99 can certainly be traced back to then. But the point at which war became inevitable was probably reached in the late 1980s, when Slobodan Milosevic realised the political benefit that Serb nationalism was likely to deliver. Acting as president of the Yugoslav republic of Serbia (not then a sovereign state the way today's Serbia is), Milosevic in 1989 rescinded the autonomy of the mainly Albanian province of Kosovo and began a programme of imposing Serbian culture. The move sent shock waves through the Croats and Slovenes. They feared they would be next and, when the 14th congress of the Yugoslav Communist Party voted in January 1990 for a multi-party system, the nationalist parties seized the initiative.

By the start of 1991 it was clear Yugoslavia was going to break up, but the Karadjordjevo agreement between Milosevic and the equally fervent Croatian nationalist leader Franjo Tudjman in March 1991 meant that a bitter struggle over the ethnically mixed areas would follow. This agreement set out how both men saw the dissolution of Yugoslavia, effectively by dividing Bosnia between them.

Three of the four wars overlapped. Skirmishes in the Serbo-Croat war of 1991–95 had begun in the early spring but in June Slovenia declared independence. For 10 days, Serbia, in the form of the Yugoslav National Army, tried to bring the Slovenes back but they soon gave up and Slovenia gained its independence before the summer was out. This was the first of the wars, sometimes referred to as 'the 10-day War'.

That spurred Croatia and Macedonia to declare their independence. The Croats had already signalled that they wanted to secede and had prepared a constitution for the new sovereign Republic of Croatia. That constitution reclassified the Serbs living in Croatia – about 12 per cent of the population, most of them living in the province of Krajina near the Serbian border – as a 'national minority' when, up till then, they had been a 'constituent nation'. As Serbia's approach under Milosevic had been that non-Serb nations could have their own republics but that all Serbs were entitled to belong to 'Greater Serbia', the Croatian Serbs announced their secession from Croatia in the hope of integration into the new Serbian state.

That triggered the second of the wars, often referred to as the 'Croatian War of Independence', although the Croatian Serbs prefer to view it as their battle for self-determination; some call it the 'Serbo-Croat War' but that can be misleading because ethnic Serbs and Croats clashed in Bosnia too. Because of the involvement of the largely Serbian Yugoslav National Army, which marched around 70,000 soldiers into Croatia, the initial victories went to the Serbs. The first act of ethnic cleansing took place that summer in the town of Kijevo, where Croats were rounded up and shot simply because they were Croats, but more ethnic cleansing followed. One particular name, Vukovar, became a symbol for the whole Serbo-Croat war. It was a peaceful town just inside the Croatia-Serbia border of around 50,000 inhabitants of mixed ethnic origin – some say there were 22 different nations represented among Vukovar's residents, making it a model Yugoslav town. By July 1991 Vukovar was surrounded by the Serbs, who bombarded it for four months; it eventually fell to the Serbs in November 1991 as hundreds of Croat patients were herded from a hospital, taken to a field and shot. Four years later, with the Croats surging west, making good the territorial losses they had suffered in the early months of the war, Vukovar was retaken and the Serbs had to flee. Vukovar is less than 20km from Vinkovici, where Dijana Djokovic's family hails from.

The bloodiest of the four wars was the 'Bosnian War' of 1992–95. Bosnia-Herzegovina was the only one of the six Yugoslav republics not to have a distinct resident nation. The ethnic mix was approximately 43 per cent Bosniak (Muslim), 31 per cent Serb and 17 per cent Croat. The early part of the war saw the Serb-dominated Yugoslav National Army bombard Bosniak territory, carrying out ethnic cleansing by killing large numbers of Bosnian

Muslims. But there were also clashes between Bosniaks and Croats, and clashes within sub-groups of the ethnic nations.

The Bosnian War lasted three and a half years and led to an estimated 100,000 deaths, with up to 50,000 women raped and around 2.2 million becoming refugees or otherwise displaced. Most of the names that stand out from the Yugoslav wars of the 1990s are from the Bosnian War, largely because it was so brutal. The Bosnian Serbs were led by Radovan Karadzic, with the Bosnian Serb military commanded by Ratko Mladic – both were indicted at the Yugoslav war-crimes tribunal in The Hague. Several place names became recurring terms in the world's news coverage – like Mostar for the destruction of its 427-year-old symbolic bridge, or Banja Luka for the concentration camp the Serbs set up there. But perhaps the two names that symbolise the war were Sarajevo and Srebrenica.

Sarajevo, the Bosnian capital, had hosted the winter Olympics in 1984 but was badly damaged in a siege that began in April 1992 after Bosnia's Muslim president Alja Izetbegovic declared independence from Yugoslavia. That independence was promptly recognised by the international community, causing the Serbs to mobilise their forces around the city. The siege lasted longer than the war itself, not ending until February 1996. Srebrenica was a small town of about 8,000 inhabitants but that population had swollen to around 40,000 because of all the Bosniaks fleeing ethnic cleansing. Supposedly under the protection of the United Nations, it was shelled and ransacked by Serb forces on Easter Monday 1993, leaving dozens dead. The UN declared it a 'safe zone' but insufficient military protection was provided and in July 1995 Serb forces captured the supposedly demilitarised town and slaughtered an estimated 8,500 Bosnian men. This was the episode that later caused the Yugoslav war-crimes tribunal in The Hague to declare the killing as genocide, and to censure Serbia for failure to prevent it.

The Bosnian war came to an end when Nato intervened, bombing Serbian positions in Bosnia in August and September 1995. It was concluded with the Dayton peace accords of November 1995, which established various ethnic rights within the borders of new independent states. The peace has held but almost in the form of a mini-Yugoslavia within Bosnian borders, such that national successes like qualifying for the 2014 football World Cup are never the source of unified national rejoicing they would be in most other countries.

So by the end of 1995, Slovenia, Macedonia, Croatia and Bosnia had all declared independence. It meant that Yugoslavia was now only Serbia and Montenegro. Yet it continued under the name Yugoslavia, and in 1997 Slobodan Milosevic moved up from being president of Serbia to being president of Yugoslavia. And he was not finished with his nationalist wars.

The fourth war came in 1998 and centred on Kosovo. This is a conflict rich in symbolism, which embodies many of the factors that cause territorial struggles in a world where travel – and thus migration – is so easy. It is also the war that has the greatest impact on the Djokovic story.

The defeat of Kosovo in 1389 marked the end of Serbia's great era of dominance in the Middle Ages and the start of the rise of the Ottoman Empire. So Kosovo had always been a poignant reminder of Serbian failure. It had remained a province of Serbia but it was never a massively prosperous area and, from the middle of the 20th century, the Serbs tended to move north where economic prospects were better. As the Serbs moved north, ethnic Albanians moved in. These Muslim migrants, referred to by the Serbs as 'Siptar' (very much a term of abuse), often bought land from the departing Serbs. More importantly, they had a phenomenally high birth rate, with the result that by the start of the 1990s Kosovo had a majority ethnic Albanian population.

For most of the four decades of Tito's Yugoslavia, Kosovo had the status of an autonomous province, but this was rescinded by Milosevic in 1989. Not only that but Serb culture was imposed – Albanian radio and television were closed, Albanian teachers were forbidden from teaching in schools and colleges and Albanians were fired from jobs in public-sector industries (which accounted for most industries at that time). In 1996 disaffected Albanians formed the Kosovo Liberation Army, which started attacking Serbia. An agreement of sorts was reached in 1998 but it was never going to hold because the ethnic Albanian population wanted independence for Kosovo while Milosevic wanted it to remain part of Serbia.

The 'Kosovo War' began in 1998. The bloodshed intensified, to the point where Nato ordered Serbia to stop its attacks in Kosovo. Serbia refused, probably believing Nato had no mandate to intervene as Kosovo was a legally constituted province of Yugoslavia. But as evidence emerged of more massacres of innocent civilians, Nato eventually responded by launching bombing raids on both Kosovo and Belgrade. For 76 days, from 24 March to 8 June 1999, Belgrade came under air attack, forcing its residents to flee to underground shelters, including the Djokovic family. Eventually, Serbia accepted the United Nations' offer for Kosovo to become a province under UN protection and the war ended.

Kosovo remained a UN-protected province for nine years. Then in 2008 it declared independence. It was recognised by most of the international community but a few states – notably Russia, China and five EU members – supported Serbia by not recognising Kosovo as a sovereign state. In April 2013 the EU brokered a deal under which the Serbs in northern Kosovo are guaranteed a community of Serb municipalities in both the north and the south of Kosovo; Belgrade denied that the deal meant Serbia recognised Kosovo's independence, saying it was just to regularise the situation in the short term so both Serbia and Albania could negotiate their accession to the EU.

These days no more than about 10 per cent of Kosovo's population is Serb but the Serbs still form a majority in about a quarter of Kosovo's land – around the city of Mitrovica where Srdjan Djokovic, Novak's father, grew up. The Serb-Albanian tensions continue to simmer but, with the two countries wanting to join the European Union and the EU saying this can only happen with 'full normalisation' of relations (whatever that comes to mean in practice), some lasting solution needs to be found. As part of 'full normalisation', the EU has insisted that Serbia should cooperate in bringing the last two war-crimes suspects (Ratko Mladic and Goran Hadzic) to justice. Meanwhile, Kosovo exists in a sort of limbo – a state recognised by many but not by enough to become a United Nations member. This means, for example, that it can't join Uefa or Fifa, so a football player such as Manchester United's Adnan Januzaj, whose parents are ethnic Albanians from Kosovo, couldn't play for Kosovo in international competitions if he wanted to – except in friendly matches – as Kosovo isn't admitted (ironically, Januzaj could choose to play for either Serbia or Albania by dint of having Kosovan parents).

It could well be that the ethnic Serbs in Kosovo will eventually join Serbia as part of a final settlement that will see Belgrade recognising Kosovan independence. Whether Kosovo then seeks to be part of a larger Albania is not yet on the agenda but it might be at some stage. What seems most likely is that Serbia and Albania will both end up as members of the EU and the resulting economic interdependence between the two might well lead to the evolution of a more peaceful solution, whether that involves a sovereign Kosovan state or not.

The four Yugoslav civil wars of the 1990s became the subject of various judicial hearings into war crimes held under a specially constituted UN court, the International Criminal Tribunal for the former Yugoslavia (or ICTY). It met in the Dutch city of The Hague, the seat of the International Criminal Court, and was also known as the Hague War Crimes Tribunal. A string of guilty verdicts early on suggested the tribunal was sending out tough signals about what was acceptable in the theatre of war, but a run of not-guilty verdicts on technicalities in recent years has cast doubt on how strong the signals will prove in the long term. The tribunal was supposed to have concluded all its work by the end of 2014 but the late captures of Mladic and Hadzic mean it will probably not wrap up until 2016 or 2017.

The tribunal's most eye-catching conclusion was that some of the atrocities did constitute genocide. Genocide was defined in the 1948 Genocide Convention (UN General Assembly resolution 260) as an act 'committed with intent to destroy, in whole or in part, a national, ethnical, racial or religious group' but, until the Yugoslav war-crimes tribunal, no state had ever been found to be in breach of the convention. The ICTY found Serbia not guilty of direct involvement in genocide, but it did become the first country to be criticised for a breach of international law by failing to prevent the genocide committed in Srebrenica in 1995. The tribunal indicted 161 persons under the Genocide Convention and convicted 69 of them for genocide or lesser war crimes. But the most high-profile defendant, Slobodan Milosevic, escaped justice when he was found dead in his cell in 2006. The assumption has been that he took his life but no definitive cause of death has ever been proven. Whether suicide, sudden illness or murder, his death robbed the world of a verdict in a rare trial of a head of state for atrocities committed under his rule.

Throughout the period in which the tribunal did its work, Serbia and the other former Yugoslav nations rebuilt their badly damaged countries. In 2003 Serbia and Montenegro dropped the pretence of being Yugoslavia and called themselves 'Serbia & Montenegro' in a three-year deal that would culminate in a Montenegrin referendum on independence. In 2006 the Montenegrins narrowly voted for it, thereby ending the break-up of Yugoslavia that had started in 1991 and taken 15 bloody years. In that time, more than 140,000 people are believed to have lost their lives in the wars, based on estimates by international humanitarian agencies.

There's no doubt that Serbia emerged from the break-up of Yugoslavia with the lion's share of the blame. The belligerent figure of Slobodan Milosevic probably has a lot to do with that, and a 1994 UN report said Serbia was trying to create a Greater Serbia, rather than trying to restore Yugoslavia. The war-crimes tribunal also said the majority of the casualties were victims of Serbian aggression, and there are accounts that Serbs who argued for a tempering of Serbian nationalism were often harassed, hounded and even killed. Yet is it really fair to tag the Serbs as the only villains, even if statistics suggest they were the biggest culprits in the four wars? Croatia's nationalism too was always 'exclusive', there are plenty of tales of the Muslim community of Bosnia whipping itself into a frenzy, and while the Muslims and Croats did indeed suffer in Bosnia at the hands of Serb nationalists, in the 1941–45 civil war it had been largely the Serbs who had suffered at the hands of the brutal Croatian fascists, the Ustase, and, to a lesser extent, the Muslim Bosnians. It makes it understandable but still tragically unnecessary. It would be wrong to spend too much time in this book on the question of blame, yet it is fair to say that a view of the Yugoslav wars that says it was all down to Serbian aggression, and that the Croats, Bosnians and others were innocent victims, is oversimplistic in the extreme.

It's also important to remember that there were many in the old Yugoslavia who had no truck with the inter-nation belligerence. Symbolically, a march in Sarajevo in March 1992 united Bosnians, Serbs and Croats in opposing inter-ethnic conflict, but it ended when shots were fired from Serb positions, and Sarajevo's first fatality was a student demonstrating for peace in that march. Such voices for peace were seldom heard.

It's easy to see the Yugoslav civil wars of the 1990s as the build-up of inter-ethnic hatred over many decades but that isn't, on its own, a satisfying explanation. The ethnic and religious differences between most of the nations that made up Yugoslavia were, if anything, much less pronounced than the differences among some of the German-speaking states that made up Germany from 1871 and continue to make up the country today. Faced with joint threats in the 1920s and 1940s, the Yugoslav states were happy to come together, first as the Kingdom of Serbs, Croats and Slovenes, then as Yugoslavia under Tito, to fashion a state that defied international threats and did rather well out of both Moscow and Washington. But once Tito had gone and Moscow's influence was on the wane, there was no longer an external threat to hold the various states together. And perhaps the fact that they had been held together pretty much from 1918 to 1990 – largely by Tito's charisma and without the crimes of the civil war of 1941–45 being fully worked through – meant conditions were rife for resentments to grow to the point where they created a powder keg just waiting to be lit.

Arguably the biggest tragedy is that Serb nationalism grew to the point where anyone who was not Serbian was relegated to second-class citizenship and ethnic cleansing was considered (by some) a legitimate means of establishing the Serbian state. The idea that Serbia had an 'inclusive' ideology in the 1850s and 1920s, viewing Croats, Montenegrins and Macedonians as people who could live peacefully in the same country as Serbs, may be a little too benign as an interpretation of original Serb nationalism. The Nacertanije document of 1844, which acted as a blueprint for the establishment of a sovereign Greater Serbian state, talked of including Montenegro, Bosnia,

Herzegovina and northern Albania in the new Serbia, and there are those who believe Serbian nationalists came to see the 1918 kingdom as a construct that they could dominate and, therefore, as a vehicle for achieving Greater Serbia by the back door. But the fact that the Serbs worked moderately successfully with their five fellow Yugoslav states up to 1990, plus the closeness of Serbian language and culture to that of many of Serbia's neighbours, suggests that an entrenched 'them and us' attitude towards national identity is not helpful today. One hopes that Serbia's application to join the European Union means 'inclusiveness' is back, if only because Serbia's economic well-being depends on it.

So Serbia went into the 21st century restored as a sovereign state but needing to undertake a massive exercise in rehabilitation. What Germany, Italy and Japan had faced after the Second World War, South Africa after apartheid, and Argentina after its era of ruthless military junta, Serbia faced after its bloody emergence from Yugoslavia. In this context, if you had to draw up the ideal ambassador to represent the still-new Serbian state on the global stage, it would probably be a passionate Serb of mixed-nation parentage who both connects with his people and has the intellect and sensitivity to understand the reservations harboured by an international community still in shock from the images of Serbian brutality it saw on its television screens throughout the 1990s. How fortunate for Serbia to have just the man.

CHAPTER FIVE

TOUGHENED BY NATO'S BOMBS

I t's hard for a generation of people who have not known the hardship of war to hear the tales of those who went through it. Those born in Europe after 1945 will have had to listen to the stories of parents and grandparents telling them how they survived the fear and privations of the two world wars, the people they knew dying around them, the uncertainty of not knowing who would be next – stories often told with a subliminal admonishing message of 'You don't know how lucky you are'.

What distinguishes Novak Djokovic from Roger Federer, Rafael Nadal, Andy Murray and many of their contemporaries is that Djokovic does know. He was 11 when Nato planes started bombing Belgrade and he spent his 12th birthday with the bombing in full swing. It didn't stop him playing tennis, although each new day often meant a different court. But spending many of the 76 nights of the bombing in a cellar robbed him of sleep, as well as allowing him to share the collective fear of the whole city and, specifically, the people he and his brothers shared the cellar with. It's he who will be boring his children and grandchildren with tales of how he survived the war.

When the bombing began, the family was together in Belgrade after the winter season in Kopaonik. They spent much of the time in Grandfather Vlada's two-bedroom flat, not because it was a spacious place to be but because it had a basement storage area where the family could flee to whenever the sirens started.

In late 2011 Djokovic allowed a camera team from the American television company CBS to come with him and Vlada and visit the cellar where they spent many nights during the bombing, including every night of the first two weeks. Even today, the basement is stark, lightless concrete. Modern warfare meant that, when the siren went, they had to go straight down to the cellar – there was no time to prepare as there had been during the Second World War – and there was no limit on the number of people allowed into the cramped space. Watching him on camera in the cellar, it's clear he has retained the child's ability to be factual about it and not to impose on to his memory the feelings that come with adult awareness. It's just what happened, and if there's any emotion attached to it, it's the schoolboy's satisfaction of not having to go to school.

Djokovic was asked by the CBS interviewer Bob Simon whether he lost his focus. 'The first couple of weeks I did,' he replied. 'We were waking up every single night more or less at two or three in the morning for two and a half months because of the bombing. But I try to remember those days in a very bright, positive way. We didn't need to go to school and I played more tennis. It made us tougher, made us more hungry for success.'

His coach Jelena Gencic, who had lived through the German and British bombings of her country and had hoped never to experience another, tried to keep up his tennis education in spite of the carnage and chaos. Because she was a leading figure in the Serbian tennis world, she could turn up at courts and they would let her play, so she was constantly looking for safe courts. 'One morning I called him,' she said, 'and I said there's a military hospital across the road from the tennis courts, so I said they probably wouldn't bomb the hospital, especially as all around it had been bombed. They went for a different bombing target every night, so when a place was bombed, it seemed safe after that to practise there. One day I made a mistake: they bombed the area where we had just been playing. We changed clubs constantly. Once we thought of practising at a club on the other side of the Danube but we didn't because we thought the bridge might be bombed and we wouldn't get back. We were all very afraid and we had very little food, so we were hungry and Novak often had to practise without having eaten enough.'

Ana Ivanovic, a contemporary of Djokovic who had visited the Djokovic restaurant in Kopaonik when she was four (her father and Djokovic's uncle Goran were at school together), tells a similar story:

It was a very tough period, not only for us as kids but for our country in general. The 1990s were very hard anyway, the economy wasn't great and I remember the bombing starting on 24 March – it was actually my cousin's birthday, so she was very sad because she couldn't celebrate it as everyone was going into the shelters. For the first few weeks we didn't practise because we didn't know what to expect, so we'd stay at home, but later on, when the danger was not there, when the sirens were off, that's when we started practising. Most of the time it was six to eight in the morning, or maybe seven to nine. We'd try to live as normal as possible. I remember towards the end that they had an under-12s tournament and they even had a rule that, if the matches were on and the sirens came on, the match had to be finished but no new matches were called to start! I never played a match when the siren went off but I was there once when it went off.

Ivanovic also tells the story of her and Djokovic having fun at tournaments around that time. 'We shared lot of fun moments,' she says. 'We played lots of tournaments, under-10s, under-12s, in Serbia. We used to play hide and seek. You play two, three matches a day. In between you have nothing to do, so you play games.' Without ever having been an item, Djokovic and Ivanovic are very close – they are clearly very fond of each other and many who know them suggest Djokovic holds something of a candle for Ivanovic but not to an extent that has ever threatened his relationship with his fiancée Jelena Ristic. It may be more of the shared history of both Kapaonik and surviving the bombing that creates a 'bunker' solidarity and thus transcends any conventional idea of friendship, sexual or otherwise.

The Serbian coach and Davis Cup captain Bogdan Obradovic remembers that lunchtimes, rather than early mornings, were the safest time to practise during the bombing. He says he did most of his coaching between noon and 2 pm 'because nothing really happened then'. The time is almost immaterial – the fact is they were constantly adjusting their life and practice courts to keep clear of the best aircraft Nato had at its disposal.

The impression someone from western Europe could get from such tales is that there was a string of tennis clubs dotted around Belgrade, but that would be a slightly misleading picture. There were several courts but many of them were in a very modest state of repair. Tennis had never been particularly big in Yugoslavia and this was a time when the Serbian economy was in a particularly parlous state. Often, it was a case of making a court out of any available space. The most notorious example was the court at the Jedanaesti April club (the '11 April' club) where Ivanovic and Janko Tipsarevic played. The club had an Olympic-sized swimming pool but it was too expensive to maintain, especially when people weren't into swimming. So the pool was emptied, a carpet put in it and a singles court was marked out – there wasn't enough room for a doubles court. These days it's a pool again and it has proper courts where Tipsarevic runs his academy. But that illustrates the lack of facilities available to budding tennis players in Serbia throughout the 1990s.

In a rare interview, Dijana Djokovic told the *Guardian* newspaper in January 2008 that it was Djokovic's tennis routine that saw the family through the Nato bombing. 'All our family were here in Belgrade during the bombing and all day we were on court,' she said. 'And this is what saved us. It wasn't any more or less safe than any other place in the street, but if you're sitting at home in the basement, thinking they are going to bomb your home, you're going crazy. It's not good. We were practising all day and at seven o'clock we would go home and sit with the curtains closed, everything closed and dark the way it had to be.'

Ana Ivanovic echoes this philosophical approach to the threat:

We were underground for the first night and then my parents said, 'You know what? If it's going to hit, it's going to happen,' so we just stayed at ground level. We had a two-floor house, so we just took the back room and that's where we basically lived. Once we got into the bombing, people would say they had an idea of where would be bombed that day – they said it was targeted but we never really knew. A few times we heard really loud explosions and it's not the best feeling. For me, it wasn't about missing school, it was that everyone was together. As a kid, I never wanted to sleep on my own, so during the bombing we all slept in the same room, so for me, that was paradise – my parents and my brother, we all stayed in one room. We always had grandparents and other people coming over to stay, we were always hanging out, so I was never on my own, which was perfect. There was one very scary moment. We used to live across from this large post office and one night they came and said this would probably be bombed that night. This was 10 o'clock in the evening and we were ready for bed, so my parents said, 'Right, we're going to go to [your] grandparents,' who lived about 10 minutes away. So we took a car, we drove there and we had to pass by a really tall building, which was about 500 metres as the crow flies from where my grandparents lived and, literally 15 minutes later, there was a huge explosion – they'd bombed the tall building, the building we'd driven past 20 minutes earlier. That was the worst moment. As a kid, your parents tried to protect you a little bit. I remember one time sitting in the living room and a plane went through the sound barrier, and there was a very loud noise like an explosion. And I said to my dad, 'Oh my God, what was that?' and he said, 'Oh, nothing, a truck fell in a hole in the street.' These kind of things – they try to protect you and it's only later that you realise that was actually quite scary.

Djokovic himself has talked of that time as 'the period that nobody in our country likes to remember' but he goes further. 'It is a very powerful memory from my childhood that really shaped my character,' he says. 'It was a devastating and helpless time for my country; those three months of not knowing who and what is next, and you have nowhere to hide for real. Many innocent people died, a lot of infrastructure was destroyed and even now is still in ruins… It takes time for a country to recover after such a big destructive force. We were at first hiding at the basement thinking we would be safe there, but the reality is that even some people hiding in basements were dying when the bombs crashed, so there was no point. So, after those first few weeks of panic and disbelief, we went back to standard routines, even though the bombs were still falling all over. My family was at first all together, but then each of us went back to our duties. My parents went to Kopaonik to work, I went back on court to practise.'

Like Ivanovic's cousin, Djokovic was unable to do much celebrating when his 12th birthday arrived on 22 May 1999. 'I celebrated on court, like every other birthday,' he says with a smile, 'except that by then there were no more bombs flying over my head, only fireworks.'

During the 2013 US Open, Djokovic ventured a very strong opinion on whether the US government should support air strikes against Syria, whose government was suspected of using chemical weapons against its citizens. His vehement reaction (see page 249) stems directly from the lessons he learned from the Nato bombing of Belgrade. But when it was happening, when the 11-year-old boy was playing tennis by day and dodging the bombs by night, did he realise why it was happening? He is very clear about this. 'That is the first thing everybody asks when things go wrong, and something bad happens. Why me? Why us? I did ask and got a very simple answer: *Because they can*. And that was the truth. Now as a grown person, I can always give you a straight answer: there is no valid justification for any act of violence that for a consequence has the death of many people. What answer can justify the fact that many children died, many families were torn apart, many cities destroyed, many left sick? No war is good and thank God many people are now fighting against it.'

This is powerful stuff. His 'because they can' appears to strip bare the morality of the foreign policy of countries in the developed world. Although he doesn't use these words, his statement could be read as implying that there are all sorts of injustices in the world and no shortage of despotic regimes, yet the countries either side of the North Atlantic choose which of them to attack and which to leave well alone on the basis of feasibility. As a *cri de coeur* from the developing world, it is very resonant, whether one agrees with it or not.

The bombing clearly didn't help, but the 1990s were hardly a propitious time for budding tennis players in Serbia anyway. With war going on from 1991 to 1995 and then again 1998–99, and economic sanctions to boot, the Serbian economy was in no position to recover and, with Slobodan Milosevic's state-controlled economic policies still in place, there was little incentive or possibility for foreign firms to invest in Serbia. That meant it was very hard to finance a professional tennis career.

Dusan Vemic was born in 1976. He turned professional at 16, just as the wars were reaching their height, and he struggled to find both sponsorship and the help he needed. He says,

Companies didn't have money for sponsorship and we needed to get a visa for every country – we'd spend whole mornings standing in line for a visa, not knowing if we'd get it. We skipped one or two European championships because they were in Switzerland and we couldn't get a visa in time. The federation was extremely poor, so we had to do a lot ourselves. Fortunately, there were some satellite tournaments in Serbia and nearby, so we could play a few tournaments. We were fighting for our livelihoods so we appreciated any help we'd get from anyone but it wasn't much. In Serbia we had no great players except Bobo [Zivojinovic] and he was a businessman at that time so not able to do much for us. We didn't have enough coaching, we didn't do enough fitness work – I can't say whether that would have made a massive difference to our results but it would have helped us if we'd had proper coaching.

Vemic can thank tennis for taking him out of Belgrade during the bombing – he left the day before it started to play a handful of Challenger tournaments in the USA but it was hardly good for his peace of mind. 'As I arrived, I saw Belgrade on fire on the TV. It didn't exactly feel great. I tried calling home to my parents in Belgrade but I couldn't get through for a few days. I wouldn't wish that on anyone – not knowing what's going on [with] your loved ones back home. Somehow, I'm able to use sport as my escape from reality, I was able to be in the moment playing but it wasn't a nice experience, even if it gave me a bit more of a spark. I was probably luckier than many of my friends who were back home.'

It was against this background that Srdjan Djokovic was having to find money for Novak's tennis. Plenty of top-level athletes and artists have come from unlikely places but there was normally some money there. There was no obvious funding stream for Djokovic.

There are different views as to how much money the family actually had at its disposal. The Djokovics did have two restaurants that were doing reasonably well, which is enough to feed one line of thinking that questions the 'boy from modest surroundings' line. In fairness, Srdjan has never claimed the family were poor; he said they always had enough to live but that didn't leave much over for additional expenses like coaching and travelling to tournaments. Indeed, as the head of a family with three children, it would have been irresponsible if he had thrown everything into one child's potential career. And he had to be patient and beware the risk of teenage burnout. The tennis wayside is littered with the tales of children whose parents thought their playing ability was the key to untold riches that would benefit the entire family – many such children burned out, if only because they couldn't handle being the family's cash cow.

So when Srdjan tells the stories of having knives held to his throat and dealing with loan sharks charging massive rates of interest, it's very easy to believe him.

It also raises the question of whether the tennis careers of Marko and Djordje were sacrificed because finding the cash for one player was putting the family at full strain. In a rare television interview, Srdjan said of his second and third sons, 'I tried to discourage them but to no avail. Their own brother is the greatest idol to them. They don't have to look elsewhere. I am convinced they are going to be good tennis players. How good I don't know but they're trying hard and want to be like Novak.' Jelena Gencic backed this up, noting that 'Djordje was very good but Srdjan told me he didn't want to have two or even three tennis professionals playing in his house – for him, Novak was enough. He didn't stop me working with Marko and Djordje but he told me not to make them the best. I said it was probably too late anyway.' And Dejan Petrovic, who coached Djokovic for 10 months in 2004–5, says, 'Djordje has a lot of the same qualities as Nole' without ever having the full package his elder brother has. The general feeling among tennis observers is that Marko would never have made it as a touring professional but Djordje might have done. Gencic, Petrovic and others never believed Djordje was in Novak's league but then there are many players who could make a good living from tennis without ever coming close to that.

Gencic also made one observation that suggests that Djokovic was sensitive to the role money played in the family. She recalled that

When Novak started to be famous, Grandfather Vlada came to watch and Novak asked me if I'd seen him. I told him where he was and, when he found him, he asked his grandfather to lend him some money. Novak knew that Vlada didn't have much money and Novak did – he was in the world's top 20 by then – but Novak recognised that it was very important for both of them for him to ask to borrow money, to show what an important person his grandfather was. It was a matter of pride for his grandfather to be able to lend him some money. The next day Novak gave me the money to give back to his grandfather, which was always going to happen, but he'd given him the satisfaction of being able to offer him the sum. Novak was sensitive to that.

The issue of money never fully resolved itself until Djokovic was 16 and a deal was struck with a management company that brought a guaranteed income into the Djokovic coffers (see page 83).

The period from age 12 to 14 is the time when Jelena Gencic started to relinquish control of Djokovic, but it was a gradual process and it doesn't lend itself to a neat chronology. A feature of this time is that there are a number of people who worked to a greater or lesser extent with the young Djokovic, some overlapping. Most of them – understandably – claim their slice of the Djokovic cake. Perhaps this is heightened by the fact that the Djokovic family doesn't always rush to acknowledge the help they received from these coaches – sometimes all people want is recognition yet sometimes that recognition is very hard to give.

Gencic and others around Djokovic felt he needed a more competitive tennis environment if he was to continue his progress to the top. Gencic said,

In the morning he did his technical practice but in the afternoon I felt he needed a practice match over three sets, four afternoons a week. He was about 11 or 12 at this stage and I couldn't find players who wanted to play with him. I asked boys a couple of years older but, if they lost the first set, they said, 'I have to do my homework,' or some excuse because they didn't want to lose against this little boy. So I said he could play with older players with ratings and at the beginning it was good because everyone wanted to play with the little boy, the older ones didn't mind. But he then beat all the older ones too. So I said to Srdjan and Dijana, 'We must send him somewhere where he has sparring partners.'

The obvious place to go was America but Gencic urged them not to send him there. She recognised that he was a very family-orientated boy who couldn't be away from his mother and brothers for too long; that the closeness of the family was central to his personal security. At the time, Spain was emerging as the leading European country for tennis coaching, largely because in much of the country you can play outdoors for most of the year, and the Sanchez-Casal academy in Barcelona had created a worldwide reputation for itself (Andy Murray was later to spend two years there). But the wish was for somewhere even closer to home.

Gencic hit on the idea of Nikki Pilic, the controversial Yugoslav left-hander whose refusal to play a Davis Cup tie in 1973 because of a professional commitment had unleashed the furore that led to 81 male professionals boycotting Wimbledon that year. Just three years younger than Gencic, the two had played on the circuit together. He had later moved to Germany and had set up an academy in Munich, which specialised in players aged 13 and over who were looking to make the transition from junior tennis to the full pro tour.

'So I called him,' Gencic recalled, 'and said, "Niko, I have a very good young player. He's 12. Can I send him to you?" He said, "Oh no, Jelena, you know I'm not working with players that young." I said, "Please, only one week, just one. Have a look at him, and if you don't want to work with him, he'll come back to me and you can give me one or two suggestions as to how I can help him. But please remember, they don't have money. He will return your money for the camp because I'm sure he'll be the best one day." He sighed and said, "Oh, Jelena, Jelena – all right, send him."'

A week after Djokovic had arrived at Pilic's academy, he called Gencic and said, 'Jelena, why didn't you send this boy earlier to me?' Gencic said she answered, 'Oh, Niko, if I'd sent him earlier, you'd have said, "I've discovered and made this great champion!" and I didn't want that to happen.'

Pilic's version of that story is, perhaps not surprisingly, slightly different. He says of Gencic,

She had been asking me for some time but I told her we should wait a bit. So Novak didn't come to me until he was 12 years and 10 months. He came with his uncle Goran and I didn't think much at first. I saw that he had a little bit wrong with his game. He had wrong grips – he had an extreme western grip and his backhand grip was also extreme. He was moving OK, his coordination was OK, his serve was OK but nothing special and he didn't volley much. I had to show him what I wanted to see on the forehand and backhand and, for a guy with that coordination and such fine motor skills, and good eyes and good legs, he picked it up very quickly. We also played soccer and he was very good at that.

It would be easy to conclude from this account that Gencic's coaching was not all it was cracked up to be, that Djokovic was a talent when he went to Munich but very much a rough diamond in need of a lot of polishing. While broadly true, that would be a slightly unfair interpretation. The technique taught to youngsters aged 5–12 is frequently different in subtle ways to that taught when they have teenage growth spurts. In addition, Pilic admits that he's naturally cautious on first viewing: 'I'm not that impressed with anyone at the beginning,' he says. 'There are thousands of people who play great tennis but they don't make it because they don't have character, they don't have mental strength, they don't have the will to win. There are lots of components to really winning. But I think nobody could be that impressed [with Djokovic] because he didn't have great technique.' Is there, perhaps, also that universal element that makes it easy for any specialist to believe their first job is to undo the work of the last specialist?

Yet even the hard-to-impress Pilic realised after about four months that he had someone a bit special on his hands. Pilic's wife Mija is Serbian, so she often got Novak into conversation, especially in the early visits when Djokovic lived with the Pilics (only when he moved to Pilic's academy full-time did he live in separate accommodation). And it was as much in conversation as on the tennis court that Pilic realised that the boy had 'incredible focus'. Pilic says, 'He was very professional and always early for training. I remember arranging to hit with him at two o'clock and, 20 minutes before two, my wife saw him and asked him where he was going. He said he was going to warm up and she said, "That's very good," to which he replied, "I don't want to risk my career!" This at 13 years and two months.'

Djokovic paid several visits to Munich for the first couple of years, before basing himself permanently there. That meant he was coached by Pilic part of the time but also had coaches in Belgrade.

One of them was Bogdan Obradovic, who was based at the Partizan club in Belgrade when he wasn't travelling with Nenad Zimonjic. With Gencic also based at Partizan, Obradovic got to see Djokovic for the first time in 1997, when Djokovic was 10. 'He was so professional,' Obradovic recalls. 'You didn't need to say anything to him about preparing for tennis – he got there early, did his warming up, his running, a total professional at 10.' Obradovic liaised closely with Pilic, which gave a degree of continuity to Djokovic's tennis education, especially as Obradovic also recognised the need to make adjustments to the boy's technique.

Obradovic coached Djokovic to his first international title, the Under-14 European Individual Championships in San Remo. While there, Djokovic was interviewed by an Italian tennis magazine, which asked him who his coach was. He could have replied Jelena Gencic, as she was very much still on the scene, but he replied Bogdan Obradovic and later proudly showed Obradovic the article in which the quote was faithfully reported.

In April 2000, just as the Milosevic regime was on the wane, an industrialist Djordjo Antelj founded a tennis club about 500 metres from the Marakana football stadium called TK Gemax (sometimes written Gemaks). Gemax was a construction company that had built roads and buildings, and Antelj had become one of Serbia's richest men. He was also big into tennis, so founding a club was both a business proposition and a hobby. More than that, he offered financial support to all the Davis Cup and Fed Cup players with free winter court hire, and this extended to supporting all the Serbian players that were any good, or might be in the future.

Barely a year after establishing the club, Antelj identified three 14-year-old boys he wanted to sponsor: Branko Kusmanovic, Bojan Bozovic and Novak Djokovic. That same year (2001), Ladislav Kis, a Serbian-born player who had emigrated to Australia at 15, returned to Serbia as coach of the country's top woman player, Dragana Zaric. But as she was struggling for funding after failing to break the top 150 by the age of 24, Antelj approached Kis and asked if he wanted to coach the three boys. More importantly, he offered Djokovic a deal that effectively made Kis his coach. Bozovic had his own private coach (with whom Djokovic had been working informally) so, effectively, the Gemax club began funding Kis to coach Kusmanovic and Djokovic.

Kis says Djokovic approached him on their first session and said, 'You've just lived 10 years in Australia, right? I really want you to coach me in English.' When Kis asked why, given that Serbian was the mother tongue for both of them, Djokovic replied, 'Well, I'm going to need English when I'm No. 1, I'll have to do all my interviews and press conferences in English, so it's good if I practise my English now.' Even today, when Djokovic runs into Kis, he will greet his former coach with, 'G'day, mate!' out of affection for Kis's Australian twang.

'It's every coach's dream to work with a player like that,' says Kis.

He was such a good student. You could even tell him to do something wrong and he would do it so well that the wrong might turn into a right – he was that capable. And his confidence and self-belief were amazing; no matter what you asked him to do, he would do it. He was so focused. Once he had a shoulder problem and the physio asked him to put his finger in his belly button, just to open up the shoulder muscles. After about 10 minutes the physio started working on Novak's legs but Novak kept his finger in his belly button. Eventually, the physio asked him why his finger was still in his belly button, to which Novak replied that the physio had asked him to put it there and hadn't told him to take it out! Whatever I asked him, he did to perfection. I used the old 'suicide drills' to see how tough a kid is – you get a basket of balls and move him left and right, front and back, until he gives up. We'd need Srdjan at the back picking up balls and throwing them back into the basket because Novak would always go more than a hundred balls – this at the age of 14. As a coach, you need to monitor that his legs aren't collapsing because there's a risk of injury if you let them go on too long, but no, this kid just went on and on and on. After about 120 balls, he'd throw his racket aside and say, 'I'm done,' which was good because I was close to telling him to stop. That's what you see these days with his ability to run and run.

Kis was also taken by Djokovic as a person: 'He was fantastic, and he still is, even if these days he's torn between a million people who all want a piece of him. I was 24 at the time and I wasn't totally aware then that I had a future world No. 1 on my hands. I think I got the opportunity to work with him because I was a new face at Gemax, so I was lucky enough to get the honour of coaching him. He was a gift, he's a gift to any coach because, to be honest, he'd be this good whoever was coaching him.'

The story of how Kis's coaching relationship with Djokovic came to an end is told on pages 94–6 but the six months they spent together offered Djokovic a degree of stability when he was starting to make his way on the international junior circuit. When it ended in early 2002, Djokovic spent the rest of the winter playing at the Partizan club under the eye of Bogdan Obradovic, before moving to Munich full time.

Pilic noted the same massive willingness to learn that Gencic and Kis had picked up. Djokovic constantly asked Pilic questions about tennis, in particular about the top players Pilic had worked with – Boris Becker, Michael Stich, Goran Ivanisevic and others. In November 2000 Ivanisevic came to Munich in a terrible state – he had lost 13 first rounds that year and had ended his tournament schedule with the embarrassment of defaulting in a match in Brighton after running out of rackets in the final set against the Korean Hyung Taik Lee. Pilic told Ivanisevic he had a kid who would be 'at least top five' and told him to 'hit with this boy for a few minutes'. They hit for half an hour and Djokovic didn't hit one ball into the net. Pilic says Ivanisevic was hypnotised and Ivanisevic himself admits he was seriously impressed. 'I hit half an hour with him,' he says, 'and you could see he was talented, he had that something that he needs to be where he is now. You couldn't say if he was going to be one, five, 10, 15, but you could see his potential.'

Pilic's wider contacts in the tennis world meant others got to see the promising Serbian boy. One was Ivan Ljubicic, the cerebral Croatian player who worked with Pilic when Pilic became Croatia's Davis Cup captain. 'Nikki is unbelievable in reading the potential of players,' Ljubicic says, 'and he said he was definitely going to be top class. He was mentally ready for it from the beginning.'

It wasn't until July 2001 that Pilic began to be seriously impressed. Just two months after his 14th birthday, Djokovic won the 14 & Under singles and doubles titles at the European Junior Championships. That was when Pilic first got the sense that the lad Gencic had sent to him might be a world-beater. 'I could see he was already playing at a very high level – he needed to improve his serve and use his volleys more but from the back he was very strong. I used to hit with him myself, I knew how good he was from his reactions, from how he sees the ball, how he reacted to drop shots – you can see all those things. He was very coachable, a good worker and had in his head where he wanted to go. He was very professional in all respects.'

Djokovic was based at the Pilic academy for almost four years – two years part time, two years full time. Gencic's assessment that Novak should never be too far from his family meant he often returned to Belgrade, even if it put a further strain on the family's fragile finances. 'When Novak came back to Belgrade,' Gencic said, 'we'd work at Partizan, or he'd play some matches at Gemax and then, after three or four days, I'd ask him whether he felt able to go back to Belgrade and he'd generally say yes.' The trips back to Belgrade allowed him to catch up with his school friends, many of whom remain his friends today, as they offer him an escape from the tennis world.

One of his closest tennis friends during his early teens was Bojan Bozovic. 'We became best friends because we spent the whole time together,' says Bozovic from his home in Zurich, where he now runs a tennis academy but remains in regular contact with Djokovic. The two boys were not just friends but also doubles partners, winning the European doubles gold medal at under-14 and under-16 level. So what was Djokovic like as an early teenager? Bozovic says,

I could see that his only wish was to be No. 1 and he sacrificed everything for that goal. He didn't want to do anything else, only to be the best. You could see that he only had tennis on his mind. He had one goal and everything he did was directed at achieving that goal. I remember when he won the singles at the European Championships, we were given 10 days off afterwards but he was still going to bed at 9.30 or 10 o'clock. Everyone else went for a walk or went for an ice cream but Novak went to bed no later than 10 because he didn't want to lose the rhythm. At 14 he was practising six hours a day. He had no time for other stuff, although he did like football and skiing. He hasn't really changed from then to now; he's stayed the same. He always had great charisma. I don't care that he's No. 1. He's my friend and I have a lot of trust in him.

One figure who played a more prominent role in the rise of Serbian tennis than is widely appreciated is Nenad Zimonjic. These days, the studious-looking Zimonjic with his greying goatee beard is thought of largely as an ageing doubles specialist, but he is in some ways the quiet godfather of Serbia's tennis golden age. And his role in the Djokovic story began around this time.

Born in 1976, Zimonjic broke into the world's top 200 in singles at the end of 1998 and the top 100 in doubles a couple of months later. In 1999 he reached the third round of the Wimbledon singles.

Amid the dearth of Serbian talent in the post-Zivojinovic and post-break-up era, he was the shining light. Although a man of great, if softly spoken, self-confidence, he was never going to set the tennis world alight, but having been Yugoslav national champion at under-16 and under-18 level in singles, doubles and mixed, he was the leading player to emerge from Serbia in the 1990s and he, Dusan Vemic and Dejan Petrovic were the only Serbs playing regularly on the global pro tour. When the swimming pool at the '11 April' sports club that had fallen into disrepair was refurbished as a carpeted singles tennis court, Zimonjic played an exhibition match at the official opening (the court allowed Ana Ivanovic and Janko Tipsarevic to continue practising during the Belgrade bombing and to learn something about playing on hard courts, as almost all the courts in Belgrade at that time were clay – see pages 62–3).

How good Zimonjic might have been had he not had diplomatic obstacles put in his way is open to question, but in some ways his contribution to Djokovic comes from what he learned from the post-1999 privations. He says,

At first we had one of the best passports in Europe but then, when the war started, I had to practise somewhere else. I was in the US and I saw how Serbia was being presented in the media. All the media talked about us as being really bad and then I'd be on the phone to my parents and they would tell me a completely different side of the story. And then you'd listen to what they talk about on CNN or hear about your country, about your people, something you can't imagine. If you hear stories like this and you don't know Serbia, you would think, 'What kind of people are these Serbians?' At first, we couldn't compete, you couldn't travel – when we got to borders, officials looked at us as if we were some kind of terrorists. And then there was the 1999 bombing and your family is there –

that was really difficult. Sometimes I was there, sometimes I was outside but it wasn't pretty at all. People went through really tough times. I felt I learned a lot through my own experience – I made a lot of mistakes, I didn't have much support, but I learned a lot and I wanted to pass it on, so it wouldn't take others as long as it took me to learn about life on the tour.

Zimonjic became aware of the promising Novak Djokovic before he was a teenager. 'Srdjan used me a lot,' Zimonjic adds. 'He asked what I thought about the idea of Nole going to the Pilic Academy. I said I thought it was a great thing to do. Pilic was a great player, he coached a lot of guys. We didn't have the high-quality coaches, so you can only benefit. If you look at all our players, they all practised outside Serbia.'

Zimonjic began to see a great Serbian generation coming around 2000. In early 2001 Serbia had the world's top two juniors in Jelena Jankovic and Janko Tipsarevic, Djokovic had been spotted, as had Dejan Katic, who was the Orange Bowl under-12s champion in December 2000. And there were other promising juniors, such as Ilija Bozoljac, Viktor Troicki and Ana Ivanovic, all born between 1985 and 87, plus Boris Pashanski, a player already on the Futures circuit. Not all of them would make it, but if a handful did, Zimonjic could see it creating a golden era for Serbia.

In 2001 Zimonjic, by then a top-20 doubles player, invited Djokovic to practise with him at the Gemax club. He recalls,

We did two-on-one drills and I remember, even at 14, if he didn't have to move or run, he would never miss a ball. He was already consistent then. He was incredible. I knew he was going to be a very good player but I had no idea he was going to be this good, mentally so strong, and to have the career

79

he's had. He did some work there with Ladislav Kis, then at Partizan with Marco Nesic, then with Bogdan Obradovic, so with a variety of coaches. He was working with the same fitness coach I had, Zoran Grebovic, and they used the same physio I had. They were trying to see what I was doing as a top player, to watch someone who was very professional and to copy that. The next stage was to see what the best in the world were doing in singles and, since he was 15 or 16, he always had a physio travelling with him. He was with Milos [Jelasavcic], who was my physio as well. I got Milos into the Davis Cup team. All this shows you how professional Novak was. He thinks of all the small details and the prevention of small injuries. Although he is doing incredible things like sliding on hard courts, you see how flexible he is and how well his body is taken care of. He didn't miss much because of injury.

Zimonjic was in the driving seat when Tipsarevic made his debut in the Davis Cup at 15 in Tunisia. For two years (2003 and 2004), Zimonjic was the Serbian team's player/captain and gave either debuts or sparring opportunities to Djokovic, Bozoljac and Troicki. His ultimate reward came in December 2010 when Serbia won the Davis Cup. Zimonjic, by then 34, was very much the elder statesman in a team made up of the 23-year-old Djokovic, the 24-year-old Troicki and the 26-year-old Tipsarevic, and no doubt some saw him as just an elder brother brought in to stop the young pups from going overboard. But while Djokovic was the clear team leader and Troicki scored the winning point, Zimonjic had done much to lay the foundations for his country's greatest tennis achievement as a nation.

While Zimonjic gave Djokovic his first chance in Davis Cup, Pilic gave him his first chance in tournaments. Pilic revelled in the title of

'Master Coach' of the German tennis association DTB. That made him not only the head of a network of around 11,500 coaches but he had wildcards (entry to the draw for tournaments) to give out for tennis events on German soil. As Pilic had a Futures tournament in Oberschleissheim (the suburb of Munich where he had his academy) in the first week of January, he gave one to Djokovic in 2003. That allowed Djokovic to play his first match in a professional tournament. He lost to the German Alex Radulescu 7–5, 7–6 but that was not a bad start for a 15-year-old.

Pilic also had influence outside Germany and requested a wildcard for Djokovic to play in four Futures-level tournaments in Belgrade in June and July. In late June, when the cream of the tennis world was at Wimbledon and Roger Federer was preparing to win his first major title, Djokovic beat Cesar Ferrer-Victoria 6–4, 7–5 in the final of the tournament at the Red Star Belgrade club. It was his first professional title and it was a source of great pride to all those who had helped Djokovic that it should have come on Serbian soil.

Based on what today's juniors are put through, Djokovic played very few international tournaments in those days. His first one was the under-14s event in the French town of Tarbes known as 'Les Petits As' (the little aces) in February 2001, when he came up against a Scottish lad aged just a week older called Andrew Murray. Murray won the match 6–0, 7–6. These days, when asked what he remembers of the match, Djokovic says, 'Andy's curly hair and the fact that I was crushed.' Whether losing the second set on a tie-break is really a crushing is open to debate but Djokovic clearly felt it was. Despite that defeat, Djokovic ended 2001 at the top of the Tennis Europe Junior Tour's '14 & Under' rankings, one place ahead of Murray at No. 2.

He only played three junior Grand Slam tournaments and, while he had a trip to Florida in late 2002 for three tournaments culminating in the Orange Bowl, most of his events were in Europe, with a large number in Serbia and Germany for practical and financial reasons. He got a taste for representing his country in team-tennis events when he led Serbia & Montenegro to victory in the Copa del Sol, the 14 & Under European outdoor team event. And in 2003 he competed in the Junior Davis Cup in Germany. He won all his five matches as 'Yugoslavia' (in effect Serbia & Montenegro) finished fifth.

His three Grand Slam junior events were the French and US Opens in 2003 and the 2004 Australian. He reached the third round in Paris, lost in the first in New York and was a semi-finalist in Melbourne. A decade on, it's interesting to see who has made it from those who posted wins against the future world No. 1: his conqueror in Paris was Daniel Gimeno-Traver, in New York it was Robert Smeets and in Melbourne Josselin Ouanna. He also lost to Gael Monfils in the third round of a warm-up event in Melbourne. Gimeno-Traver, Smeets and Ouanna have all gone on to have modest careers with occasional moments in the limelight but none has got anywhere near Djokovic's achievements. It's a salutary lesson that a list of the world's most promising juniors is no guide to world ranking lists of the future.

The weekend that Djokovic reached the semis in Melbourne, Serbia won its first Grand Slam main-draw title as Serbia (even though, technically, it was still Serbia & Montenegro, the last two remaining Yugoslav republics – the acronym YUG had been replaced by SCG in 2003, as opposed to today's SRB for Serbia alone; any temptation to opt for S&M was resisted). Nenad Zimonjic partnered the Russian Elena Bovina to victory in the mixed doubles, beating the defending champions Leander Paes and 47-year-old Martina Navratilova 6–1, 7–6 in the final. Zimonjic had invited the 16-year-old Djokovic to sit in his box for the final and it was a natural extension for the player to invite the youngster to join the celebrations. At the party they held in a Melbourne nightclub, one of the revellers was Marat Safin, Djokovic's idol. A year later they were to be rubbing shoulders in Melbourne again but this time on the Rod Laver Arena in a match with great significance for both of them.

On 22 May 2004 Djokovic turned 17. He was ranked 515 in the world but, having just won back-to-back Futures and Challenger tournaments in Hungary, he was guaranteed to jump 177 places to 338 just a couple of days later. Impressive enough, but what had become of Gencic's prediction that he would be in the best five in the world on his 17th birthday? 'Maybe I got it wrong,' she said without much sheepishness, 'but he had two very important years when he should have been in international junior competition in Europe and the Americas but they hadn't got money to send him, so he didn't travel. It would have been when he was 14 or 15. So yes, he was a year late but I still believed he'd be the best. I explained to Novak and the family, "Don't worry, be patient, he'll be the best."' (Actually, by her prediction, he was three years late: Djokovic didn't break into the top five until 30 April 2007, but that was the time when a shift was taking place which meant the top players tended to mature later than had been the norm a decade or two before.)

One of the most significant milestones in Djokovic's career had come about six months before his 17th birthday.

Over the years when Srdjan had been seeking funding for his son's burgeoning career, he had become gradually more successful as Novak's results started to justify all the promise. A meeting with Amit Naor proved particularly fruitful. Naor was an Israeli agent who was ploughing an independent furrow in player management and representation, not an easy job in a market cornered for many years by three big players: IMG, Advantage International (now Octagon) and ProServ (later SFx, now Blue Entertainment). Naor was already working with Ivan Ljubicic, the thoughtful Croat whose star was in the ascendant in 2003–4 after several years of steady but unremarkable results, and was keen to recruit someone from the next generation.

The deal Naor did together with his business associate Allon Khakshourian and the German coach-cum-agent Dirk Hordoff effectively ended the family's financial worries. The negotiations were slightly comical, in that Srdjan had refused to learn any English, so Bogdan Obradovic had to interpret during discussions in an upmarket hotel. But the substance meant Djokovic and his family were provided for. The deal was reported to provide around €250,000 a year. The sum has never been confirmed and such figures have to be treated with caution, as they are normally a media construct based on maximum payments in an arrangement that pays more if certain performance targets are met. But whatever the exact figure, from then on, the player and his family were effectively in the clear.

In some ways, the deal should have come five years earlier – that was when the Djokovics needed the money, whereas by late 2003 Novak was on the point of starting to earn decent prize money. But the deal added to the sense of progress. For example, Djokovic got a wildcard into the ATP tournament in Bangkok in September 2004, an event where Khakshourian was the tournament director.

In 2008 Naor and Khakshourian entered an arrangement with the Hollywood talent agency CAA, which effectively took Djokovic to CAA. The agency was also keen to break the IMG/Octagon/SFx stranglehold, and Naor and Khakshourian recognised they had a better chance of succeeding as part of a bigger entity than on their own. Djokovic stayed with CAA until the end of 2012, when he switched to IMG, but the big deal for him was the first one done by Naor, Khakshourian and Hordoff.

After all, at that time there was no guarantee he would go on to post the body of work he has subsequently posted. In fact, if ever there was a time in Djokovic's career when he was in danger of drifting, it was just before and after his 17th birthday. He had left Pilic's academy and had worked with a number of coaches in Serbia, but it wasn't until September 2004 that he had his first touring coach.

Dejan Petrovic was an Australian of Serbian parentage who was born and grew up in Adelaide. He reached 116 in the doubles rankings but never cracked the top 150 in singles. However, having opted to play for Serbia, rather than Australia, he played three Davis Cup ties, profiting from the relative lack of Serbian players in the post-Yugoslav break-up era. He was, therefore, a largish fish in a smallish pond.

He had first met Djokovic at the Gemax club in Belgrade when Djokovic was 14 and being coached by Ladislav Kis, with whom Petrovic had played doubles in Australia. Another person based at Gemax was Milos Jelisavcic, the physiotherapist who worked with the Serbian Davis Cup team and later went on to travel with both Djokovic and Viktor Troicki. Jelasavcic knew Petrovic well and suggested he 'come and look at this kid and tell me what you think'. Petrovic says, 'What struck me was his will to win, and his self-belief was incredible. The first time we hit, he played a Futures at Red Star Belgrade and he won it. For him at that age, it was phenomenal. I never saw anyone have so much passion to win. He liked to joke off court but when he was on court, he was totally focused. And he had a willingness to learn – he's the best student I've come across, in all aspects.'

Petrovic was still on the tour, hopeful of advancing up both the singles and doubles rankings, so his meetings with Djokovic were sporadic. They practised together at the Partizan club and, at 16, Djokovic went to Adelaide for a week before the Australian junior tournaments that culminated in the Australian Open boys singles. 'We played a lot,' Petrovic recalls. 'He made semis of the Australian

Open juniors and then, during the year, he came back to Belgrade for a week or so before a Futures and Challenger in Hungary. He won them both, so Srdjan kept contacting me, asking if I would work with Novak. At that stage, I was still professional and playing Davis Cup for Serbia, so initially I said no.'

But Petrovic had long-term plans. He planned to settle in Serbia and open a tennis academy. At 26, he had a couple of injuries and was struggling to improve on his best singles ranking of 157, yet he had been one of the highest-ranked Serbs since Slobodan Zivojinovic. Even though tennis wasn't that popular, he felt his status as a Serb who had competed at all four Grand Slams could help him be successful. But suddenly the landscape was a little different – perhaps the best thing he could do for his post-playing career would be to invest in a player he felt could be an icon of Serbian tennis? True, the opportunity to do so had come a few years earlier than he'd hoped, but here was this 17-year-old who Petrovic believed was going to be 'the next big thing in Serbia' and, if he made it to the top, what better advertising for the hoped-for academy?

Petrovic therefore gave up his playing career to become Djokovic's first travelling coach. 'I had an agreement with Srdjan for three years and a contract for one,' he says. 'I was very aware that I was doing it for Novak, that I'd be very happy if I could one day see him in the big scene but I also knew that, to get tennis started in Serbia, we needed a superstar. Srdjan first approached me in May [2004] and I didn't really hesitate, although I guess it took me about three months to formally say yes to the offer. Coming from Adelaide, I'd known Lleyton Hewitt as a kid – Lleyton lived 500 metres from me, he was the youngster and I was the leader of the pack, and I saw a lot more in Novak than in Lleyton.'

The 10 months that Petrovic and Djokovic worked together saw a massive improvement in the player's fortunes. In statistical terms, he went from 272 in September 2004 to 94 by July 2005. More importantly, Petrovic helped Djokovic negotiate the often tricky passage from the 'Futures' tournaments (the lowest level of professional competition, though still with a very high level of play), first to the 'Challengers' (the intermediate level for players ranked between about 60 and 250) and then to the full tour, including Grand Slams. Petrovic had experienced that transition as a player, so he was one of the few Serbs who knew what it took.

Djokovic's progress in the first four months was considerable. He beat the former Australian Open runner-up Arnaud Clement in three sets in Bucharest for his first tour-level victory – Clement's best days were behind him but he was still ranked 67 to Djokovic's 272. He was hammered 6–1, 6–1 by Wesley Moodie in the first round of qualifying for another tour-level event, the Swiss Indoors in Basel, but a month later he qualified for the Aachen Challenger and won it. OK, so he didn't beat any big names of the time (he did beat Stanislas Wawrinka in the first round but Wawrinka was only 19) but he'd won eight matches in little more than a week and dropped just two sets. More importantly, he had broken into the world's top 200 before the end of the year. In addition, Petrovic used the fact that he himself still had a reasonable doubles ranking to get him and Djokovic into the doubles of the Helsinki Challenger – the coach-and-pupil pairing reached the semi-finals.

Mark Woodforde, the doubles legend who was later to work with Djokovic, tells an interesting story from January 2005. 'I was co-tournament director of the South Australian Open,' he says, referring to January's tour-level tournament in his home city of Adelaide.

Novak was working with Dejan. I knew Dejan pretty well and I remember him coming into the office and saying, 'Look, Mark, I've got this youngster who I'm practising with who's been here in Adelaide. Have you seen him?' He told me his name but it meant nothing to me. So he asked me if I'd be able to get him a wildcard into the main draw. I said to Dejan, 'Look, I can't give a foreigner a wildcard,' because my job was to use the wildcards to promote local interest and help young Australian talent. But he was very forthright and said, 'What about qualifying?' I said, 'Because I'm working for Tennis Australia running this tournament, I can't do that. You know how short we are on player opportunities.' But he persisted, saying, 'But this guy is going to be good.' This is a story you hear a lot as a tournament director, so I said, 'Yeah, that's great.' But Dejan said, 'No, you don't understand, he's *really* good.' And I said, 'OK. I'm sorry, it's definitely not going to happen in the main draw. As for qualifying, if there's no one that comes because there are other tournaments going on, it's a possibility, but it's a long shot.' So he asked me how he could get Novak a wildcard into other tournaments. I told him he was following the right path by coming to me and asking me directly because there aren't too many people who would go up and boldly predict that their player is going to be that good. So I suggested he call Colin Stubs [the former Australian Open tournament director who was in charge of the pre-Australian Open exhibition tournament at Melbourne's Kooyong Club] and call the other tournament directors, because if they don't know that he's after the wildcard, word of mouth isn't going to happen. But still he persisted: 'But Marco, I was really hoping you might be able to help here because of the Adelaide connection.' Nole was just around the corner, so he introduced me and I shook hands with this youngster. That was the first time I met him and it meant I had Dejan's words in the back of my mind when Novak asked me to do some work with him just over two years later.

As it happened, Petrovic's persistence paid off. Djokovic did get a wildcard into the Adelaide qualifying tournament, and while he lost to Brian Baker in straight sets, the experience served him well for his next qualifying tournament, the Australian Open. After beating Francesco Piccari and Stanislas Wawrinka, he came up in the final round of qualifying against Wesley Moodie, the South African who had crushed him in Basel just 10 weeks earlier. This time Djokovic was ready and, on a 6–4 final set, he reached the main draw of a Grand Slam tournament for the first time.

And who should he be drawn against but the man who had been celebrating with him in Nenad Zimonjic's entourage a year earlier, his idol Marat Safin. It's easy to dismiss Safin as the tennis circuit's wild child, and for much of his career he was. But approaching his 27th birthday, Safin had begun to realise that, if he was going to add to his sole major title (the 2000 US Open) before hanging up his racket and going into politics, he needed to get a move on. He had teamed up with Roger Federer's former coach Peter Lundren during 2004 and had very nearly beaten Federer in the semi-finals of the Tennis Masters Cup in Houston, losing on a memorable 20–18 tie-break. So he was up for doing something big at the 2005 Australian Open and Djokovic was a bit like a hedgehog caught in the path of an oncoming juggernaut. Djokovic won just three games but he'd been given star billing on the first night session of the centenary Australian Open on the Rod Laver Arena. It was a landmark match for both men – Djokovic's first main draw at a major, Safin's first step towards his first and only Australian Open title.

There's a saying in tennis – and in various forms in all walks of life – that you learn more from defeats than from victories, and Djokovic suffered a much more painful defeat two months later. Playing for the first time in Euro-African Zone 1 of the Davis Cup, Serbia's experienced player/captain Nenad Zimonjic said he couldn't do both duties, so he remained a doubles player and was replaced by Petrovic as Serbia's Davis Cup captain. Their first match was a comfortable 5–0 win over Zimbabwe in Novi Sad, but then in April came the match in Belgrade that would have seen Serbia into the playoff round for the 2006 World Group. Belgium were the visitors and it was no embarrassment for Djokovic to lose to the 33rd-ranked Olivier Rochus on the first day. But with Janko Tipsarevic having come back from two sets down to beat Rochus in five to level the tie at 2–2, Djokovic, by now ranked 142, faced Belgium's Kristof Vliegen, a man ranked just 38 places higher, in the live fifth rubber. Vliegen won it in four sets, having never looked in danger, and Serbia were left with another year in the second tier of the team competition (two, as it turned out).

Despite winning the Challenger tournament in San Remo in May – the scene of his 14 & Under European Junior Championships triumphs – Djokovic's ranking was still not high enough for him to get automatic entry into the main draw of the French Open and Wimbledon (a player's ranking needs to be 104 to be guaranteed entry into the main draw of a Slam but 110 will normally suffice given a few injuries to higher-ranked players), so he had to go into the qualifying tournaments. In Paris, qualifying took place in the week of his 18th birthday, on 22 May 2005. And as with the Australian Open, he came through his three rounds comfortably.

Knowing his birthday would clash with French Open qualifying, Djokovic rescheduled his party, which took place at the Calling Club in Belgrade. It was a big party and one which showed that Serbia's business community had started to get wise to his potential. He got a car from a sponsor, albeit one he had to return a couple of months later, and one of Serbia's leading movie actors, Sergej Trifunovic, was present to sing a song he had composed about Djokovic beating Roger Federer and Rafael Nadal, the lyrics indicating that the time would come when he would beat these guys.

It was not to come at the 2005 French Open or Wimbledon. At

Roland Garros, Robby Ginepri became the first man to lose to Djokovic in a Grand Slam main draw, before Djokovic retired at one set all in his second-round match against the previous year's runner-up Guillermo Coria. At Wimbledon, Djokovic beat Brian Baker, Jimmy Wang and Wesley Moodie to qualify for the main draw and then beat Juan Monaco and Guillermo Garcia-Lopez (the latter from two sets down) before losing to Sebastien Grosjean in the third round.

The story of how Petrovic's time with Djokovic ended is told on page 102. It is arguable that Djokovic would have made more progress between 18 and 20 if he'd stayed with Petrovic than he actually did – he talked at the time about a 'golden team' of himself, Petrovic and the physio Milos Jelisavcic. But given that Djokovic was a Grand Slam champion by the end of January 2008 and was the all-conquering world No. 1 in 2011, it's hard to make a case that the decision to part company was wrong. True, he seemed to stagnate, certainly in ranking terms, during the subsequent eight months working with Riccardo Piatti and Ivan Ljubicic, but in retrospect it's clear he was learning things from the Italian coach and Croatian player that were to help him in the long run.

Petrovic remains endearingly relaxed about his stint coaching Djokovic. 'That 10 months was a great time,' he says.

We have a great relationship, Novak is like a son to me. Yes, it was nice playing Davis Cup and it was a wrench to give up that part of my playing career, but to have had that 10 months working with him – I don't regret it at all. He appreciates it and that's the most important thing for me – I don't need any financial reward, I'm just happy with the fulfilment of being a piece of the puzzle at a crucial period of his playing career and in helping him move up to the top 100 so quickly. Players like Becker, Federer, Nadal and Novak – they're one in a million, not really from this planet, so I feel blessed to have been able to work with one of them.

So was Djokovic's time with Petrovic the last chapter of his childhood or the first chapter of his professional career? It's hard to say and ultimately it doesn't matter. Djokovic had a path dotted with stepping stones and Petrovic clearly escorted him to a very important place. But it's possible to argue that the laid-back Petrovic could only have taken Djokovic so far and that, eventually, he would have needed a stricter and more focused team. By qualifying for the Australian Open, qualifying and winning a round at the French Open, and qualifying and winning two rounds at Wimbledon, Djokovic had laid the launch pad for the explosion in his career that was to start within a year.

CHAPTER SIX

FATHERS
AND SONS

The period in Djokovic's development from about 2001to 2010
– from the ages of 14 to 23 – features a recurring theme. Or
perhaps that should be a recurring sore because it adds an
unsavoury element to the Djokovic story but one without which the
story cannot be properly told. The theme is the role played by his
father, Srdjan. It is a difficult topic on which to remain scrupulously
fair but which is ultimately understandable in context. All the
elements of a turbulent Russian novel are there – pride, family
loyalty, hate and a lust for revenge.

Srdjan Djokovic was always going to do his best for his eldest
son, but it would have been a lot easier for him if that son's gift was
in football or skiing. Because he knew nothing about tennis, he was
to a certain extent out of his depth. Yet faced with wise counsels
telling him he had not only a very gifted tennis-playing child but
potentially a world-beater, he set about trying to do what was
necessary to fund Novak's rise. Ultimately, he succeeded but, having

gone through a number of harsh learning experiences along the way, his abrasiveness left its mark on many of those who were crucial to Djokovic's rise. If Srdjan had been blessed with his eldest son's benevolent temper and willingness to see the good sides of people, he would probably have had an easier ride. But the combination of an indifferent – sometimes hostile – environment and the insecurities of his own temperament meant that, at several stages in the Novak Djokovic story, his father was the villain in the background, and sometimes the villain in the foreground.

There are many who witnessed Srdjan's stormy *modus operandi*. Some are more willing to speak about it than others. Many say he was right, or mostly right, but in the wrong way. All speak more in sorrow than in anger. None seems to take any satisfaction from the volatile father of Serbia's favourite son, and many are willing to recognise an element of bravery in his single-minded pursuit of his son's career. As one victim of Srdjan's tempestuous reactions put it, 'He stuck his head where most people wouldn't put their feet, all in the best interests of his son.'

The case for the defence comes later but it's worth outlining some of the episodes that led to Srdjan Djokovic becoming such a divisive figure.

One of the first people to be aware of Srdjan's impetuosity was Ladislav Kis. Kis was Djokovic's coach at the Gemax club in Belgrade under an arrangement funded by Gemax's founder and owner, the industrialist Djordjo Antelj. What exactly the arrangement entailed is not known as it was a private agreement, but it appears to have been a generous one by any standards, especially by the standards of Serbia's precarious economy just two years after the Nato bombing. It is thought to have involved Djokovic getting three meals a day in the club's restaurant, massage, all his coaching, plus trips to tournaments with Kis and one accompanying parent – all paid for. Kis was contracted to coach

Djokovic and another promising junior of the same age, Branko Kusmanovic. Kis recalls,

I was being crucified. I was on court in the morning for two hours with Novak and then two hours with Branko, and then in the afternoon it was another two hours with Novak and two hours with Branko. I was starting to get seriously tired – these boys could play, it wasn't like doing basket drills all day long. So I asked to adjust the daily schedule so Novak could hit with Branko. Novak was the better player but it wasn't like Branko couldn't train with him – whenever they did play a training set, it was always close, even if Novak won five out of six on average. So the schedule was changed to put them together three days a week for two hours in the afternoon. But Srdjan didn't like it: he said his boy wasn't playing with a kid that's weaker than him. I said this is an arrangement that everyone has approved and it's better having me fresh for all the lessons, but he just threw the piece of paper on which the agreement was set out back at me. When you think about it, it's nonsense! Who does Novak practise with now he's No. 2 in the world – with Rafa? No, you don't need always to have better people to practise with. Branko was good for him and Novak didn't mind, but Srdjan wasn't having his son practising with weaker players, and Novak had no word in it.

According to Kis, Srdjan then went to Antelj and asked for Jelena Gencic to be allowed to accompany the Djokovic team on his next trip. Antelj said it was out of the question – he was paying a lot of money for one coach (Kis) and one accompanying parent, so he wasn't going to fund a second coach, especially one who had coached Novak before he was 12. Srdjan is reported to have stood his ground, whereupon Antelj threw him out, apparently with a letter saying all the Djokovic family were banned from Gemax except Novak. 'Novak was crying his eyes out when he left that day,' says Kis, 'because we really did work well together. But that was the end of the working relationship.'

Another person to get a tongue-lashing from Srdjan around the same time was Vojin Velickovic. Velickovic is the tennis correspondent for *Sportski Zurnal*, Serbia's national sports daily newspaper (similar to the French daily *L'Equipe*), and he attended a junior tournament in 2001 because there were two promising Serbian boys, Dejan Katic and Djokovic. Katic had won the Orange Bowl under-12s competition the previous December (the Orange Bowl is the most prestigious junior tournament outside the four Grand Slam junior events and the culmination of the junior year), so was ahead of Djokovic at that stage. 'Because Katic had won the Orange Bowl and Novak hadn't won anything, I put Katic in the headline,' says Velickovic. 'When he saw it, Srdjan called me. He was furious because he thought his son was always to be No. 1 in everything. He was very angry about that – that was my first contact with him.' For the record, Katic never made it into the big time – he broke into the world's top 600 but never graduated beyond the 'Futures' satellite circuit.

Something similar happened at the 2004 Australian Open. Djokovic had done very well to reach the semi-finals of the boys' singles but the mixed doubles was won by Nenad Zimonjic, partnering the Russian Elena Bovina. 'OK, so it was just the mixed,' Velickovic recalls, 'but it was the first Grand Slam title of this generation and Novak had only reached the semi-finals of the boys singles, so we could easily have put Zimonjic on the cover. But we decided to put them both on the front page. The editor of my newspaper then got a call from Srdjan. He was furious because his son was given equal status as someone who had won the mixed – "What is the mixed?!" he was saying. With him, there's always something happening.'

Another member of the Serbian media to meet Djokovic at the age of 12 was Nebojsa Viskovic. A regular commentator for the state-funded national television service RTS, Viskovic saw the potential of Djkovic and wanted to do all he could to help. At one stage he tried to use his work for a government project to leverage $100,000 for Djokovic. It came to nothing as the letter he wrote was ignored, but he tried. He also took Djokovic's middle brother Marko on some trips to Geneva when working for RTS. Viskovic says,

I was working on a TV magazine programme and I did a number of features with Novak. I felt he could be a great player, he had a good position in the junior rankings, and I just sensed it. People I spoke to who were experts said, 'There is something about him that could be very special – he has great potential.' There were no tournaments in Serbia, so he had to travel a lot within Europe, so I didn't have much chance to watch him playing. But everyone whose opinion was valued was saying good things about him. We had had no quality players since Bobo Zivojinovic, so I felt it would be a good investment to get to know Novak while he was still a young junior. He told me I was the best in the business and he valued my opinion, which was nice for me – I suppose he'd heard me on TV.

Viskovic certainly felt he had a good relationship with both Djokovic's parents, but he was to learn that, the moment Srdjan felt someone had been the slightest bit critical of his son, he or she became *persona non grata* and all previous help was forgotten.

The first public sign of conflict came when Serbia travelled to Geneva in September 2006 to play Switzerland in a Davis Cup playoff round tie. A month before, Srdjan had made comments in the Serbian media denigrating Roger Federer (whether that added to Federer's venom in his final press conference that weekend is not clear – see page 166). Srdjan then told Viskovic that he wanted him to cheer for Djokovic like a supporter when commentating. 'He wanted me to just ignore the opponent's good moves, or to be silent,' recalls Viskovic. 'Basically, he wanted me to be a fan, which is totally different from my point of view of what a commentator has to do. A commentator has to be objective. Of course, when a Serbian player is on court you do move the boundary a little because I want him to win and my viewers do, but you still have to be objective.'

Viskovic's refusal to change his commentary style meant further clashes were always likely, and the next flashpoint came during the semi-finals of the 2008 Hamburg Masters when Djokovic – by now Australian Open champion – faced Rafael Nadal.

Viskovic was commentating on his own from RTS's studios in Belgrade. The first set was keenly fought, Nadal eventually taking it 7–5. As Viskovic signed off for the two-minute end-of-set break, Srdjan stormed into the commentary booth, screaming at the security guards, 'I'm the father of Novak Djokovic!' Viskovic recalls, 'He marched in, he told me it was a disgrace that I'm a Serbian commentator and that I'm obsessed with Nadal, or something like that. I just told him to walk away, or something similar. The microphone was off – he was sufficiently sensitive to know he couldn't do it when the microphone was live – but it was very aggressive and I found it was really hard to concentrate after that. I was really upset and, as I happened to have some sedative pills in my bag, I took one.'

The following Monday, Viskovic got hold of Alexander Tijanic, the editor-in-chief at RTS, and said he wanted him to listen to the recording and judge what had happened. 'I wanted protection,' Viskovic says, 'but I didn't get it. The editor told me he would handle it in his own way, which meant doing nothing to offend Srdjan.'

Viskovic obviously felt he was on moderately safe ground, for he ignored Tijanic's request to say nothing to the media. The media got to hear about Srdjan's invasion of the commentary box and it became a big story. A Facebook group entitled 'Support for Nebojsa Viskovic' was set up and, for a few days, it reached 10,000 followers. Whether that protected Viskovic's position within RTS is hard to tell – it must have been tempting for Tijanic and co to fire a commentator who was increasingly at loggerheads with the father of the country's emerging sporting hero. But Viskovic was being portrayed as the good guy in the media, and the station's failure to protect him was looking somewhat shabby.

Not that it made much difference in the long run. Nine months later, the inaugural Serbian Open took place at the 'Novak' club in Belgrade. It was a low-ranking ATP tour-level tournament built on the back of Djokovic's success. Srdjan, who was a leading light in the tournament organisation, asked RTS to exclude Viskovic from the RTS commentary team at the tournament – it was not just a request for Viskovic to be banned from commentating on Djokovic's matches, but any match. Srdjan backed up his request with a threat that he would give the TV rights to another broadcaster if Viskovic was allowed to commentate. The RTS editor conceded, whereupon Viskovic quit. Viskovic says RTS, probably fearing a media backlash, offered him more money, but he said no, saying there would only be more problems in the future.

One could argue that the tactic backfired on Srdjan. Viskovic had been doing a bit of moonlighting for an emerging independent sports station, *Sport Klub*, which had started in 2006 and was looking to expand its rights portfolio. So *Sport Klub* snapped up Viskovic as one of its leading tennis commentators.

Interestingly, Viskovic says Srdjan tried to put pressure on the editor of *Sport Klub* not to give Viskovic Djokovic's matches, but counter-intuitive as it may seem, it was the private station that stood up to Srdjan in a way the state-funded broadcaster hadn't. The result has been that Viskovic now commentates more matches than when he was with RTS, and far more of Djokovic's. *Sport Klub* has the rights to show 54 ATP tournaments a year, including all the Masters-1000 Series and the ATP World Tour Finals, so Viskovic commentates on almost every match Djokovic plays outside the four Grand Slam tournaments (Wimbledon is the only major for which *Sport Klub* has rights).

There was one final skirmish between Srdjan and Viskovic. In April 2010 the Serbian Tennis Federation asked Viskovic to be master of ceremonies for the Fed Cup home tie between Serbia and the Slovak Republic. When Srdjan found out, he told the federation that this was not possible. Given the dependence of the federation on Djokovic's willingness to play Davis Cup (and Serbia had not won the cup at that point), it was hardly surprising that Viskovic was stood down. He was given his agreed fee but told he could not work as MC. The story again got into the media, with one newspaper, *Kurir*, running a double-picture on its front page with Viskovic as the good guy and Srdjan the bad guy. Djokovic clearly saw it, but Serbia's Davis Cup captain Bogdan Obradovic, who was both a former coach of Djokovic and a good friend of Viskovic, explained exactly how the problem had come about and that Srdjan was largely the cause of it.

Since 2009–10, Srdjan and Viskovic have acted as if the other doesn't exist. 'Voja Velickovic doesn't speak with Srdjan,' Viskovic says. 'Every journalist in Serbia has a problem with Srdjan, I just had the biggest problem.'

Yet it wasn't just coaches and members of the media who Srdjan fell out with. In April 2004, three months after Djokovic had reached the Australian Open boys' semi-finals, the Serbian Davis Cup player-captain Nenad Zimonjic picked the still-17-year-old to be the fourth member of his Davis Cup team for the tie against Latvia. The tie was played on a fast indoor carpet at the Gemax club in Belgrade. Zimonjic was still playing singles and had won a

Challenger-level tournament a few weeks before, he had the young Janko Tipsarevic for second singles, who by then was inside the world's top 200, and he had Dejan Petrovic, who had been top 150 in doubles. So he didn't need Djokovic, but having had him as a hitting partner for a couple of Davis Cup weekends, Zimonjic named him in the team for experience.

Djokovic fully expected to play and was very disappointed when he didn't. 'It was amazing,' Zimonjic recalls. 'He thought he was going to play on the first day. I remember him telling me he was so disappointed he couldn't play. I said, "Listen, you'll get the chance to play but you have to start gradually. It's a lot of pressure in Davis Cup, you're still young, there's plenty of time for you, even when you play a dead rubber it's going to be tough for you to handle this." He was talking about, "When am I going to have a chance to play, what do I have to do to earn a chance to play?" He was never afraid of the challenge. I've never seen him afraid of anybody, or of having this responsibility, whoever it was. That was incredible, even then.' Djokovic accepted the decision and was ultimately happy to make his Davis Cup debut in a dead rubber against Janis Skroderis, a match he won 6–2, 6–2 to see Serbia to a 5–0 win.

Less accepting of the decision was Srdjan. 'He thought it was my biggest mistake that I didn't play Novak on the first day,' says Zimonjic. 'He didn't approve and from that point on we didn't talk at all. The next time we really said hello was over a year later, when Novak invited me to his 18th birthday party and his parents were welcoming the guests. Novak asked me six or seven times, "Please come." That was the first time I said hello to Srdjan after that Davis Cup tie. Once Novak turned 18, it was a lot easier to deal with him because I could do most things directly and not through Srdjan – I have respect for Srdjan and he has respect for me but I don't really communicate that much with him.'

Dejan Petrovic tells a similar story. He was Djokovic's coach from late summer 2004 to just after Wimbledon 2005. He was brought in to see Djokovic through the Futures and Challenger tournaments and into the realm of tour-level and Grand Slam draws. During the 10 months they worked together, Djokovic moved from 272 to 94 in the rankings, at that time the highest-rising player on the ATP circuit.

'No one quite knows why it ended and there's no satisfactory explanation,' Petrovic says. 'Srdjan plays a huge part in the story. He always was the boss. Huge credit goes to him, whether you like him or not. He always tried to give Nole everything, the best that he possibly could. Nole knows that. Srdjan shares Nole's hunger for victory but Srdjan is a very hard man. The downfall for him is that he burns bridges. During the time you're with him, you can't really complain that much. He's a nice man to have a beer with. If he likes you, it's fine, but if he doesn't like you, well, he doesn't like you and there's nothing you can do about it. I think he regrets a lot of those things.'

Petrovic says he had a verbal agreement to work with Djokovic for three years, and a contract for one year, yet never received any compensation for his employment being terminated early. Not that it seems to worry him – he has the non-confrontational laid-backness of the Australian more than the wounded pride of the Serb and is happy to have been a helping hand on Djokovic's route to the top. Although he gave up his playing career to coach Djokovic, his long-term aim was always to set up an academy in Serbia, and he has one now in Kragujevac, about 130 kilometres south of Belgrade. Djokovic's presence at the top of the world rankings is the biggest boost to Petrovic's welfare that he could want, and he also coached the next rising Serb, Nikola Milojevic, for a while, so he has a hand in two players who could enhance the standing of tennis in Serbia.

But Petrovic only hints at the language used by Srdjan when Djokovic Sr fired him:

> My culture is never to hate anyone and, in that sense, I don't really understand the way Srdjan finished with me. It wasn't very nice; the words he used were not acceptable for somebody who stopped their career and basically gave their heart to his son. It wasn't an appropriate way to finish. He fired me but there was no need to do it like that. My culture, coming from Australia, was always to do things in a nice, diplomatic way and I was never an aggressive person, so to this day I don't understand his philosophy. But I understand that's how he ends all relationships. Srdjan has his own philosophy and he's got a short fuse. If he had a bigger fuse, if he had time to think about it, he wouldn't say some of the things he does. But he gets fired up. And he never apologises. Apologising isn't in his system. I understand that if someone speaks badly about his son, he would automatically be in conflict. But when someone means the best for his son and would almost do anything for his son – that I didn't understand and, to this day, I don't understand his philosophy in that regard. It's something Novak has changed because Srdjan was ruining his reputation.

Djokovic has, indeed, become more the boss since becoming an adult but he has done so slowly and subtly. And the way Petrovic's time with him came to an end illustrates that he was never going to go against his father until he could stand on his own feet. Petrovic says,

> We were in this house for the [Wimbledon] qualifying tournament and, when he qualified, I said, 'OK, it's time for a beer to celebrate qualifying for Wimbledon.' So he had a very

rare beer to celebrate. That's when I announced that this would be the last tournament we'd be working together. I'd had a meeting with Srdjan after Roland Garros and knew that Wimbledon would be the last one ... We both had tears in our eyes and we hugged each other. I said, 'Let's make sure we finish on a high.' And he got to the third round that year, so we did go out on a high. Srdjan was the boss, so Nole couldn't make the decisions. He knew how much the family had made sacrifices for him, so there was no question of him saying, 'No, I don't want to switch from Petrovic to Piatti.'

So was Srdjan a monster? Almost certainly not, even if he did often behave in a way that left people feeling he was pretty monstrous.

Srdjan himself has never given an interview in English and he rarely gives interviews in Serbian. But he did agree to an hour-long interview with Serbia's B92 television station two months after Serbia had won the Davis Cup in December 2010. Disaffected with the leadership of Djordjo Antelj and Slobodan Zivojinovic in the Serbian Tennis Federation, Srdjan was part of a coup to oust the industrialist and the former Wimbledon semi-finalist. Most of the interview is about the federation and the coup, but in the last few minutes he talks about himself and the role he played in doing his best for his eldest son:

I don't think I'm arrogant. I don't think I'm unpleasant. I only say what I think is right and just. I say what I mean. We as a family have nothing to be ashamed of. And I as head of this family have nothing to be ashamed of. Nothing to cover up. If something hurts me, I talk about it. I expect people to accept what I say in a right way. And believe me, ordinary folk in cities across Serbia not only accept it in a right way but accept it with enthusiasm because I say what I mean. I don't hide behind the fancy statements of some marketing agency. They know very well how difficult our life as a family has been for the last 17 years. We lived in rented apartments, we had to borrow money since we didn't have enough ourselves, even though we had reasonable income for the times. Novak's expenses for his career were more than we could afford. We borrowed money from loan sharks at 10, 12, 15 per cent monthly interest rates. And we struggled to repay these loans – it was bloody hard. It even happened on numerous occasions that we didn't have money to buy our daily bread. And then we sold all the gold jewellery that my wife and I owned. And then we slept on a sofa bed in a living room of one of those rented apartments for 10 years. We couldn't afford a new mattress; instead we used old blankets to cover the springs which were poking into our chest and back.

Asked whether it was all worth it, he said, 'Of course, but without any help from anybody. Not the country, or the city officials, or the tennis association.'

Some context is needed here. Serbia in the early 2000s was a country recovering from a bloody civil war and the loss of its pre-eminent position in a country where it was the most influential of six federated states. Needless to say, not every business transaction that took place in Serbia was entirely clean, much business was conducted under the table, and many people in Serbia who did well at that time would not welcome too much scrutiny of their business affairs. It was in this environment that Srdjan saw it as his job to finance the launch pad for his son's career. He sold his Belgrade restaurant around this time to free up cash for Novak to fund his travelling as a junior, and he eventually got rid of the pizzeria in Kopaonik, albeit in a long lawsuit involving complications over the fact that he had used the premises rent-free for many years. No suggestion of impropriety is made here, but some understanding is needed of the difficult economic climate in which he was operating, one in which it would probably be unfair to condemn those who sought merely to find a level playing field.

The problem is that Srdjan's abrasiveness not only created enemies but means he is sometimes judged by reputation. He has told the story of having gone to a government official to ask for money and been turned away empty-handed. But there is a version of that story that suggests Srdjan was the architect of his own undoing. According to this version, the official concerned had a habit of recording all conversations. Srdjan had gone in with a couple of friends and, at one stage in the interview, the official had left the room, ostensibly to check something but in reality to listen in to the conversation being held in his absence between Srdjan and his friends. As Srdjan's tone had changed from polite benevolence to disparaging comments about the official, the interview came to nothing – in fact, the official is alleged to have confronted Srdjan with what he had said during his absence. Whether the story is true is not certain but that's almost irrelevant – Srdjan's reputation for interpersonal skills was such that most people who knew him could believe it was true, so he was judged by his past record, whether or not he bad-mouthed the government official.

What's notable is that most of those who have been on the wrong end of Srdjan's behaviour have a very sympathetic explanation for it.

Vojin Velickovic, the gentle, almost avuncular tennis correspondent of *Sportski Zurnal*, says,

The first thing to say about Srdjan is that he was a very good father. He brought his three boys up to be polite and patriotic. Srdjan was very sure Novak was going to make it and he was very angry because no one else saw it. He expected the country, the federation, everyone to help, because he saw the future in his son. But to him, it seemed that no one cared until Novak became really big and that made Srdjan a bitter person, and that was the main reason for his reactions to be too furious. It's true the federation did nothing to help him in his early years but they had no money, no interest, no ideas – they were just not able to do anything. For them, it was a big step if they had three boxes of balls. That was fine for many players but not for the likes of Djokovic, Jankovic and Ivanovic. So I understand Srdjan's frustration, I understand his character. For me, he's like a sportsman who gets angry in a game and then goes for a beer afterwards and it's all OK – only with Srdjan, it takes a long time for it to be all OK.

Despite the high-profile run-ins, Nebojsa Viskovic has a similar assessment.

His father made him, nobody else did. Here there was no infrastructure, there was no money, he had no help from the government, from the federation – everything was from his family. From that point, I totally understand Srdjan but he doesn't know how to deal with it. He can't stop and enjoy it, he still hates everybody – he has so much hate inside him. People like Novak because he represents Serbia in such a beautiful way, but his family is down in the public's estimations because they represent Serbia in a very different way. The hate comes from the time when he was asking for money and no one wanted to help. And he said, 'OK, one day, when Novak is No. 1 in the world, then you'll see.' Now Novak is No. 1 – for Srdjan, it's payback time.

The Belgrade-born Viskovic throws in one other hypothesis. 'They are from Kosovo,' he says. 'It's less cosmopolitan than Belgrade, it's a little less modern, and the typical family from there is very paternalistic. Srdjan accused me because I wasn't patriotic enough. Perhaps it has to do with Kosovo. Maybe people from Belgrade are not as passionate about Serbia as the people from Kosovo are, or perhaps it seems like that to people from Kosovo.'

A common theme running through comments about the way Srdjan conducted himself is that most of the decisions he made came good. Ivan Ljubicic says, 'Srdjan is most of the time right but the way of showing it and trying to get it is wrong. He has also changed lately but obviously his manners are what they are.'

Bojan Bozovic was Djokovic's doubles partner when the two were European junior doubles champions in their early teens. He believes at least part of the antipathy towards Srdjan is jealousy.

Srdjan had a very, very tough time, in his own life and in fighting for Novak, and in Serbia lots of people don't forgive success. In Serbia there are a lot of people who haven't been successful themselves and are jealous of others' success. The federation didn't help Novak when he was the best junior in Europe and Srdjan was very pissed off. Now they're all happy to take money from his success and Srdjan doesn't like that. Novak wants to play for his country but isn't that bothered about the federation. Srdjan is a strong character who had a big role in Novak's life. He gave up everything so that Novak had what he needed. They sacrificed everything for Novak. Everyone in the family has their own job – mother, father, Uncle Goran. Marko and Djordje suffered a bit but that's normal in any family with a gifted first child – the second child always suffers a bit. But I liked Srdjan. He was very funny, he still is, and he had a lot of moments with my father that were very funny. But he had a goal and he didn't care for other people – he just had a goal.

Dejan Petrovic makes a similar point.

> The only thing that really concerns Srdjan is Novak, and sometimes, when you're realistic about Novak, Srdjan doesn't accept it. He has his own view and that's it. He never tried to do a Richard Williams [father of Venus and Serena Williams] and coach, he only came to three tournaments in the 10 months I worked with Novak. He would ask questions sometimes but he never interfered. But until he got what he wanted for his son, he would never stop. The hunger for success and always the battle – that's what made Novak what he is now. Serbia lacked coaching staff, so they were always striving to find someone better. Srdjan saw in me the possibility of taking Novak further. I got on well with Novak, I knew a lot about tennis, I had great coaches myself and, until then, Srdjan never left Novak's side, he was always with him – he told me I was the only person with whom he would say, 'Here's my son, you can travel with him.' I understand that at some point he would feel I had outlived my usefulness and he'd part company with me – I just don't think it helped Novak for him to do it the way he did.

Ladislav Kis, the other coach who 'lost' Djokovic thanks to Srdjan's intervention, says, 'You can say many things about Srdjan but he was good for his kid. I don't think Srdjan ever had any self-awareness, he never believed he'd done anything wrong. But he saw very early what Novak was and he went all the way until he got what Novak needed. Srdjan also never interfered in the coaching, so I have no complaint in that regard.'

And in an era in which two of the former Yugoslavia's six republics are members of the European Union and others are applying to join, it's easy to overlook the harsh reality of the economic and political situation in which Djokovic was a teenager. 'Srdjan was in a situation that was pretty bad,' says Nenad Zimonjic, the veteran of Serbia's golden generation, who was born in 1976 so was an adult throughout the break-up of Yugoslavia. 'The economy was bad, we'd had sanctions, you couldn't get visas for certain countries. I was in a similar position as a junior. I could not really compete, I couldn't play some junior events because I couldn't enter the countries where they were taking place. These were tough times! Srdjan was fighting to get sponsors, fighting to get attention, so when he objected to journalists not giving Novak the coverage he felt he deserved, maybe it was just to get Novak more publicity, which would help get the funding. He certainly used me a lot, asking my advice on things, like whether to send Novak to the Pilic academy.'

Jelena Gencic made the point that Djokovic would never criticise his father. In public, that was true – the paternalistic nature of the Djokovic family has rubbed off on Novak to the extent that it would go totally against the grain for him to criticise his father in public. And there is also the fact that he is intensely grateful for what his dad has done for him.

But what happens behind the scenes is a different matter. It's known that Srdjan is no fan of Djokovic's long-term girlfriend and now fiancée Jelena Ristic, yet that has never undermined the relationship. So it's quite possible Djokovic has had words in private with the family to tell his father to calm down. And on at least three occasions, he couldn't keep them to the privacy of the family.

The first came at the 2008 Australian Open, when his family were cheering a little too loudly for many people's liking. Djokovic picked up on this and muttered something to his box, after which the cheering was markedly more muted. What he said exactly, no one seems to know, but it was noted for the significance of him calming the cheerleaders. The second came just over a year later at the first Serbian Open in Belgrade. This was much less subtle – in fact, some say Djokovic veritably exploded at Srdjan. He certainly told him in no uncertain terms to leave, an instruction witnessed by several members of the media. Srdjan duly did leave and was seen strolling down the river bank a short while later, smoking a big cigar. The third came at Wimbledon in 2009 when Djokovic was playing (and losing to) Tommy Haas. Djokovic asked his complete entourage, including Srdjan, to leave the players box. Only his uncle Goran returned later in the match. When asked to explain what had happened, Goran's only comment was that this was a family matter and there was nothing to say publicly. Djokovic may well have been tacitly happy for these incidents to have been witnessed but he would never say or do anything that would humiliate his father, or indeed any member of his family, in public.

There's one other person in the Srdjan Djokovic story whose role is crucial because it's so low-profile: his mother Dijana. She has not had it easy, having to play the calm rock that holds the family together while her husband is often making headlines of an unwanted kind in the national press. It's not a set of circumstances that makes her role in public particularly comfortable, and she seldom speaks to the media. She made an exception on her 50th birthday when she gave an interview to the Serbian newspaper *Blic* about her role as a mother, but by and large she is seen, not heard.

Djokovic's doubles partner from junior days, Bozan Bojovic, says, 'Dijana is a very strong and positive woman. She looked after a lot of Novak's behind-the-scenes stuff. She had to be very tough.' And Dejan Petrovic says of Dijana, 'She was a great mother. I guess being in the house with four boys, she had to be. She was the one who made sure Novak had the right things to eat, the right clothes – in that respect she did a great job, hats off to her. And the two younger brothers are good kids. It's not easy for her but she has a very strong relationship with Novak. In fact, in some ways, Novak probably holds his parents together.'

It would be nice to feel that, at some stage, Djokovic will have achieved enough that Srdjan can relax and doesn't feel the need to exact revenge or payback on those who didn't recognise his son's talent many years ago. That moment ought to have come by now – by September 2011 Djokovic was the runaway world No. 1 and held three of the four major titles plus the Davis Cup. Srdjan could easily claim to have had the last laugh. Yet a year later he was in intensive care in a Belgrade hospital with a respiratory infection. For a while the doctors struggled to diagnose his illness and for a few days his life was in danger. But he pulled through and Djokovic ended the year by beating Federer in the final of the ATP World Tour Finals in London

Many have said Srdjan has emerged from his illness a calmer man. Maybe – he will have to be tested before we can be too sure, and remarks he made to the Serbian daily *Kurir* in July 2013 suggest the fire remains undimmed (he accused Federer of trying to discredit Djokovic and said Nadal only wanted to be friends with Djokovic while he, Nadal, was winning). Now that he has a respectable home and a comfortable mattress to sleep on, it would be nice to think Srdjan can enjoy the remaining years of Djokovic's playing career without feeling the world is his enemy, but maybe that's just not in his character. And for those of us who have not had to fight for everything and become as hard as nails in pursuit of our escape from oppression, drudgery or whatever we want to escape from, are we really entitled to condemn someone for an apparent inability to lose the mindset that was so essential to his son's astonishing success?

There is no doubt that Srdjan played the pivotal role in his son's rise to the top. To make an omelette, you have to break eggs and he was always going to break several eggs on his eventful journey. But did he really have to break so many? The question may well be unfair, but it does linger after even the fairest assessment of the volatile personality of Srdjan Djokovic and his so much calmer and more dignified eldest son.

CHAPTER SEVEN

THE MANIA BEGINS

The switch of coach from Dejan Petrovic to Riccardo Piatti in July 2005 had already been negotiated by Srdjan before Djokovic left Paris for the grass of London. From the perspective of the time, it was a very smart move and there was no question Djokovic was walking right into a winning culture.

Ljubicic was having the year of his life – he'd started it by very nearly beating the undisputed world No. 1 Roger Federer in three finals and had gone on to beat the US Davis Cup dream team of Andre Agassi, Andy Roddick and the Bryan twins almost single-handedly in Los Angeles in the Davis Cup first round (he needed Mario Ancic's help in the doubles but it was very much Ljubicic's tie). In those first few months of 2005, it was easy to make the case that Ljubicic was effectively the world's second-best player behind Federer.

Amit Naor, the Israeli agent who had signed up Djokovic, was also Ljubicic's agent. He, Piatti, Ljubicic and Djokovic all sat down and worked out that they could work together. 'I never had a problem with Riccardo working with other players,' says Ljubicic. 'I just don't mind it, I've never felt that I need a coach 24/7, I just needed certain things. The way Riccardo works is not to tell you what you need to do but to explain things and get you to understand, so there's always a time when you need to sit back and work out all the information and, once you understand, you are your own man, you make decisions, and that makes you a better player.'

It was easy for Ljubicic to be relaxed about the arrangement because he was the senior player. 'It is really important within a team to know who is No. 1 priority and who is No. 2,' he says, 'because you cannot coach two top players. The perfect combination is one top player and then a younger player who can learn from the top guy, possibly already ranked high enough that they can play the same tournaments, so in that case it works without any problems. It does take some understanding by the younger player.'

Logically all fine and dandy, but what happens when the two players come up against each other? This is a perennial problem for the coaches hired by sportswear companies who suddenly find themselves with two players they coach going head-to-head – in that case, the coach generally doesn't sit in the stadium. That was Piatti's response when Ljubicic and Djokovic played each other in the Croatian capital Zagreb in February 2006. He opted to watch the match on television. It was Djokovic's first tour-level semi-final and he took the first set on the tie-break, before losing 6–7, 6–3, 6–4. 'I remember it was mentally really difficult,' Ljubicic recalls, 'but at the end of the day, it's a tennis match and you have to adapt.'

Djokovic spent nearly a year working with Piatti and Ljubicic. In that time he made modest progress, rising from 94 in the rankings to 63. But it was behind the scenes that a lot of progress was being made that would help him later.

In one of their early practice sessions, Piatti noticed something. 'I felt he was watching the ball in a strange way,' the Italian says. 'I can't remember what was strange about it but I was aware that Goran Ivanisevic had had some problems with his eyes, and when he sorted them out, he won Wimbledon. So I asked Novak if he'd ever had his eyes tested. He said he hadn't, so I suggested that when he next went back to Serbia he get them checked out. He did and found there was a serious problem which needed correcting.' Since then, Djokovic has worn contact lenses and occasionally some stylish glasses in off-court situations. Also early on, Ljubicic suggested to Djokovic that he change the strings he was using. He was using synthetic on both his main strings and his cross strings. Ljubicic said to Djokovic, 'Listen, all the best players except Rafa use a combination of synthetic and gut!' The Croat suggested Djokovic use a hybrid of gut and synthetic and choose a better quality of synthetic string than the one he was using. Djokovic took the advice.

And in May 2006 Djokovic had a foot injury. Naor sought help from an Israeli physiotherapist Rafi Virshuvski, who in turn sounded out a contact, Tamir Kfir. Kfir is a life-long amateur tennis player who made his professional name in making orthotic insoles and orthopaedic prostheses. After analysing Djokovic's movement, Kfir decided to design three different sets of orthotics: one for grass, one for clay and one for hard courts. Given that Djokovic relies heavily on the flexibility of his ankles, in particular to play powerful shots when at full-stretch (almost doing the splits) when most players would be happy just to get the ball back into play, the significance of Kfir's analysis and solution can't be overstated. After beating Roger Federer and Andy Murray in straight sets in back-to-back matches to win the 2011 Australian Open with some outstanding footwork, Djokovic threw his racket, his shirt, his socks and his shoes to the crowd – but before throwing his shoes, he took out the orthotics. When asked whether he had special insoles, he said, 'Yes. That's the secret to my footwork. You got me there!'

Ljubicic recalls,

What struck me is that he really knew what he needed. He had physical needs, which he recognised. We shared a fitness coach but very quickly he figured out he needed a different approach to fitness work. The fitness guy we worked with, Salvador Sosa, is based on pure strength, explosive strength and power, whereas Novak always felt he needed to be more flexible, more soft, which you see on court. He was always about stretching, how flexible he is, and Sosa wasn't working like that. I think he was really mature really soon. I think every tennis player reaches the moment where he becomes a man and, to him, it happened really quickly. With me, it happened when I was 23 or 24, with him it happened when he was 17 or 18, which is why he went up so quickly. He wasn't really a joker. He wanted to become as good as he can. Once he realised who he really is and he was going in the right direction, he relaxed more and let go more that side, which is his personality. But when he was younger, he was more professional in the sense that he wouldn't waste time on unnecessary things. He was 100 per cent focused on what he wanted to do.

Piatti says, 'It was very easy to see the potential. When we started working, I noted his flexibility, his attitude on court, his technique, his mentality. He was so focused and so determined. Yes, he was young but in some ways very mature. He was also ready for the top level. Technically he was ready, physically he was good. I felt sure he was a No. 1 of the future; his parents had built him in the correct way for that role.'

Such determination and focus is all well and good but it still needs to be channelled in the right direction. Ljubicic believes Piatti did that channelling. 'Riccardo helped Novak grow up. There were moments when he was lost. Now that he's king of the world, it looks like he always knew what he was doing but, back then, it wasn't really like that. He was a character. He travelled with a friend to Australia and Riccardo said maybe that was not the right thing to do. That was Riccardo's way; he tried to think what was right for Novak. Novak was 18, he had to explore the world, but it didn't take him long to work it out. I think he learned about himself. He learned more and more what he needed, he gained from the experience of being close to a top player, because I was No. 3 in the world at that time, so he could see what was needed to get there. He never needed to talk about forehands and backhands, though we did work a lot on his serve – he wasn't really using his serve and, while we were working together, Riccardo and I were giving him tips.'

The link with Ljubicic is an interesting one for the subject of nationality. In 2005 Ljubicic cemented his place as a national sporting icon for the new Balkan state of Croatia, when he won a record 11 out of 12 Davis Cup matches (seven out of eight in singles) to bring Croatia the title. Djokovic's equally impressive singles record when Serbia won the Davis Cup in 2010 can be put neatly alongside Ljubicic's achievement. Indeed, the two friends have arguably done more to put Croatia and Serbia on the map than any of their compatriots (with the possible exception of Croatia finishing third in the 1998 football World Cup). But one other thing binds them – they were both sounded out about playing for a different country.

Ljubicic escaped the carnage of the disintegrating Yugoslavia, fleeing his home in the Bosnian town of Banja Luka and spending time in war-torn Zagreb before fleeing to the safety of a family in

Italy willing to provide shelter to a gifted young tennis player. A Bosnian Croat, Ljubicic could have opted for Bosnian or Croatian citizenship but, after five years residency in Italy, he would have had the option of playing for Italy. Because the club where he played cancelled his residency card when he left after three years, the option never materialised, although Ljubicic did play under the Italian flag when entered for tournaments by his club. He says today, 'At some point I would probably have had a chance to decide if I wanted to become Italian, but the truth is I don't really think I would have done it.'

Djokovic's offer appears to have been much more concrete. In April 2006 Serbia & Montenegro, the last two remaining states of the former Yugoslavia which had given up the name 'Yugoslavia' in 2003, beat Great Britain in a Euro-African zone Davis Cup tie in Glasgow. Shortly after, it emerged that negotiations had taken place between the Djokovic family and the British tennis authorities during the tie about the possibility that the three Djokovic boys might qualify for residency and thus play Davis Cup for Great Britain. Details of the negotiations are sketchy and it's not known who approached who. A spokesperson for the Lawn Tennis Association (the British national tennis governing body is the only one in the world that does not have the country's name in its title!) said at the time that Dijana had approached the LTA, while it is generally accepted that the LTA offered the Djokovic family a lot of money to switch to Great Britain.

It's important to understand the background for both sides. The British were facing another potentially humiliating situation in which they had the most prestigious tennis tournament in the world, which gifted a surplus of £25–30 million a year to the LTA, but no players to challenge for the title. They had enjoyed the Henman-Rusedski era. Both Tim Henman and Greg Rusedski had reached fourth in the world rankings at their respective peaks but both were in the twilight of their careers and, while there was a promising Scottish boy called Andy Murray on the horizon, there were (and are) no shortage of promising British juniors who never make the transition to the full tour. There had been a lot of fuss among British tennis traditionalists when Rusedski switched from Canada to Great Britain in May 1995, but it became muted fairly quickly (especially after he reached the US Open final in September 1997). Rusedski had clearly been of massive value to the LTA in helping to promote tennis to British youngsters and the British public, and his rivalry with Henman probably made both of them into more successful players than they would have been ploughing a lone furrow. Therefore, offering a sizeable sum to a player who could play the same mutually beneficial role with Andy Murray as Rusedski had played with Henman must have looked like good business for the affluent LTA.

From the Djokovic family's perspective, it was a lucrative offer. Serbia had no tennis tradition, the country had shrunk from the six-state Yugoslavia to the two-state Serbia & Montenegro, and was about to lose Montenegro whose citizens had voted to secede. Srdjan had been knocking on doors for several years looking for funding and had come up with considerably more rejections than expressions of interest. Under International Tennis Federation rules (the ITF owns and runs the Davis Cup), living on British soil for three years would have been sufficient for Djokovic to play Davis Cup for Great Britain, even if the family hadn't got British citizenship, and that qualifying period might have been even shorter if someone could have successfully argued that the break-up of Yugoslavia meant the country Djokovic was born in no longer existed. So the offer of funding and practice facilities in a mature tennis country must have been attractive.

But by then, Djokovic already had his contract with Amit Naor and Allon Khakshourian, so the financial need was no longer quite

119

as pressing. In addition, the family had absolutely no connection with Great Britain. There was no emotional pull to Britain the way there had been with Rusedski, whose mother had lived the first six years of her life in the Yorkshire town of Dewsbury, and Rusedski himself had a British passport and had been living in south London for several years before opting to play for Great Britain. In the end, the offer was politely and quietly declined.

The offer to play for Great Britain may seem a small detail in Djokovic's career, even a pedantic one – after all, there are lots of people who could opt for different nationalities on the basis of parentage, grandparentage or residency, and Djokovic himself could have played for Serbia, Montenegro or Croatia. But it's important for Djokovic's status as national icon. If he went actively seeking a different nationality, that would surely undermine his credibility as a Serbian flag-carrier. Yet all the evidence suggests that he listened to the offer but never really wanted it.

Speaking to the British tennis journalist Neil Harman in 2009, Djokovic said,

Britain was offering me a lot of opportunities and they needed someone because Andy [Murray] was the only one, and still is. That had to be a disappointment for all the money they invest. But I didn't need the money as much as I had done. I had begun to make some for myself, enough to afford to travel with a coach, and I said, 'Why the heck?' I am Serbian, I am proud of being a Serbian – I didn't want to spoil that just because another country had better conditions. If I had played for Great Britain, of course I would have played exactly as I do for my country but, deep inside, I would never have felt that I belonged. I was the one who took the decision.

All of which rings true except that last part – Srdjan is likely to have had the lion's share of the decision to reject the offer, as Novak's move towards greater independence from his father came later (even as late as January 2007 Srdjan only allowed Djokovic a credit card, not a cash allowance, so he could monitor his son's spending).

Djokovic's first touring coach, Dejan Petrovic, who was still Serbia's Davis Cup captain at the time of the offer and who has dual Serbian and Australian nationality himself, believes the finances and functionality of the British approach could never replace the emotional pull of Djokovic's Serbian nationality. 'The LTA made a big offer,' he says, 'and the family thought about it very seriously. It was very attractive and I'm very happy he didn't accept it. Novak being who he is, he's very patriotic. From the 10 months I was travelling with him, I know how much Serbia means to him. After winning the first Australian Open [in 2008], he stood up on the balcony of the city hall in Belgrade to wave to thousands of well-wishers who had turned up on a cold winter's morning, and I remember him telling me that was the ultimate for a sports person. He could never have had that as a Briton.'

A trawl through the newspaper reports of the time suggests Djokovic had been saying behind the scenes that he was considering the possibility of a move. But the British press doesn't have the most reliable record for accuracy and frequently bases stories on rumour and is thus vulnerable to leading figures and their spin doctors floating ideas through the press. More importantly, Djokovic was well aware of all the sacrifices his family had made for him, so he probably felt it his duty to at least listen to what was on offer. Had the offer come a year earlier, who knows what he would have done, but both he and Srdjan were ultimately against it.

Nenad Zimonjic, who was the senior professional in the Serbian team that played in Glasgow, believes the LTA's offer may have been engineered by the Djokovic family. 'Maybe it was a way of saying to our country, "Listen, you have an unbelievable talent here, you should help it." He used it as a lever, perhaps. And that's OK – deep down, I don't think he was thinking of taking different citizenship but I think he was expecting more support from his country, certainly more than he was getting at that time. He had unbelievable support from the people but the Serbian association didn't help him. In fairness, it didn't have much to help him with – I had to fund all my own travel.'

The most likely explanation is that the family's attraction to the offer was based on what it would offer the younger boys, Marko and Djordje. They were both gifted tennis players, albeit not in Novak's league, but Srdjan had made it clear that he couldn't handle more than one world-beating prodigy in the family. Therefore, if Marko and Djordje were to get any chance of making it as tennis professionals, they would need some help from outside the family, the kind of help that just wouldn't have come from Serbia. It's interesting that the approach to the LTA is reported to have come from Dijana – as most of Srdjan's efforts were directed towards Novak, it was left to Dijana to make sure the couple's second and third sons weren't left out, so the family's motivation might well have been based on them, rather than Novak. Only when the story of family conversations round the dinner table is revealed will we know the answer.

With the benefit of hindsight, the decision to remain Serbian was a good one. While Djokovic was the youngest player in the world's top 70 at the time the negotiations in Glasgow took place, there was no guarantee that he would scale the heights he has since scaled. To that extent the decision was a brave one and leaves his standing as a national icon for the nation of Serbia well and truly intact.

By the end of 2005, Djokovic was making sufficient progress that the equilibrium Ivan Ljubicic speaks of – between the top player and the younger No. 2 who is learning from the more established professional – was beginning to creak. Piatti was always clear that Ljubicic was the top priority, and Djokovic was beginning to feel he needed a coach who was focused solely on him.

The first friction came at the last regular tour event of the year, the Paris Masters, when Srdjan approached Piatti and said he wanted the Italian to devote more time to Djokovic. Piatti said Djokovic would be a great player to coach, but his priority was Ljubicic who was at the peak of his career. That was effectively the beginning of the end because Srdjan was, from then on, on the lookout for a new coach. 'I saw Novak was not happy with me,' Piatti says, 'but I was with Ivan and he was No. 3. I didn't want Novak to lose time, so I fully accepted his wish to find his own coach. I've been in tennis for 30 years and he's the best player I've worked with. It was an unbelievable opportunity to work with him.' Djokovic stayed on for another six months, but after the Rome Masters of May 2006 he broke from the Piatti-Ljubicic stable.

Ljubicic recognised Djokovic's needs too, and when the split came, it was entirely amicable – Ljubicic and Djokovic have not only remained good friends but they talk with each other several times a week. And their friendship can survive a lot of ribbing. At a particularly stressful meeting of the players at the 2007 Australian Open, when the subject of anti-doping measures was occupying everyone's minds, Djokovic broke some of the ice when he complemented Ljubicic on an incisive question and suggested his bald-headed friend be given a bottle of shampoo as the prize for the best question.

Djokovic's run to the French Open quarter-final in May 2006, where he retired with breathing problems against Rafael Nadal after losing the second set, took him into the world's top 50 and further emphasised the need for an individual coach. Interestingly, Djokovic received a phone call from the Serbian Prime Minister Vojislav

Kostunica to congratulate him on his achievement – it's easy to forget now just how big it was for Serbia to have a Grand Slam quarter-finalist in those days.

In the run-up to the French Open, Djokovic's agent presented him with a list of several possible coaches. One of the names on the list was Marian Vajda, a Slovak born in 1965 who had reached 34th in the rankings in 1987 and had won a couple of rounds at the 1991 French Open. He had gone on to coach the Slovak Davis and Fed Cup teams, and various individual players. His last one was his fellow Slovak Karol Kucera, who had retired after losing to Ljubicic in the 2005 Davis Cup final, so Vajda was a free agent. Djokovic picked his name off the list and asked to meet him.

Vajda tells the story that he was in two minds about whether to make the trip to Paris to meet Djokovic and his entourage but was persuaded to do so by his 10-year-old daughter Natalia, who was a keen tennis player herself (she has since competed on the junior Grand Slam circuit – as a woman, her surname is Vajdova). The two hit it off and thus began one of the most enduring player/coach relationships in modern tennis history.

Vajda got a sense of the potential and the challenge within a few weeks. After reaching the fourth round at Wimbledon, where he lost to Mario Ancic, Djokovic won the title on the Dutch clay of Amersfoort and then went to Croatia to play in the holiday resort of Umag. He reached the final on his ninth consecutive victory since Wimbledon but retired with breathing problems in the first set tie-break, gifting his opponent Stanislas Wawrinka with his first tour title. Whatever the tennis world may have made of it, it was pure melodrama. Djokovic paused several times to get his breath back during the first set, he sought medical advice at the start of the tie-break and had to be held around the chest to help him to breathe normally. After four points of the tie-break – and leading 3–1 – he suddenly fell to the ground and lay motionless. His father and a doctor ran out, checked him out and carried him to his courtside chair while his Croatian mother sat weeping in the stands. The crowd bore him no malice, warmly applauding the apology he made in his presentation ceremony speech. After all, he was half-Croatian and the first set had lasted 73 minutes, longer than some finals that are won decisively in straight sets.

The Davis Cup tie in September 2006 against Switzerland in Geneva was one of the first indications of some of the sideshows that were to accompany Djokovic for the next few years. It was Serbia's first attempt at reaching the competition's elite 16-nation World Group (you can't win the Davis Cup if you aren't in the World Group). It was only the second time Djokovic had come up against the runaway world No. 1 Roger Federer and it was the first time Srdjan got involved publicly in a matter that impacted on his son. In the run-up to that tie, Srdjan made some comments in the Serbian press denigrating Federer. Most of it could be put down to the kind of kidology that characterises the build-up to all sorts of one-to-one sporting contests, but it probably added a little to Federer's keenness, especially as the Swiss maestro had by then rather lost the appetite for winning the Davis Cup and had begun to view the competition as a set of isolated weekends that he could take or leave as a way of spending a bit of time with his tennis mates, rather than as a series of ties leading to one of the most prestigious trophies in tennis.

After Federer beat Tipsarevic in straight sets in the opening match, Djokovic went two sets to one down against Stanislas Wawrinka in the second singles. If Serbia had lost that one, the tie would have been lost on the opening day, but Djokovic came back, winning the fourth set on a 7–3 tie-break and the fifth 6–4. Yet on several occasions he called for the trainer, which severely angered Federer. With Federer and his former flatmate Yves Allegro winning the doubles in straight sets over Zimonjic and Ilija Bozoljac, everything was set for Federer to play Djokovic in the first reverse singles. Federer was clearly pumped, and while the result might have been the same even if he hadn't been because he had the ability to play sparkling tennis whatever the circumstances, this was a rare occasion for Federer when it was personal. Djokovic won just eight games and was the subject of Federer's 'he's a joke' tirade in the post-match media sessions (the full story is on page 166).

In retrospect, that tie was the last of an era for Djokovic and his country. It was the last tie contested by Serbia & Montenegro – henceforth, it was to be just Serbia. By the time Serbia played again seven months later, Djokovic was a top-10 player and the expectations were massive. It's also interesting to note that the team that played Switzerland in September 2006 was the exact same team that saw Serbia to the final against Canada in September 2013 – in essence, Serbia has used just five players in its rise to the top of the team-tennis standings: Djokovic, Tipsarevic, Troicki, Zimonjic and Bozoljac. Sometimes having a small nation with not a great pool of players to choose from can deliver a settled squad that doesn't happen when there's a greater pool of riches.

From Federer's tongue-lashing in Geneva, Djokovic moved on to Metz, where he won the tournament and with it acceded to the world's top 20. He was a quarter-finalist at the indoor Madrid Masters, a tournament that allowed him to mend some fences with Federer, and he finished the year ranked 16. He picked up another title in Adelaide (the one Dejan Petrovic had tried to get him a wildcard for three years earlier) but then came up against Federer in the fourth round of the Australian Open. Although hyped by the media as a grudge match, Federer's only concern was to show that he hadn't beaten Djokovic on anger in Geneva, and he posted another straight-sets win, Djokovic this time winning 10 games.

There are various points where the Djokovic story shifts into a new gear and the two American hard-court Masters Series tournaments in March 2007 were clearly one such point. 'The whole mania began in 2007 when Novak won in Miami,' says Nenad Zimonjic. 'It created such interest at home that, within a few months, we had the [Davis Cup] tie against Australia when 19,000 people came – when we won that tie, we qualified for the World Group. For me personally, starting from the bottom, from the fifth group, to go through a couple of different generations and now to have the opportunity to win the Davis Cup in front of your own crowd, it was incredible.'

At Indian Wells in the California desert, Djokovic beat Andy Murray in the semi-finals to set up a final against Rafael Nadal. Nadal beat him 6–2, 7–5, but when the two met in the quarter-finals in Miami 11 days later, Djokovic notched up his first-ever win against Nadal, 6–3, 6–4. He went on to beat Murray and the wily Argentinean veteran Guillermo Canas to take the title. That took him into the world's top 10, and when he went to Belgrade for his next official match, the Davis Cup tie against Georgia, he was ranked No. 7.

This period in Djokovic's rise is marked by the first of his forays into seeking outside help. He had been working with Marian Vajda for eight months when the two men – plus Srdjan – felt Djokovic needed some additional guidance on getting to the net. There was not a lot wrong with his volleys, but playing an aggressive game of tennis is not just about being willing to go to the net, it's also about going there at the right time and with the right approach shot.

They looked at a number of possible people to come in and help but eventually alighted on Mark Woodforde. The softly spoken South Australian is known as a doubles specialist because of his record-breaking partnership with Todd Woodbridge, but Woodforde had been a distinguished singles player – he reached the Australian Open semi-finals in 1996, often beating more powerful players by getting his tactics right at the right time. Woodforde was a contemporary of Vajda and they had played against each other a few times, so his first thought on being approached by Djokovic's co-agent Allon Khakshourian was about where Vajda fitted into the picture if Woodforde was being summoned.

'I said to Marian the first time we sat down that I'd be uncomfortable if he wasn't on board with this,' Woodforde says. 'I said it has to be an association, I wanted to make sure he was comfortable with what we were trying to achieve. Khakshourian had explained that Marian was going to be there, Marian confirmed that he was still the coach but was worried that that transition from baseline to net was a vital part of Novak's game that he wasn't consciously able to call on and bring it into play when he needed to, so they wanted my help to work with Marian. I was cool with that. I just had no idea at the time about the strong influence that Srdjan had.'

Woodforde joined the Djokovic set-up in March 2007, just before the tournament in Indian Wells. The Australian remembers the impression Djokovic created from the first day. 'He was like a sponge,' Woodforde says. 'He had a thirst for information. He was never shy about stopping and asking someone. Srdjan understood that if you could take little things from people along the way, you'd build what you need. You have to give him [Srdjan] credit. The goal was to be No. 1 – it was so overpowering, it really shocked me, and picking up things along the way was all part of attaining the goal. Whilst it was nice to be tapped – and I did have the experience of being a pretty decent volleyer in my time – I was well aware I wasn't the only person he was seeking advice from.'

Off court, Djokovic had elements of the fun teenager (he turned 20 during Woodforde's four months working with him). 'He enjoyed night time,' Woodforde recalls.

He let his hair down in the evening. I could see he was heading in such a strong and healthy direction but I think we all have our moments. He was always on a quest to get fitter, stronger and to outlast Roger and Rafa – not just to compete with them but to outlast them, but there were a couple of nights in our time when he did enjoy himself. I wasn't a clubbing person even when I played but I went out with him a couple of times and he loved the fact that people recognised him – he kind of revelled in that. He wore his glasses once or twice and he looked really stylish in them. I once asked him, 'What are you – half-blind or something?' And he said, 'No, but they look good, don't they?' I thought they looked very scholarly.

Woodforde had very little to do with Srdjan, largely because he didn't speak much English. When he was around, he would talk with his son in Serbian and with Vajda in a mixture of Serbian and Slovak. 'Dijana was much more comfortable with her English,' Woodforde says, 'and I was struck by Nole's very impressive command of the English language. He's obviously a very smart guy.'

Djokovic had come to realise that he couldn't beat Federer and Nadal solely from the baseline – he had to use his net game more. Yet Vajda explained to Woodforde that Djokovic would come to the net, get passed once or twice and say, 'I'm not going there again.' It wasn't just hitting the volley that was the problem but the movement forward, the positioning, picking the right time to go in. The Djokovic camp appeared to be gearing up for the short but prestigious grass-court season, albeit making some adjustments on hard and clay along the way.

Woodforde says, 'I felt he was capable at the net but I wasn't a fan of his backhand volley. There were little details. He would come in willy-nilly at times, so we sat down and talked, not just about being on the court but how he felt about coming to the net. If you don't enjoy coming to the net, you're not going to do it successfully when you need it.'

Results-wise, the period after Woodforde joined the team was a dream. The run to the Indian Wells final, the victory over Nadal in Miami, which was of huge psychological significance – OK, so it was on Nadal's least favourite surface, but Nadal had beaten Federer in Miami a couple of years earlier, so it was a genuinely morale-boosting result – then the title in Miami, a hero's welcome at home in Davis Cup and a title on clay in Estoril. Things were going so well that Khakshourian sounded out Woodforde to ask if he would be willing to spend increasing amounts of time with Djokovic.

But Djokovic's run of victories presented problems, as all players face when they get on a productive run of form. Players, male and female, plan their schedule based on hoping to play around 60–70 matches a year; so if they expect to play an average of three matches per tournament, they will enter around 20 events. But if they then find they win back-to-back tournaments, the schedule becomes unsuitable and counterproductive, but by then the player has committed to the tournaments and can't pull out without incurring a fine (unless they have an injury, or a doctor who'll say they have an injury).

It meant Djokovic approached the most intense period of the tennis year – the French Open and Wimbledon period – with his body starting to show signs of the physical battering it had taken. Woodforde says,

Everything Novak did was in comparison to Rafa and Roger. He'd been experiencing all these great results in the Slams but he was breaking down in the quarters and the semis; physically, he was not at the same level from day one. So he was asking the questions: how can they last five sets? How can they back up after a punishing match? How can they sustain their fitness through a two-week tournament? He was starting to realise he needed to spend more time on the physical but he had put in a lot of work in the run-up to the French Open and then he got to the semi-finals, so he was pretty fatigued by the time he lost to Rafa in Paris. All this time, I'm trying to get him to work on new skills on the practice court, but it's hard to pull the guy on to the court to get him to do another hour or two hours of work when he's very tired from his run of matches.

Djokovic and his camp wanted to take the week after the French off and then play a lower-ranking grass-court tournament the week before Wimbledon. Woodforde persuaded him to go to London, play his scheduled tournament at the Queen's Club and then take the week before Wimbledon off. The thinking was that he'd be tired either way but, by playing Queen's, he would get some decent matches on grass and then rest before Wimbledon. Unfortunately, it didn't work out that way. Although Djokovic only played two matches, losing to Arnaud Clement, who was a much better grass player than he was ever given credit for, there was a lot of rain, so it took five days to get through the tournament. He then roused himself for Wimbledon, got through to the semi-finals but in a series of marathons that saw him play nine tie-breaks in four matches, leaving him as dead meat against Nadal in the semis (the story of how he very nearly pulled out of that match because of the inflamed toe that was the legacy of all his marathon matches is told on page 171).

It had been a great four months since the start of Indian Wells, and at the end of Wimbledon, Woodforde was approached about working with Djokovic for another couple of months, at least until the end of the US Open. But it never happened. Woodforde was back at home in the USA and could sense there was some hesitation from Djokovic's agents. Most of the top players take at least three weeks off after Wimbledon before returning on the North American hard courts, but Djokovic had committed to playing in Umag, Croatia, and didn't want to pull out of the tournament in the country of his mother's ethnicity, especially after being given a wildcard. In the second round, he lost to Viktor Troicki on a 7–5 final set. As the match wore on, the tiredness caught up with Djokovic. He went to the net more and more recklessly to keep the points short and was eventually picked off by his fellow Serb.

'I was led to believe that Srdjan was irate that he'd lost,' says Woodforde philosophically, 'and wanted to know why Novak was going to the net recklessly.'

This wasn't part of the plan but it makes sense – when you're tired, you don't try to elongate the points, you try to shorten them, so he had this desire to rush to the net and was exposed. I was the guy who was brought in to help him get to the net and this happened. Suddenly, I got a message from the agent saying, 'Thanks, we think we've got what we needed,' and that was the end of it. These days I see him going to the net at the right time, and I know I was part of that. I don't look at him and say, 'That was me,' because I was one of many who helped him. But the end seemed odd – it was certainly abrupt and I think Srdjan directed the whole scenario at the end. I wish I'd got more court time but I was aware of the accumulated work-load he'd had at that time and I didn't want to overdo it. Looking back, if I'd had a bit more court time, would it have happened sooner? You never know.

Woodforde also notes that Djokovic was 'always after information to make him a better player' and Djokovic sought his next outside information from one of the greatest names in tennis, John

McEnroe. In the three subsequent tournaments he played – Montreal, Cincinnati and the US Open – McEnroe helped with advice on volleys. And again the results were good.

He won the Masters Series title in Montreal, with a run-in of Roddick in the quarter-finals, Nadal in the semis and Federer in the final – that final was his first victory over Federer and a psychological milestone over the newly crowned Wimbledon champion (for the fifth time). After losing to Carlos Moya in Cincinnati, Djokovic then had a reasonable draw at the US Open. He beat Moya in the quarters, then in the semis, instead of coming up against Nadal, he beat David Ferrer, the man who had beaten Nadal in the fourth round (at that stage in his career, Nadal was known for running out of steam on the North American hard-court swing). His straight-sets victory over Ferrer took him into his first major final, where Federer awaited him. So did Maria Sharapova and Robert de Niro, who were in the crowd cheering for the 20-year-old newcomer.

A more experienced Djokovic would probably have beaten Federer that day. The Swiss was, in theory, at the peak of his career, going for a third major in a year for the third time, undisputed as the world's best player and already being talked about as arguably the greatest of all time. But he was looking vulnerable. Many were shocked when he was taken to five sets by Nadal in the Wimbledon final and some of the confidence was missing from Federer's game in the US final. His forehand was all over the place in the first set, in particular when Djokovic broke him to lead 6–5 and 40–0. But Djokovic, who'd had two set points at 5–4, missed five more and double-faulted on Federer's first set point in the tie-break. Djokovic had two set points at 6–5 in the second set but lost the set on a second tie-break. Djokovic had chances in the third but, by then, Federer was away, Djokovic was looking increasingly ragged, and Federer ran out the winner in straight sets.

Many were saying after that final that Djokovic had shown he wasn't up to taking his opportunities when they presented themselves. That was a bit harsh for a man in his first Grand Slam final and still only 20 years of age. But when Federer admitted after the match that he had been nervous because of a stomach upset that had left him with 'nervous shaking and cold hands' before the final, it did seem as if a rare opportunity to beat the Grand Master had been offered and declined.

Federer revealed later that, in the two men's chit-chat at the net after the match, he had told Djokovic to 'keep it up' and that the two men would have lots more battles in the future. They were to meet in another major just four months later, and Djokovic was to show that he had indeed learned something from his US Open missed opportunity.

It was around the middle of 2007 that Djokovic made a name for himself in a way that he has slightly struggled with since. Though a very serious and studious man on the court, he has a great sense of fun off it and is clearly a very sharp observer of people. He must also have some innate acting ability because it emerged that he was highly proficient at impersonating other tennis players.

Like the best comedians and impressionists, he had a few classic acts with which he built a reputation, and they really were very good. A BBC camera caught him doing Maria Sharapova, Rafael Nadal, Goran Ivanisevic and Lleyton Hewitt on a practice court at London's Queen's Club just before the 2007 Wimbledon championships, after which word got around. His highest-profile performance came after beating Carlos Moya in the 2007 US Open quarter-finals, when the on-court interviewer asked him to do some impressions. With the crowd still in good number, Djokovic offered them Maria Sharapova, Rafael Nadal and Andy Roddick, and brought the house down. But perhaps the more revealing footage is a private video that made its way to YouTube, which shows Djokovic doing a handful of impressions in the men's locker room. Some of the players he impersonates are not household names, so the impersonations would be lost on all but players and tour groupies, but the attention to detail is remarkable. Like the best cartoonists, he takes a gesture or nervous tic and exaggerates it, which sometimes creates a very different impression of the person being impersonated. His impersonation of Roger Federer overdoes the effeminate gestures that are part of Federer's on-court persona but the overall sense is still very much that this is Roger Federer he's portraying.

After doing his Sharapova impression at the 2008 Australian Open, Djokovic rather shut down the show. 'I was serving at 4–4, 30–30 in an important match,' he told CBS television, 'and a guy goes, "Hey, Novak, do the impersonation of Sharapova, we like that, make us laugh."' That sent a message that the sideshow was threatening to usurp the main act. He also said he had received some bad responses from his fellow professionals and he didn't want unease in the locker rooms and player lounges. He admits that Rafael Nadal was offended when he did the tugging-at-the-under-pants gesture Nadal seems unable to shake off. Of course, Nadal won't thank anyone for making fun of him, but he is known on the tour as a bit of a practical joker himself and he's able to laugh about it, as he had to on the podium after beating Djokovic in the 2009 Rome Masters final – Djokovic, the loser, was asked to imitate Nadal after both men had received their trophies; Djokovic obliged but was clearly embarrassed to be doing so in front of Nadal. Djokovic has said publicly he doesn't want to offend Nadal twice.

The impersonations may have an important role to play as a form of release for Djokovic. 'He's very serious when he comes to tennis,' says his former coach, the Australian-raised Dejan Petrovic, 'but he's not the type to be serious all the time. It's in his blood that he likes to joke. That's a bit of the Serbian mentality – we Serbians like to joke a lot. He possesses something phenomenal, that when it's on a tennis court in a match, he's serious 100 per cent – not one thing enters his mind but winning the match. With him, the mind just doesn't wander.' And the Serbian tennis commentator Nebojsa Viskovic says, 'He needs the jokes, it's his release valve.' One could equally argue that the increasingly baseline-orientated sport of tennis needs the parallel humour of seeing a top player's sense of fun.

Djokovic says today, 'I felt that it became too forced at times – people would force me to do it when I didn't quite feel like it. I was doing those impersonations on practice courts at first, at the end of my training sessions. It was a way to relax and have fun and entertain the crowd that came to watch me. The word spread and all of a sudden they asked me to do it in front of the cameras on stadiums. The first couple of times it was fun, but then it started being too forced and I just didn't want to do it any more. And I didn't want to have people guessing if I am offending someone or not, because that was never the motive behind it. I'm glad my colleagues got that part right and joked with me.'

Perhaps a feeling that he'd got his message across allowed him to resume the act when the mood took him. Certainly, by 2013 his willingness to do the impersonations was returning. He did Sharapova at a pre-Wimbledon exhibition tournament, an act that had extra spice given that he did it during a match against Grigor Dimitrov, the Bulgarian who had just begun dating Sharapova. Dimitrov loved it but Sharapova admonished Djokovic gently in her pre-Wimbledon press conference, saying she had eliminated many of the gestures that were the staple of his impersonation. That's obviously the problem – his imitation makes a player aware of their tics, which prompts the player (well, some players) to eradicate them.

Given the following the former Iranian professional Mansour Bahrami developed on the seniors' tour for his impressions of John McEnroe, Boris Becker and others, there will always be a market for Djokovic's impersonations, certainly when he retires from top-level tennis. But his strict demarcation of business and pleasure means there will always be limited scope in his schedule for performing them.

The victory over Georgia in April had taken Serbia into the playoff round for the Davis Cup World Group for the second year running. But this time the Serbs were drawn at home against Australia, for whom Lleyton Hewitt was still the leading player. This tie, in effect, marked the birth of Serbia as a modern Davis Cup powerhouse, not because the Serbs were particularly dominant against Australia but because they discovered a venue that became not just their default venue for big home ties but their spiritual home.

Djokovic's victory in Miami in early April had created a massive burst of interest, so faced with a home tie to get into the World Group, the Serbian Tennis Federation opted for the Beogradska Arena (Belgrade Arena), a new venue whose troubled construction history reflected the rollercoaster ride that Serbia as a country and Serbia's players as individuals had all been through. It was a gamble because the capacity for basketball was 20,000 and for tennis it would be very close to that. Having played in front of just a few thousand spectators in a compact, makeshift indoor court in April, it was an act of faith to hope that around 17,000 tickets could be sold just five months later. But Djokovoic's run to the US Open final increased the anticipation, and a full house christened Serbia's natural Davis Cup home.

The arena was conceived in the late 1980s as Belgrade applied to host the 1994 world basketball championships. In 1989 it was awarded the championships, on condition that the new arena was built. Construction work began in 1992, but with Yugoslavia falling apart and economic sanctions imposed on the country, Belgrade was stripped of hosting rights for the basketball in 1993. Yet the project had begun, and on some of the prime business real estate in New Belgrade, an area being developed for business just across the Sava river from the historical centre of the city. So there was a strong will for it to be completed, and when Belgrade was chosen to host the 1999 world table tennis championships, work on the arena resumed. But those championships were also withdrawn after the Nato bombing of Belgrade in the spring of 1999, leaving the arena with an air of being jinxed.

It had by then been built sufficiently to stage some events, and the first one that took place there was a political rally for the 2000 Serbian presidential election. In an attempt to show he was the architect of the modern Serbia, Slobodan Milosevic held his final rally of the election campaign there. He went on to lose the election, and while he tried to cling to power, he was forced to resign after his continuation in office was made impossible by a series of street protests that culminated in a march of 100,000 people and the setting on fire of the state television building. That appearance in the Beogradska Arena proved to be Milosevic's final speech in public.

When the International Basketball Federation awarded Belgrade the 2005 European basketball championships ('EuroBasket'), it acted as the incentive to get the arena properly finished. It opened for basketball in 2004, hosted EuroBasket and the European volleyball championships in 2005 but then had to close because it didn't meet the necessary safety requirements of a modern indoor venue. So when it was chosen for the Serbia v Australia Davis Cup playoff tie, it had only hosted about half a dozen public events. It has since gone on to become a major tennis venue, with Serbia's women setting a Fed Cup attendance record when Ivanovic,

Jankovic and colleagues attracted around 19,000 spectators for the visit of Japan in February 2009. Since then, it has also hosted judo and handball along with other sports and a string of musical events, notably the 2008 Eurovision Song Contest, after Serbia's Marija Serifovic won it in 2007 with the song 'Molitva'.

These days the arena is sponsored by a bank, Kombank, so is officially called the Kombank Arena. But its position right by the main highway from Belgrade to Novi Sad and Budapest makes it a sight from the ground, as well as from the air, as many routes into Belgrade's Nikola Tesla Airport fly within easy visual distance of the arena.

In the run-up to the Serbia-Australia tie, Serbia changed its Davis Cup captain. Whether Srdjan Djokovic used his influence behind the scenes to effectively engineer the change is not certain – he clearly had something to do with it but the impetus seemed to come more from the players. Dejan Petrovic had become captain in early 2005 after Nenad Zimonjic decided that being player and captain was too much for a team just one level below the World Group and very much aspiring to get there. Petrovic remained captain when Srdjan fired him as Djokovic's coach in the summer of 2005, but with the impending tie against Australia and Petrovic having played the early part of his career under the Australian flag, there were questions about whether he was the right man for Serbia. He was also thought of as too laid-back to be the ideal captain – he was liked by the players, but some of them found him a little too relaxed. So on Tipsarevic's initiative, Bogdan Obradovic was approached. Obradovic, who had worked with all the Serbian players, took on the job, with Nikki Pilic as team supremo (the captain of a Davis Cup team has to be a national of the country but the other members of the team don't, so Pilic was able to help Serbia; he has dual Crotian and German nationality and is the only man ever to have captained two nations – Croatia and Germany – to the Davis Cup title).

The tie itself was never close and Djokovic never needed to play his best tennis. Australia were effectively a one-man team, relying on Hewitt to win two singles and team up with the veteran Paul Hanley to win the doubles. Although the score after day one was 1–1, Janko Tipsarevic had done Serbia's spadework by keeping Hewitt on court for five sets. Hewitt won the match, but when he and Hanley lost to Djokovic and Zimonjic in four sets on Saturday, the game was up. In fact, Hewitt couldn't appear for the first reverse singles and Djokovic had no difficulty blunting the big serve of the Australian left-hander Chris Guccione. His 6–3, 7–6, 7–6 win unleashed joyous scenes in the arena. Serbia was in the team-tennis elite for the first time as Serbia (as opposed to Yugoslavia) – it had a young team that looked like getting better and it had an arena to act as its fortress.

Elsewhere in Belgrade, the Djokovic family were starting to make plans for cashing in on Novak's success. Having spent much of his youth scrabbling for money to fund the investment, it was now time to underpin that effort by investing in the future.

The first outward sign of it came in a restaurant, 'Novak', which opened one block removed from the Beogradska Arena. It still exists today, adorned by the statue of Djokovic presented to him at the 2007 Tennis Masters Cup in Shanghai – all eight qualifiers were given statues looking approximately like them in the style of the ancient Chinese terracotta army, and Djokovic brought his home to stand outside his first eatery.

A second restaurant followed as part of the tennis centre that he opened in the historic part of Belgrade, which formed part of his plans to create a tennis legacy. He had wanted to open a tennis academy but he initially had difficulty getting a piece of land in Belgrade. So he was offered a piece of land in Kragujevac, a town about 130 kilometres south of Belgrade. The mayor of Kragujevac

Above left: Novak Djokovic at six – he was always one of the smaller boys. This and the next photograph are stills from Jelena Gencic's videos.

Above right: The young Djokovic and Jelena Gencic were a perfect match, and she coached him as much in life skills as in tennis.

Below: The European 14 and Under doubles, San Remo, 2001. Djokovic and his tall friend Bozan Bozovic won; in third place (right) sporting a blond rinse is Andy Murray.

(© *Jonathan Jobson/Tennis Europe*)

Left: Djokovic brings the 2011 Wimbledon trophy to Jelena Gencic's home; a still from a Serbian TV programme in the *Agape* series, *Novak Djokovic i Jelena Gencic*.

(©*Studio B, Belgrad*)

Right: Djokovic had always admired Gencic's trophy collection, so enjoyed adding his Wimbledon trophy to it on the same visit. She died 18 months later aged 76.

(©*Studio B, Belgrade*)

Left: When he was seven, Djokovic insisted on buying Gencic a birthday present: this painting, which he found in a market. She displayed it proudly in her house.

(© *Chris Bowers*)

Top: Djokovic was given his Davis Cup debut by Nenad Zimonjic (right) and has always been proud to wear his red Serbia shirt. *(© MN Press)*

Above: With his friend and fellow Serbian tennis star, Ana Ivanovic, whom he first met when they were both four. *(© MN Press)*

Left: Administering a head massage in a charity exhibition match to Serbia's other top female tennis star, Jelena Jankovic.

(© MN Press)

Above: Vladimir Djokovic, Novak's much loved and admired 'Grandfather Vlada', who was almost a third parent at times.   (© *MN Press*

Below: From left to right: Dijana, Djordje and Srdjan Djokovic, Novak's parents and brother, arrive at the memorial service for Jelena Gencic in 2013.   (© *MN Press*

Left: Bogdan Obradovic and Marian Vajda, two coaching figures who have played a big part in Djokovic's career, pictured during Serbia's Davis Cup glory year of 2010. (© *MN Press*)

Right: Miljan Amanovic, Djokovic's Croatian-born, ultra-professional physiotherapist, who plays a vital role given the importance of fitness in Djokovic's game.

(© *MN Press*)

Left: Novak's long-time girlfriend and now fiancée, Jelena Ristic, waves the Serbian flag during one of the country's Davis Cup matches against the USA in March 2010.

(© *MN Press*)

Above left: Djokovic in glasses – many fans don't know that he wears them.   (© *MN Press*)

Above right: Djokovic, oblivious to the fact that he has been 'crowned' by the flag behind him, after winning in Miami just a few days short of his 20th birthday, the title that launched the mania back home.   (© *MN Press*)

Below: At UN headquarters in New York with Vuk Jeremic (centre), President of the UN General Assembly, and Jacques Rogge (left), outgoing President of the International Olympic Committee, August 2013.   (© *Niu Xiaolei/Landov/PA Images*)

Above left: Djokovic's first-ever main draw match at a Grand Slam ended in defeat to his idol Marat Safin at the Australian Open, January 2005. (© *AFP/Getty Images*)

Above right: Posing in Melbourne with the Australian Open trophy after his first major title, January 2008. (© *Getty Images*)

Below left: Cradling the Wimbledon men's singles trophy after his victory over Rafael Nadal, July 2011. (© *Getty Images*)

Below right: The sporting statesman – Novak Djokovic at UN headquarters in New York, with Jelena Ristic, August 2013. (© *Dennis Van Tine/ABACA USA/Empics Entertainment*)

Djokovic lets out the animal within after beating Rafael Nadal in the longest final in Grand Slam history at the Australian Open, January 2012. (*Getty Images*)

thought he was on to a winner when he teamed up with the Djokovic family, but, as the piece of land was a public park used by lots of families and children, the mayor found himself up against the wishes of the people. The people won, leaving Djokovic back at square one. He then bought a piece of land in Belgrade, which he used as a bargaining counter to secure some city-owned land where the University Games had taken place. The city agreed to invest in the complex, so Djokovic now runs his Novak Academy and restaurant on land he rents from the city of Belgrade. The site was also the location for the Serbian Open, an ATP tournament that ran from 2009 to 2012. The academy concentrates not just on tennis but on the development of the students' character – that may sound a little trite, or from a good PR manual, but given how much sport in Serbia found itself in the grip of gangsters and other corrupt and dubious folk during the 1990s, and Djokovic's own personal philosophy, the point has some resonance.

Cynics may look at the academy as a money-making exercise for the Djokovic family, rather than an attempt to invest in Serbia's tennis future. Both are true: in fact this is what business is meant to be – both sides profit! Serbia's elder tennis statesman Nenad Zimonjic says, 'We need to use this generation we have of incredible players to invest in the future,' and in many ways, that is what Djokovic is doing. And while Serbia's economy is in better shape than it was in the mid-1990s, it is still a long way from providing large sums of money to invest in non-essential services like tennis facilities. It therefore makes sense for Djokovic to invest money for the benefit of tennis in Serbia, and if it ends up benefiting him and his family, then everyone ought to be happy.

It's easy to think of Djokovic as the new golden boy of Serbian sport in the middle of 2007. He was, but there were two golden girls who were slightly ahead of him that year.

Jelena Jankovic and Ana Ivanovic are thought of by many tennis observers as two of a kind. Striking, with outgoing personalities, they reached the top relatively quickly but then slipped back and have lived in Djokovic's shadow ever since.

Jankovic is nearly three years older than Ivanovic. She was the world's top girl in 2001 (at the same time as Janko Tipsarevic was the world's top boy) but had a much slower route to the top. She was 21 when her run to the US Open semi-finals in 2006 announced her as one to watch. In 2007 she notched up Serbia's second Grand Slam title (after Nenad Zimonjic's mixed-doubles triumph at the 2004 Australian Open), when she and Jamie Murray won the mixed at Wimbledon. By the end of the year she was third in the rankings.

Ivanovic was very much a contemporary of Djokovic. Just five and a half weeks younger, she had announced her potential as a 16-year-old, winning a round at the 2004 Zurich tournament and impressing everyone with her poise and confidence, wrapped in a shell of captivating politeness and good looks. She burst on to the scene on the clay in May 2007, winning what was then the leading women's warm-up event for the French Open in Berlin and going on to reach her first Grand Slam final, when she lost to Justine Henin at Roland Garros. A run to the semi-finals at Wimbledon meant Serbia had a player in the world's top five by mid-July, and the end-of-year women's rankings in 2007 show both Jankovic and Ivanovic in the top five, a remarkable triumph for a country still piecing its way out of the traumas of the 1990s.

With the benefit of hindsight, it's easy to see both Jankovic and Ivanovic as something of a pacemaker for Djokovic. That was never their intention – they were out there for themselves – but Ivanovic especially played that role. In a glorious weekend for Serbian tennis, Ivanovic reached the final of the 2008 Australian Open and, despite losing to Maria Sharapova, climbed to second in the women's rankings, while Djokovic won the men's title the following day and climbed to third. Ivanovic then went on to beat Jankovic in the semi-finals of the French Open, in what was a direct eliminator for the new No. 1 ranking, and followed that up by beating Dinara Safina in the final to join the Grand Slam and world No. 1 rolls of honour in one fell swoop. But Ivanovic sustained an injury to her right thumb in the days after winning in Paris, lost her momentum and was never the same player again. Despite several years of considerable effort and isolated good results, she has never really looked like getting back into the world's top 10, let alone the top three or winning another major title. Even if she doesn't win another tournament, she has still achieved a tremendous amount, but her rapid demise suggests an awful lot of her success was down to belief, that fragile commodity that somehow deserted her after her ascent to the top in June 2008.

For Jankovic, it was a similar story. Her best year was also 2008, when she reached the top of the rankings in August, got to her first major final at the US Open and ended the year as the world's best female player. But she never had a really big shot the way Ivanovic could crush opponents with her big forehand; Jankovic wore opponents down with her retrieving and counter-punching, and having expended masses of effort to get to the top of the rankings, she seemed exhausted when she got there. Four weeks into 2009, she lost the top spot and has never regained it. She has had more success than Ivanovic in recent years and finished 2013 in the top 10, but she remains one of three women players to have been ranked No. 1 without ever winning a Grand Slam singles title, a status she has never seriously looked like losing (the other two are Caroline Wozniacki and the now retired Dinara Safina).

Djokovic's subsequent achievements have since dwarfed those of Ivanovic and Jankovic, but the two women deserve more than a footnote in his success story. One of the biggest problems for rising athletes in any discipline is the hope and expectation invested in them by their fans and countryfolk. For Djokovic to have had two stalking horses who were capturing a lot of the limelight when he was fighting to break through into the top echelon of men's tennis was clearly a major benefit for him. And the fact that he gets on with both of them – especially Ivanovic, thanks to their time spent together as kids – means any competition between them was a friendly and constructive rivalry, rather than a bitter fight for the national attention.

Winning the title in Montreal in August had taken Djokovic to third in the world rankings. That effectively made him leader of the chasing pack behind Federer and Nadal, but such was the duopoly those two held over the rest of the tennis world that not even reaching the US Open final could get close to improving Djokovic's ranking position.

At least Djokovic was guaranteed a place at the year-ending Tennis Masters Cup in Shanghai (now the ATP World Tour Finals). He won another tournament en route, beating Stanislas Wawrinka in the final in Vienna, and then lost to David Nalbandian in the semi-finals of the Madrid Masters. But he failed to make any impression in the season-ending finale, losing all his three group matches to David Ferrer, Richard Gasquet and Rafael Nadal. He left Shanghai with his terracotta statue but with a year that had brought him five titles rather fizzling out. He was glad of the break at the end of his most successful year, a break he extended to eight weeks by opting not to play a warm-up tournament for the Australian Open.

There's no question Djokovic was a worthy winner of the Australian Open but the old adage that even the best need a bit of luck was well and truly proven. A week before the tournament began, there was real doubt about whether Federer could play – he spent a night in a Sydney hospital with a stomach complaint that defied diagnosis but was later confirmed as mononucleosis. The fact that Federer made it to the starting line-up in Melbourne at all is a considerable achievement, but there was something of El Cid about Federer's appearance – like the Spanish mythical hero who was paraded in battle despite being severely wounded, just to instil fear in the enemy. Federer had reached the semi-finals or better in his previous 14 Grand Slam tournaments and ended up holding the trophy in 10 of them. It was certainly worth a try and, by the time the tournament was down to the last four, it looked all set to be another Federer-Nadal final.

But once again it was Janko Tipsarevic – once the leader of the Serbian new generation who had been totally eclipsed by Djokovic, Ivanovic and Jankovic in the previous 12 months – who did some of Djokovic's spadework for him. The previous Saturday, Tipsarevic had taken Federer to a 10–8 final set in a 63-game, four-hour, 37-minute third-round match. Federer had come through it thanks largely to 39 aces that saved him having to do too much additional running, but it had taken a lot out of his already depleted body. Not that he would be a pushover for Djokovic, and when Federer served for the first set, few would have expected an upset. But Djokovic won three games on the run and Federer started to make a number of unforced errors. Once Djokovic had saved a set point on his own serve in the third set, he stormed to a 7–5, 6–3, 7–6 victory. One of Djokovic's post-match comments stands out: 'I'm just very amazed I coped with the pressure today,' he said, revealing perhaps that the way he had lost to Federer in the US Open final four months earlier had indeed built up a concern about his match temperament in the minds of others, and perhaps also his own.

The other massive stroke of luck was that Nadal had been beaten a day earlier in the first semi-final by the flamboyant Frenchman Jo-Wilfried Tsonga. This was effectively the unseeded Frenchman's coming-out party and he was on fire against Nadal, allowing the

Spaniard just seven games in a thumping display. So after three years of Grand Slam singles finals dominated by Federer and Nadal (it was the first major final since the 2005 Australian Open not to feature one or both of them), the tournament had a final of the young pretender against a largely unknown newcomer.

Suddenly Djokovic was the favourite. Not only was he the third seed and world No. 3 but he had the experience of the US Open final four months earlier; for Tsonga, it was totally uncharted waters. Yet when Tsonga hit two stunning forehands to win the first set – one a passing shot winner off a Djokovic smash, the other a lob at full stretch as Djokovic surged to the net – it seemed the tide was with the Frenchman.

For a match not remembered as a great final, it had periods of outstanding tennis and a wonderful atmosphere, characterised by two expressive players and their passionate supporters. That in itself is interesting. Both at the time and in retrospect, this final is thought of as something of a blip in the glorious rivalry that Federer and Nadal had created. Perhaps the fact that both men were wearing black didn't help. They weren't exclusively in black, both had patterns down the front of their shirts, but from the main television camera angle, it looked like both were wearing the same shirts (they were both with the same clothing supplier at the time) and the world's colour therapists might mull over whether the final would have left a more positive memory if either or both players had worn a warmer colour. Perhaps also there was, for the first time since Lleyton Hewitt had played David Nalbandian in the 2002 Wimbledon final, a major final featuring two players who played pretty much the same way with pretty much the same technique, a foretaste of the Djokovic-Murray matches to come that were always fascinating but not always easy on the eye. For whatever reason (or reasons), it wasn't always easy to tell the two players apart during the rallies while watching on television, and perhaps that explains why some of the great tennis the two men offered hasn't helped the final to stand out in tennis's collective consciousness.

It was a bit of initiative-seizing that allowed Djokovic to turn the match round. In the seventh game of the second set, a scorching backhand return allowed him to break and, a few minutes later, he served out the second set. Throughout the third, Tsonga tried to serve and volley more, a tactic that had served him well against Nadal three days earlier, but Djokovic's returns were well grooved by then and the Serb broke twice to take a two-sets-to-one lead. Djokovic had to have treatment on his thigh after five games of the fourth set, and with Tsonga's buccaneering style having claimed the hearts of most of the neutrals in the Rod Laver Arena, a fifth set was a distinct possibility. When Tsonga had a break point on the Djokovic serve at 5–5, the atmosphere was electric. But Djokovic guessed right after playing a short volley, saved the break point with an angled volley and sealed the title on a 7–2 tie-break to win 4–6, 6–4, 6–3, 7–6.

As Tsonga's in-to-out forehand landed in the tramlines, Djokovic fell to the ground and, in his moment of victory, lay sprawled across the word 'Melbourne' at the back of the court. It was a mildly symbolic image – Melbourne had been the scene of his first main-draw Grand Slam match; it was now the scene of his first major title. And it was to become his fortress, the tournament at which he has had more success than at any other. Serbia had its first Grand Slam singles champion, and of either gender, given that Monica Seles had played under the name Yugoslavia and was ethnically Hungarian and Ana Ivanovic's French Open title was still four months away. As Srdjan, Dijana, Marko and Djordje hugged each other in the players' enclosure while Djokovic and Tsonga hugged each other at the net, they had the ultimate confirmation that all the sacrifices they had made to give Novak a chance of getting to the top had been worth it.

CHAPTER EIGHT

MODERN-DAY SERBIA

I n 1989 Europe had 27 countries, if you don't count Iceland, the two Mediterranean island states of Malta and Cyprus, and the handful of tiny states such as Monaco, Andorra, Liechtenstein, San Marino, etc. On the territory of those 27, there are now 42, thanks to independence from the old Soviet Union for Ukraine, Georgia, Belarus, Armenia, Azerbaijan, Moldova, Kazakhstan, Estonia, Latvia and Lithuania, and the break-up of Yugoslavia into six independent republics (Czechoslovakia broke into two but West and East Germany reunited so, numerically, they cancel each other out). People can be forgiven for having difficulty keeping up with the new countries and it's often only through sporting events – like European championships and World Cup football qualifying matches – that the new states get the chance to wave their flag across a wide geographic area.

Serbia still counts as one of the smaller countries in Europe but one of the larger of the 'new' states. Its population of just over 7 million is comparable to that of Sweden and Switzerland but the average in the European Union is 18.5 million. And its GDP is barely a seventh of the EU average. Since the privatisation of the largely state-controlled economy over the last 25 years (in reality, over the past 15 years since the wars of the 1990s were such a disincentive to investment by outside firms), Serbia has done reasonably well, attracting a lot of investment and a reasonable level of economic growth in the 2000s. However, the country slipped back into recession in 2012 and its largely service-based economy remains fragile. The EU is Serbia's biggest trading partner but that isn't all good news for the Serbs, especially with the euro-zone countries having been in turmoil since 2011.

Serbia has applied to join the EU and if accession negotiations go well, it is likely to be part of the Union by the end of the decade. But the biggest obstacles to a smooth integration appear to be less economic and more an adaptation to some of the human character norms that are taken for granted across the bulk of Europe. There are specific issues, like smoking: not that joining the EU would force Serbia to ban smoking in public places, but that is generally the norm in western Europe these days, and a day sampling Belgrade's cafes and restaurants testifies to how far Serbia is from that. On a general and more important level, do the Serbs have the national mentality to be at home in an economic community dominated by the Germanic peoples of northern and western Europe (Germans, Britons, Danes, Dutch), with the southern European peoples providing the economic problem cases? That question has certainly caused its fair share of angst for the Greeks and the Iberians in recent years.

If Serbia is to become integrated into the EU, it will have to put aside residual anger towards the Croats and ethnic Albanian Kosovans. On a personal level, this won't be a problem, as Serbs, Croats, Bosnians and even Kosovans have lived side by side for

150

generations and many are good friends today. But the still-simmering tensions between Serbs and Albanians, especially in the Kosovan capital Pristina, are evidence of a conflict in which closure has still not been achieved.

And when the Serbian and Croatian football teams play each other, it always seems like war by another set of rules.

In 1999 the two nations played each other in Belgrade for the first time (Serbia still under the name 'Yugoslavia' but by then only in conjuction with Montenegro, and the team was largely Serbian). The match took place in an atmosphere described by all who were there as incredibly hostile. Serbian fans shouted 'Ustase' at the Croatian fans – not entirely inaccurately, in the sense that Croatia's red-and-white *Sahovnica* chessboard motif, which forms a big part of the design of their team kit, was originally the Ustase's emblem when its members set about slaughtering hundreds of thousands of Serbs in the early 1940s. Amid the already heightened tension, the floodlights went off during the second half, creating near-panic in the stands and on the pitch. They eventually came back on and the match finished 0–0, much to the relief of the security forces. The two teams played again in Zagreb two months later, with both sides needing to win to keep alive their chances of qualifying for the 2000 European championships. The home fans unfurled a massive banner saying 'Vukovar 91', as a warning to the Serbs that this was an atrocity to be avenged, and there was a parade of Croatian war heroes on the field before the match. The match was characterised by the sending-off of Zoran Mirkovic of Serbia, who grabbed the testicles of Croatia's Robert Jarni after Jarni shouted an insult at Mirkovic. In most countries Mirkovic would have been castigated by his fans for letting the national team down in a vital qualifier, but Mirkovic was hailed as a hero, especially after giving Serbia's three-fingered salute as he left the field. He had been insulted and had sought revenge, and that was fine by his compatriots, regardless of the state of the qualifying campaign.

One could argue that those matches took place in 1999, the year the Kosovo war ended, and things have moved on since. Yet when Serbia and Croatia met twice in World Cup qualifiers in 2013, little had changed. In the first match in Zagreb in March, Serbian fans had been barred from the Maksimir Stadium to prevent clashes between home and away supporters. The Serbian national anthem was greeted with cries of 'Vukovar, Vukovar', and in an orchestrated piece of chanting, fans in one stand screamed 'Kill, kill' while those in another chanted 'the Serbs'. If that was all unofficial, the Croatian authorities must have sanctioned – or at least turned a blind eye to – the massive banner that read, 'Through the rough times and through angry fighting, we defended our homes with honour. Those who defended our land did not die in vain – here in our land, our flag flies.' Croatia won that one 2–0, which probably limited the post-match fallout. Six months later in the return match, both sides ended a bad-tempered affair with 10 men, Croatia's Josip Simunic being sent off for a particularly brutal and premeditated foul on Serbia's Miralem Sulejmani late in the game. Serbian fans, who had chanted insults at the Croats throughout the match, threw missiles at Simunic as he left the field. That match, which did involve some away fans, ended goalless: another good result for the security forces.

It would be wrong to imply that such intense rivalries don't happen elsewhere in Europe – they clearly do – but the founding fathers behind what is now the EU were motivated, at least in part, by creating a culture of economic interdependence, so that rivalries like that between the Serbs and Croats would become secondary to both countries' self-interest. This is perhaps another area where Djokovic can help by setting an example that the odd painful defeat can still be suffered with dignity, as opposed to a need for revenge.

It's also important to point out that football has a different status in Serbian culture than other sports, and there is nowhere near the same tension when Serbs compete internationally in other sports. Only once since the Yugoslav wars of the 1990s have Serbia and Croatia played each other in the Davis Cup: that was in Split in July 2010, when Serbia won in the fourth rubber, Djokovic beating his good friend Marin Cilic in straight sets to give Serbia a 3–1 lead. There was plenty of passionate support for both teams but it never got remotely out of hand. Serbia's veteran doubles specialist Nenad Zimonjic says, 'Nole never had a problem playing in Croatia. He played the tournaments in Zagreb and Umag, so although the Davis Cup tie against Croatia was a high-risk match, there was security from both Serbia and Croatia, and we all got along really well. All the athletes were true athletes through fair play and sportsmanship. The crowd was not happy that we won but they acknowledged us. It's a different crowd than football. It's always going to be a rivalry but I think it's all about respect and sportsmanship.'

Tennis is often accused of being something of a genteel sport, yet in this case, the gentility of the tennis supporters allowed for a dignified sporting spectacle to emerge from a fiercely contested rivalry. This is perhaps another reason why Djokovic is a different type of national hero than his equivalents in Serbian football, not just because his character is so different from, say, that of Sinisa Mihajlovic (the former Serbian footballer and now national team coach) but because Djokovic plies his trade in a sport where losing with good grace is part of the deal.

Having said that, it would be wrong to gloss over the violence that has erupted between Serbian and Croatian fans at the Australian Open in recent years. In 2007, 150 people were thrown out of Melbourne Park after clashes in the garden area of the grounds, including some glass bottles being thrown in an area popular with families and tourists. The only trigger was that Marin

Cilic of Croatia was playing Ilija Bozoljac of Serbia that day. And there were further clashes in 2009 and 2010; one on the day Janko Tipsarevic of Serbia played Cilic, the other by the court on which the Serb Viktor Troicki was playing Spain's Alberto Martin. 'Serbian' and 'Croatian' participants in the 2007 brawl interviewed on Australian television that night all spoke with well-entrenched Australian accents, which rather suggests that the violence had little to do with modern-day Serbia and more to do with tribal clashes among ex-patriots. But they may reflect the tribal undercurrents that still exist in Serbia.

The subject of racism is one that frequently crops up with Serbia but needs to be tackled sensitively.

Serbia was heavily censured by Uefa after its Under-21 football team lost to England in Krusevac in October 2012, a match that featured persistent racist chanting and a mass brawl involving players and coaching staff at the final whistle. The England player Danny Rose was subjected to monkey chants throughout the match and screams of 'Kill him, kill him' whenever he got the ball, and there were several other less directed incidents. Uefa issued punishments to four Serbian players (and two English ones), fined the Serbian football association €85,000 and ordered the Serbs to play their next Under-21 match behind closed doors. Some in western Europe (particularly England) chose to see that as a very lenient punishment, which it might be, but some context is called for.

The sports writer Jonathan Wilson, who has made eastern European football his area of specialisation, says false distinctions are sometimes drawn between anti-black racism and anti-Roma (anti-gipsy) racism. He says that Serbia, as a nation that never had an empire or was involved in the slave trade, has never had much exposure to black people but has a long history of discrimination against gipsies, travellers and Romany, both as victims and aggressors. 'Western European nations can't understand the casual attitude to anti-black racism,' Wilson says, 'but they are as guilty of underestimating anti-Roma racism as the Serbs are of turning a blind eye to anti-black sentiments. Neither ought to be acceptable. All racism, surely, is equally deplorable: the racisms to which western Europeans are more attuned cannot be given precedence and nor can the FSS use what it perceives as lack of action on anti-Roma racism to justify not pursuing anti-black racism.'

This is backed up by the BBC's correspondent in Belgrade, Guy De Launey. Shortly after the infamous Serbia v England Under-21 international, he concluded, 'There can be a different attitude towards racism here. After the Krusevac match, I talked to well-travelled, English-speaking journalists who said, "Oh, come on, a few monkey chants towards a black player isn't really racism – they're just trying to put the player off." I found that astonishing but maybe that's from a British perspective.'

Although the role of sport in Serbia is dealt with in a later chapter of this book, it's another sporting example – the case of Sinisa Mihajlovic and Patrick Viera – that best illustrates the complexity of the racism issue in Serbia, even if this very public row happened in a highly charged situation outside Serbian territory.

The rumpus came during a Champions League football match in 2000 when Lazio of Rome played the London club Chelsea. Lazio's team featured Mihajlovic, a volatile and controversial Serb nationalist, who these days is coach of the Serbia national team. After the match, Chelsea's black French midfielder Patrick Vieira accused Mihajlovic of calling him 'a black shit' during play. Mihajlovic who, like Djokovic, has a Serb father and Croatian mother, has made some highly inflammatory comments and is something of a Serb hero, having escaped from his home in Vukovar thanks to assistance from the Serbian gangland hero-cum-warlord Arkan (see page 201) after Croats retook the town in 1995. As such, there is always the risk that Mihajlovic could be tried by reputation rather than on the evidence, but his defence is interesting.

Mihajlovic said the insult Vieira had used was 'zingaro', a word meaning gipsy but used in Italy as a general term of derision to mean both gipsies and those emanating from southern Slav nations. He told Jonathan Wilson,

> Yes, I insulted Vieira, but only as an answer to his insults. He called me a 'gipsy shit', so I answered back with 'black shit'. I am proud of being a gipsy, so I wasn't offended and I don't see how he could be offended because I called him black. Vieira provoked me from the first minute, and whatever colour his skin is, I'm not going to let him treat me like that. I am who I am and I would have reacted the same way even on the street. I've played football since I was 15 years old and in that time I have been kicked, spat upon and insulted. In football, these things happen. If I am a racist, so is Vieira.

Interestingly, Vieira was never charged over the incident, despite 'zingaro' or 'zingara' being unquestionably racist, whereas Mihajlovic was banned for two games by Uefa. This contrast in treatment backs up Wilson's point about anti-black racism being considered more of a sin than anti-gipsy racism, at least in the corridors of power of European football. Although it in no way excuses his behaviour, it's hard not to agree with Mihajlovic's basic logic that one form of racism is as bad as another. Mihajlovic went on to make a statement from the centre circle of the pitch during Lazio's next home game, saying he had been wrong, expressing regret and saying he didn't hold racist views. The statement was prompted by an extreme right-wing Italian group welcoming his racist views and he was keen to dissociate himself from them, but under Italian law he could have gone to prison for three years, so it may have been a partially tactical disavowal of racism.

Other remarks Mihajlovic made about the Vieira incident suggested his biggest beef with Vieira was that he brought a matter that should have been left on the field into the public domain by talking about it in a press conference. It seems to suggest Mihajlovic is working to a medieval, or perhaps gangland, code of ethics, in which honour has to be salvaged and insults avenged. Given the love, affection and esteem his fellow Serbs have for Mihajlovic, you wonder whether this undercurrent of tribalism is still working against the interests of a country that aspires to be a member of Europe's modern-day economic community.

But there's a wider point that Jonathan Wilson makes, which needs to be taken into account. Racism is still a problem in European football, and no doubt it is on the list of tasks for the Serbian football association FSS to deal with. But Wilson says the FSS can be forgiven for having its attention grabbed by bigger fish.

There was a European championship qualifier in October 2010 between Italy and Serbia in Genoa. It had to be abandoned after a few minutes after a delayed start because Serbian hooligans were running riot, but if you look at the context, you see a lot of what's going on in the background. There was a banner 'Kosovo is Serbian' and the match took place as Hillary Clinton [the then US Secretary of State, or foreign minister] flew to Belgrade to discuss Kosovo. There was also anger that the Serbian goalkeeper Vladimir Stojkovic had joined Partizan, having previously been with Red Star – that was seen as a major betrayal by many Serb nationalists. And there was fury over the arrest of a drug smuggler. Piece it all together and you see that, just to keep football in Serbia running, the FSS has to tackle hooliganism, organised crime, match-fixing, corruption and endemic violence – some of it against a nationalistic background that it can't control. It doesn't excuse racism, but it does explain why the FSS may have more immediate priorities.

If an element of racism still pertains in today's Serbian society, what of attitudes to other minorities? Serbian society's view of homosexuality seems old-fashioned by western-European standards, although as recent debates on same-sex marriage have shown (especially in Great Britain and France), there are many in western Europe who are still troubled by same-gender sexual relationships. When the Belgrade Pride parade scheduled for September 2013 was cancelled for the third year running, the authorities were quick to say the decision was taken for security reasons after threats of violence from right-wing and paramilitary groups had emerged from proposed counter-marches. Given that Serbia is applying for EU membership and thus the protection its legal system gives to minority rights will be closely scrutinised by the European Commission, this was probably a wise way to present it. But the fact that there was support for the proposed counter-demonstration from across Serbia, a country in which the Serb Orthodox Church still plays an influential role, suggests that tolerance of homosexuality is still somewhat embryonic.

The one national characteristic that the Serbs are often accused of – and which many freely plead guilty to – is a victim complex. Wilson says they 'revel in the role of the victims of Europe' and, in his fascinating book *Behind the Curtain*, he writes, 'Self-doubt is the defining characteristic of Serbian football: they are Europe's most consistent chokers.' He suggests the victim complex stems from Serbia's defeat in Kosovo in 1389, which left the once independent country under the control of the Ottoman Empire: 'The defeat remains central to the Serbian psyche: they are the wrongly oppressed but glorious losers.'

The BBC's man in Belgrade, Guy De Launey, pinpoints it to slightly more recent times but still says the sense of the Serbs as victims is very real.

Part of it comes from what happened to the Serbs during the Second World War. In Croatia, the fascist Ustase murdered tens or even hundreds of thousands of Serbs. That wasn't forgotten, and when Croat nationalism picked up again in the early 1990s, Serbs living in Croatia were frightened. It was almost as if the conflict resumed in 1991 where it had left off in 1945. Even when it comes to the Hague war-crimes tribunal, there's a perception in Serbia that the Serbs on trial were treated a lot more harshly than others, especially in terms of bail conditions. They saw Croatia and Kosovo spending millions on the defence of their generals and gaining acquittals, leaving the Serbs as the major villains of the piece – but they'll point out that more Serbs were displaced during the conflict than people of any other ethnicity.

De Launey also observes that 'there's an image of the Serbs as a lazy people, yet they are all mad on physical activity. There's even a risk of "boot-camping" youngsters if they show any talent at a sport, and sometimes if they don't.'

These are largely speculative points of view based on the personal experience of a sample of individuals and hardly the result of deep-rooted socio-anthropological analysis. Most visitors to Serbia will find a largely welcoming if not effusive people, many of them oppressed more by the dictates of everyday life than by any national characteristic of victimhood, racism or national identity. There is one distinctive characteristic that visitors to Serbia will encounter – a strong sense that 'this is my town and you are the guest', which can lead to locals insisting on paying the bill when it makes much more sense for visitors to do so. It's a fault that's easily forgiven because it comes from a sense of wanting to make outsiders welcome.

Serbia is in a good position to make the most of integrating itself into the European picture – it speaks the same language as many of its neighbours, so it can build bridges to neighbouring states (not just the ex-Yugoslav republics but also Russia to the north and east) without running up massive translation bills, and it has proved a target for investment among many leading global companies. With its reasonable work ethic, there seems every reason why Serbia, if it plays its cards right, could be much more successful in the European economy than nations such as Greece, Portugal and even Spain and Italy.

CHAPTER NINE

IN SICKNESS
AND IN HEALTH

In 1961 the Nobel Prize for literature was awarded to Ivo Andric. It was a belated reward for his book *The Bridge over the Drina*, written in 1945 but only translated into English in 1959. For a Nobel Prize-winning novel, it is still remarkably little known, though that may well change when Emir Kusturica's film adaptation hits the big screen in late 2014 (Kusturica is playing a similar role to Djokovic in the arts world – a Serbian film director telling the world that Serbia is not just a by-word for atrocities, although Kusturica's manner is much more abrasive than Djokovic's).

The book tells the violent story of the Bosnian town of Visegrad, just inside the Bosnian-Serbian border, in the 300 years after a bridge was built there over the river Drina in the early 17th century. It is a work of fiction but based strongly around historical facts. Many have described it as a fitting introduction to the complexity and character of the history of the Balkans, and while Visegrad is Bosnian, many of its problems and mix of population go for the whole of ex-Yugoslavia. In 1878, in the settlement that saw Serbia and Montenegro gain independence, Bosnia was transferred from the Ottoman Empire into the Austro-Hungarian Empire. In this (slightly abridged) extract from the book, Andric describes how this transfer affected the sleepy town of Visegrad:

[As the soldiers began to move away,] officials began to arrive, civil servants with their families and, after them, artisans and craftsmen for all those trades which up till then had not existed in the town. At first it seemed that they had come by chance, as if driven by the wind, and as if they were coming for a short stay to live more or less the same life as had always been lived here, as though the civil authorities were to prolong for a short time the occupation begun by the army. But with every month that passed the number of newcomers increased. However, what most astonished the people of the town and filled them with wonder and distrust was not so much their numbers as their immense and incomprehensible plans, their untiring industry and the perseverance with which they proceeded to the realisation of those plans ... It seemed the newcomers were resolved with their impalpable yet ever more noticeable web of laws, regulation and orders to embrace all forms of life, men, beasts and things, and to change and alter everything, both the outward appearance of the town and the customs and habits of men from the cradle to the grave ... Every task that they began seemed useless and even silly. They measured out the waste land, numbered the trees in the forest, inspected lavatories and drains, looked at the teeth of horses and cows, asked about the illnesses of the people, noted the number and types of fruit-trees and of different kinds of sheep and poultry.

Andric is effectively telling the story, from the residents' perspective, of how the new Austrian rulers were modernising Visegrad. One could see it as the imposition of Germanic order and discipline on live-and-let-live Balkan culture, and indeed the nice sleepy way of life that doesn't need house numbers because 'everyone knows the priest's or the cobbler's house' is very attractive as an antidote to the anonymity of big-city existence. But modern industrialised society could only ever have come about with large numbers of people whose lives were logged to some extent by civilian authorities, so what Andric describes happening in Visegrad would have happened, eventually, in all parts of the Balkans.

Why is this relevant to the Djokovic story? Because there is a feature of Djokovic that sets him apart from his fellow-Serbs. Talk to any Serbs, or indeed many people from the Balkans, and they will happily admit to a national character trait of victimisation. Then in the next breath, they might talk about how they were treated unfairly at The Hague when the war crimes of the Yugoslav wars of the 1990s came to be assessed. It's as if they need to have someone to blame, or are enjoying their victimhood. In *The Bridge over the Drina*, Andric describes a group of women waving goodbye to their sons who had been conscripted, noting about them, 'It seemed as if they loved their tears and their wailing as much as they loved those for whom they wept.' This is what the English football journalist Jonathan Wilson means when he talks in his book *Behind the Curtain* about the Serbs 'revelling in the role of the victims of Europe' and their self-image as the 'wrongly oppressed but glorious losers'.

It is probably dangerous to get too much into national characteristics and stereotypes, but it is clear that there was no room for a victim mentality, wailing or being a glorious loser in the Djokovic psyche. He worked out very early that if he wanted to get to the top in tennis, he had to be disciplined and totally professional about his approach. Jelena Gencic noted how he turned up to his first session with her at the age of six with his bag fully packed (including a banana!). Nikki Pilic arranged to hit with him at 2pm, only to find him warming up 20 minutes early. Mark Woodforde, who worked for three months with Djokovic in 2008 as a consultant, said he was 'like a sponge in his thirst for information that might help him'.

And the words of Dejan Petrovic are interesting. On seeing Djokovic for the first time at the age of 14, the Australian-raised Serb says,

> The first thing I noticed about him was his professionalism and his dedication towards the sport. The first time we met at Partizan [the Belgrade sports club where Djokovic sometimes played], I came 15 or 20 minutes earlier and I recall him running around the court, stretching – that was him; he was a perfectionist in every way. I saw that he wasn't 'from Serbia' – if he'd been a typical Serbian, he'd have come on time, or maybe even a few minutes late. You could see that he was somewhere else. He always told me that being at the Pilic tennis academy at a young age and at such a critical stage of his career did him wonders – having to know what was in his bag, being on time, warming up, stretching. But it was probably in him already.

And yet there is a theme of sickness, or not quite optimum health, that runs through the Djokovic story. It peaked in 2008–9 with the culmination of a series of mid-match treatments and retirements from matches that exploded in the on-court post-match interviews at the US Open.

If you discount the match he retired from against Mohamed Mamoun of Egypt in a Futures tournament in 2003, Djokovic has retired mid-match 11 times in tour-level matches: four in majors, two in Davis Cup, two Masters-1000s and three lower-ranking tour events. The rate has slowed down, for reasons that will be explained shortly: his withdrawal from the Australian Open quarter-finals in 2009 was his eighth and there have only been three since (at the time this book to press). But that is still well ahead of other members of the world's top 10. Tomas Berdych and Jo-Wilfried Tsonga have retired four times each, Rafael Nadal and Juan-Martin del Potro twice each and Roger Federer once (although he did concede two matches on walkovers).

There are no public statistics on the amount of times a player calls for the trainer mid-match, but by 2008 Djokovic had made a name for himself as a player who called the trainer so often it was thought to be largely tactical. Riccardo Piatti, who coached him from July 2005 to May 2006, says it was indeed often tactical. 'He had a problem with his nose,' Piatti recalls. 'Before we went to America, I warned him it would be very hot and humid, and he might struggle. In Cincinnati it was very hot and then in the first round of the US Open it was humid and he played five sets against Gael Monfils. I'd told him he might need to call for the trainer to take a break if he found himself having difficulty breathing.' Early in the fifth set against Monfils, Djokovic fell down after a rally and called for the trainer. Piatti says he did it deliberately – on the basis of Piatti's advice – to buy himself some time. He was fortunate that the trainer took 12 minutes to arrive on court; by then Djokovic had cooled down and was breathing more freely, so he got his leg massaged and went back on court, beating the Frenchman 7-5 in the fifth set.

Piatti took Djokovic to see a nose specialist in Milan, one who had treated the Italian footballer Andrea Pirlo for a nasal problem. He found Djokovic had a double deviated septum and recommended surgery to remedy it. That surgery took place in November 2005 at the start of the off-season and was largely successful, but the injury timeouts continued.

In Serbia's Davis Cup playoff-round tie against Switzerland in September 2006, Djokovic trailed Stanislas Wawrinka by two sets to one on the opening day and called the trainer after the third set to have his legs massaged. He went on to win the match in five, but Wawrinka's team-mate Roger Federer was so angry at what he saw as pure gamesmanship that he launched a stinging attack on Djokovic after he had crushed the Serb 6-3, 6-2, 6-3 to seal Switzerland's win on the Sunday afternoon. 'I don't trust his injuries,' he said during his main post-match press conference, drawing a few nervous laughs from the assembled journalists. 'No, it's not funny,' he added admonishingly, 'I'm serious. I think he's a joke when it comes to his injuries. The rules are there to be used but not abused. But it's what he's been doing many times, so I wasn't happy to see him doing it and then running around like a rabbit again. It was a good handshake for me, I was happy to beat him.' Federer later had an informal chat with the Swiss press, at which he added, 'I got irritated on Friday when he put on this show in his match against Wawrinka. Ninety-five per cent of players use these breaks fairly but this isn't fair and the rules need to be changed,'

Although Djokovic denied he had used gamesmanship against Wawrinka, and he and Federer had a chat in Madrid a few weeks later and made up, he was by now a marked man. Whenever he called for the trainer mid-match, journalists and commentators would mutter – some inwardly, some outwardly – that the injury may be for real or may be tactical. Matters reached a head at the 2008 US Open, when Djokovic twice called for the trainer to deal with hip, ankle, stomach and breathing problems in his fourth-round match against Tommy Robredo. Djokovic won the match in five sets, to set up a quarter-final against the winner of the match later that day between Andy Roddick and Fernando Gonzalez.

When Roddick won that match, he was asked by the on-court interviewer whether he felt good going into his quarter-final, given Djokovic's various ailments. When the interviewer started to list them, beginning with an ankle injury, the witty but abrasive Roddick interrupted, saying, 'Isn't it both of them? And a back, and a hip? And a cramp?' Later in the interview Roddick added, 'Bird flu? Anthrax? Sars? Common cough and cold? If it's there, it's there. There's just a lot. You know, he's either quick to call a trainer or he's the most courageous guy of all time. I think it's up for you guys to decide. I've got to feel good, he's got about 16 injuries right now.' Djokovic beat Roddick in four sets in the quarter-final, though he was lucky not to have to go to five, as Roddick served for the fourth set and double-faulted twice to let the Serb off the hook. So now it was Djokovic's turn to be interviewed on-court. 'That's not nice to say in front of this crowd that I have 16 injuries and that I'm faking,' he said. 'They're already against me because they think I'm faking everything.' Djokovic left the court to boos, this just a year after the Flushing Meadows crowd had loved him for his on-court impressions, including imitating all Roddick's nervous tics. As with most storms in teacups, it blew itself out pretty quickly. Roddick said he had meant his comments in jest, Djokovic apologised for overreacting, and that was that.

And yet the problem still didn't go away. At the next major, the 2009 Australian Open, the two men again met in the quarter-finals and this time it was Roddick who won, Djokovic retiring in the fourth set citing 'cramping and soreness in my whole body'. That made it eight retirements in less than four years for Djokovic. He may have had the charm to apologise and make up behind the scenes, but he was getting a reputation as someone who didn't have the stomach for the fight or, more cynically, who preferred to deny his opponent the winning shot by retiring before the end of the match. He was asked in the press conference after that Australian

Open retirement whether he needed to perhaps develop a greater trust in his body, so he could play through physical niggles a little more. Djokovic replied,

I mean, it's easy for you to say. If you come into my body, I'll be more than happy to hear what you think about playing. But I'm a professional tennis player for a couple of years now. There is absolutely no question about whether I have motivation and will and desire to continue the match and defend my title. There is absolutely no doubt that I have it in me. My mind wanted me to continue. I could have stopped even before in the end of the second set because I felt really bad. I continued playing, thinking that something could help me out, maybe a treatment and things like that. But it just kept coming back.

History records that over the next two years, Djokovic turned his fitness and health round, to the point where he won three of the four majors in 2011 and outlasted Nadal in a remarkable five-hour, 53-minute final of the Australian Open in January 2012. It's therefore easy to assume there was a turning point, a toughening-up of his attitude towards fitness, health and lasting out matches somewhere in 2009 or 2010 that proved the key to his ascent to the top of the world rankings. But it wasn't quite like that. If anything, what happened in 2009–10 was that he finally got on top of a series of health issues that had held him back to a greater or lesser extent since he had first started playing.

It was Jelena Gencic who first noticed that young Novak always got hay fever in the spring, when the flowers were first in bloom. His matches on clay were very difficult. 'I took him to many doctors,' she said, 'and one said he had a deviated septum in the nose. So his mother and father took him to have an operation to correct the deviation. After that it was much better. I also said, "Don't practise near ambrosia [rag weed]," as those are the flowers that set him off.' It appears therefore that Djokovic had two operations on his nose, one prompted by Gencic when he was a young boy, the other prompted by Piatti when he was 18. Some of the ailments Gencic claims to have spotted sound like something out of an old wives' epicurean handbook. 'When he was feeling very bad in Budapest, when he was playing a challenger tournament,' she said, 'there was a Marza [cat's flower] by the court and he reacted, so they asked me what to do. I said, "Spray him with salt water from the Adriatic Sea."'

More seriously, Gencic was worried that Djokovic never ate enough and, right up to her death in 2013, she was worried he was still not eating as much as he needed to. She claimed to have had lunch with him when he was an adult and would say, 'Nole, Nole, come on, eat.' And he would say, 'Jeca, don't tell people but I now eat all the Cevapcici.' (Cevapcici is a typical Serbian/Balkan meat dish, probably of Turkish origin.) She also took him to a homoeopath, who advised him not to eat gluten. It took until he was well into his twenties before another doctor suggested cutting out gluten, which was one of the turning points in improving his health. And it took until he was 18 for a coach to realise that his eyes weren't good enough and needed some assistance.

In other words, here was a boy with superb motor skills, a natural talent for tennis and a burning desire to be the best in the world but with a body that, in several important respects, was not playing ball. Many people who observed Djokovic on his rise to the top say this led to a cautiousness that was behind many of the trainer and retirement episodes that so irritated spectators, journalists and other players.

Nenad Zimonjic, who as Serbia's Davis Cup player-captain was the first to call Djokovic into the Serbian Davis Cup squad, says, 'Novak always had the No. 1 spot in the world in mind. He was thinking about winning the Grand Slams and the big tournaments, and he always thought about his health and his body, so he didn't want to push the limits when he felt like there was a slight chance of him getting injured. Finding out the problem with the allergies and the gluten, and developing his fitness level to compete at this high level, was a slow process, but he improved with everything. When he won the Australian Open for the first time he was still very young, he wasn't really strong physically at the time.'

It's a view shared by Djokovic's good friend and former stablemate under Riccardo Piatti, Ivan Ljubicic. 'He became stronger, physically. And the more you go through it physically, the stronger you are mentally. I don't see him as a different person, I see him just treating certain situations differently but it's still him. He's overcareful with himself and sometimes people think he's trying to fake or create something, when he's just trying to take good care of himself. Sometimes that's misinterpreted. I never think he faked injury, it's just that sometimes he overreacted in certain circumstances – that, I think, is OK.'

Yet even if such caution is a legitimate explanation for Djokovic's retirements and calls for the trainer, they weren't necessarily doing him any good. In early 2007 he sought the help of Mark Woodforde, the former doubles great and Australian Open singles semi-finalist, largely to help with 'transitioning' from the baseline to the net but also to gain from his experience in big matches. Woodforde was coaching Djokovic when he reached the semi-finals of Wimbledon in 2007. 'He was starting to realise he needed to spend more time on the physical,' Woodforde says. 'Everything was in comparison to Rafa and Roger – he kept asking, "How can they last five sets?", "How can they back up?" He'd been experiencing all these great results in the Slams but he was breaking down in the quarters and the semis because, physically, he was not at the same level he'd been at on day one.'

Having played five matches in a rain-affected Wimbledon 2007, which wiped out much of his recovery time late in the tournament, Djokovic developed a blister on his left little toe, which became infected. Woodforde explains,

He had retired a few times and that had called him to doubt his own integrity, but when he reached the semis at Wimbledon, he had this toe problem. I saw the toe and it was horrific – I hate to think what it was like to walk on. He was even talking about not playing the match against Nadal because he could barely walk and he hadn't slept. I wanted to implore the whole team that it was important to finish. I told Nole, 'If you keep going with this pattern that if you can't play you stop, you don't know what state the other guy is in – he may be going through the same trek as you are and he could fall over at any minute.' So I said you have to give yourself a chance. The accumulation of matches had certainly made the toe worse, there was a thought process going on in his head: 'I can't compete, and if I can't compete to win the match, don't play.' Whereas I said you've got to go out and play, at least try – this is the semifinals of Wimbledon, you can't not play! I think he had a painkilling injection, so he did play.

More than that, he won the first set, but once Nadal realised Djokovic couldn't really move, he took over, and with the Spaniard leading 4–1 in the third set, Djokovic threw in the towel.

Despite his efforts to get Djokovic to take to the court for that match, Woodforde copped a lot of flak from his fellow Aussies. 'I had friends coming to me saying, "How can you keep working with someone who retires in the semi-finals of Wimbledon? What are you saying to the guy? How could you let him do that?" Our philosophy in Australia was: when you step out on the court, you're fit. You don't stop. I had to explain that it wasn't as easy as you think. I could see this focus – he was asking, "What are Roger and Rafa doing?" because I have to do a little bit extra. But he wasn't ready at that time.'

Another two retirements came in early 2008. Having just won the Australian Open, he was feted in Belgrade, turning out on the balcony of the presidential residence to greet several thousand cheering fans. For some reason, on a cold early February day, he appeared in the biting winter air wearing only a T-shirt and light trousers. Whether that caused the cold that afflicted him when he arrived in Moscow a week later, to spearhead Serbia's first-ever Davis Cup World Group match against Russia, is not totally clear – the whole Serbian team was ill that week and a far-from-100 per cent Nenad Zimonjic had to play singles on the first day having not played singles for years. Djokovic sat out the opening day but partnered Zimonjic to a win in the doubles. Then, needing to beat Nikolay Davydenko to take the tie to an unlikely live fifth rubber, Djokovic played two outstanding sets, only to drop the third. At that point he retired, citing his cold. There had been no indication to his captain, Bogdan Obradovic, or the *chef d'équipe* Nikki Pilic that he was thinking of quitting – he just stopped. Whether he had internally agreed to play three sets and then stop, nobody knows. But it confirmed his image as someone who might give up if you could keep him there long enough.

Against Federer in the Monte Carlo semi-finals, he quit because of 'breathing problems' after five games of the second set. It led to another round of critical comments and probably prepared the ground for his spat with Roddick at the US Open five months later.

If there was a moment when Djokovic grasped that there was

something to be gained by not quitting, it came at the Australian Open in 2010. A year after his quarter-final abdication against Roddick, he played another quarter-final, one he lost in five sets to Jo-Wilfried Tsonga. This time he had every reason for retiring because he was suffering severe stomach spasms that came early in the fourth set when he was leading by two sets to one. At one stage he took an impromptu bathroom break when he wasn't allowed to. The referee Wayne McKewen signalled to the umpire that it was OK because McKewen knew that, if he hadn't let Djokovic rush to the bathroom, there might have been an embarrassing accident on court. Djokovic threw up in the locker room and returned to finish the match, losing it 6–1 in the fifth as his strength waned. History records that was the last time he lost a match in Melbourne until his defeat to Stanislas Wawrinka in the 2014 quarter-finals.

The man in Djokovic's corner at that Australian Open was not Marian Vajda but Todd Martin. Martin, a former Australian and US Open runner-up, had been brought in as a consultant to help Djokovic deal with big matches at the sharp end of Grand Slam tournaments and, with Vajda wanting to spend a bit more time at home, Martin looked after Djokovic on that trip down-under. Of the Tsonga match in January 2010, Martin says,

In my opinion, he had a responsibility. He was still able to play, to compete, but it was more important than that. In order for him to get to where he is now, he had to cross a few psychological barriers, and one of them is certainly dealing with the heat of Australia, the cardiovascular challenges at the extreme. First and foremost, he had to look in the mirror and say, 'Do I want to be third for ever or do I want to push this?' My belief, though I don't know this for sure, is that he answered in the affirmative and he started doing more work. I think I caught him at an interesting time in his career: one, because he was running into some challenges after a very steady and steep rise in the game, but also at a time when, as a child, he had worked very hard at his craft and this was his opportunity to cruise a little bit. It was really easy for him to be No. 3, he defended so well, he didn't have to learn how to play other elements of the game, but how much work did he want to put in? How much off-court discipline did he want to put in so he put his best foot forward every time he went out on the court? When he got out on the court, he did great. He poured his heart and soul into every match. But that's the easy part. You have to pour your heart and soul into your practice and into the regimentation of the rest of your day – those are the challenges, those are really big challenges that the great do very gracefully. I'd be very surprised if he's not practising more than he was when I was with him, if he's not showing better discipline of diet, of sleep, all the things that people watching on TV don't see. He's certainly dealing with the heat of Australia wonderfully now.

But it was not just an attitude shift on Djokovic's part that came about during that match. On the island of Cyprus, a somewhat alternative Serbian doctor, Igor Cetojevic, had a lull in his schedule and turned on the television. It was mid-morning and Cetojevic found live tennis, Djokovic playing Tsonga on the Australian Open night session. Cetojevic was no tennis fan but had been told by Serbian friends to have a look at this Djokovic guy. Watching the match, Cetojevic was struck by how the commentator kept saying of his country's national hero, 'Novak is struggling with his asthma again.'

Cetojevic, a doctor trained in allopathic medicine who has moved into more holistic, alternative approaches to health, says he just couldn't see how Djokovic's problems could be asthma. 'From my observations and experience with Chinese traditional medicine,' he said, 'I could see that asthma was not the issue here. I know that generally most asthma symptoms appear in the morning – and Novak's match was in the evening. Also, if he really had an asthmatic condition, he would not have been able to play two good sets before the breathing difficulties appeared. I suspected that, in Novak's case, his breathing problem resulted from an imbalance in his digestive system, specifically from an accumulation of toxins in his large intestine. In traditional Chinese medicine, the lungs are paired with the large intestine.'

The person who had suggested to Cetojevic that he look at Djokovic had links to the player and initiated contact. The result was that Djokovic and Cetojevic met in July 2010, when Serbia travelled to Split for a Davis Cup local derby quarter-final against Croatia. Cetojevic did some kinesiological muscle testing and, for confirmation, wired Djokovic up to a 'biofeedback device' which is claimed to measure stress, environmental toxins, brainwaves and food allergies. From those tests, Cetojevic concluded that Djokovic had an intolerance to gluten and, to a lesser extent, to dairy and tomatoes – just what the son of pizzeria owners wanted to hear! (Some people, including Djokovic himself, wonder if eating large amounts of pizza as a child brought on the intolerances.) It confirmed the finding of the homoeopath Gencic had taken Djokovic to much earlier, which Cetojevic knew nothing about until contacted for this book. Cetojevic put the player on a diet of gluten-free cereal, fresh berries, nuts and herbal tea. The most immediate result of the new diet was a loss of weight, and Djokovic didn't exactly have much weight to lose. But he persisted with the regime and the weight came back. Djokovic also adopted some breathing techniques Cetojevic taught him, both for stressful situations in matches and to enable him to get a good night's sleep.

It should be pointed out that, in traditional allopathic medical circles, such methods are highly speculative and Cetojevic is a controversial figure. The allopathic world would baulk at such a non-medical diagnosis, as well as his website advertising 'Energetic Medicine'. But while the mainstream medical world views Cetojevic's methods as 'alternative', they are very much at the respected end of the alternative-health spectrum. Kinesiological muscle testing is widely used by kinesiologists, acupuncturists, physiotherapists and other practitioners, and there are plenty of medical professionals who have come to the conclusion that wheat and dairy can be the cause of all sorts of bodily inefficiencies. When asked whether Djokovic found his diagnosis strange, Cetojevic chuckled, saying, 'I'm a strange doctor anyway, I take different approaches to most doctors. The problem is that people are tuned to think that food can't buy you health – it's medicine that buys you health – when that's wrong. Health comes through eating the right food.'

Cetojevic certainly believes all top-level sports people should eliminate gluten, or at least not eat any too soon before they do their sport. 'It's like putting dirty fuel into a Ferrari,' he says. 'You can do it and the car will still run but not very well. Gluten is sticky, it slows you down. A lot of tennis players still start the day of a big match with croissants and double coffee!' In traditional medical circles, his blanket rejection of gluten is at best speculative and at worst quack therapy. Yet energy exists in various forms, Chinese medicine has been around for thousands of years, and with wheat being genetically modified and mass produced for the world to consume, who's to say a lot of people aren't gluten-intolerant who are not picked up by traditional medical methods? The fact that a number of people with wheat intolerances can eat spelt, an ancient form of wheat that is not mass-produced and is genetically different to conventional wheat, suggests that the human body may be fine with certain types of wheat, or with high-quality wheat, but labours with mass-produced, genetically modified wheat.

This is not the place to get into too much speculation about the nutritional and medical properties of wheat. However, what is beyond doubt is that Djokovic felt a lot stronger as a result of Cetojevic's regime. That could be because he was genuinely gluten-intolerant, it could be purely psychosomatic, it could be a mixture of the diet and better sleep, or it could be for tennis reasons – for Djokovic to lead Serbia to the Davis Cup title in 2010 freed him up, allowing him to play the sublime tennis that saw him win three of the four majors and totally dominate tennis in 2011. Any scientist will tell you that, if you tackle a problem with two or more approaches, you can never be entirely sure what has solved it.

This is important to remember in the light of a book Djokovic brought out in mid-2013 in which he talks about the discovery of his gluten intolerance. Entitled *Serve to Win*, it's a 160-page paperback that is partly an explanation of the problems gluten causes and partly a recipe book, with a few of Djokovic's life experiences thrown in for illustration. Even allowing for its rather lame title, it's an unsatisfying book, largely because you wonder who wrote it. Djokovic's name is on the cover and no ghost-writer is credited, but the 'voice' of the narrative is simply not Djokovic's – it's rather breathless, whereas he is a very calm speaker, and some of the corny references to tennis in passages about nutrition would never have come from him (wheat and dairy are at one stage listed as 'the mixed doubles team from hell' – ouch!). There is a lot of research quoted but it's almost all American and Djokovic has never lived in America, and he certainly didn't have time to do this much research in the period when the book was written, because he was playing a punishing schedule of tennis tournaments.

The book has a foreword by Dr William Davis, a medical doctor and the father of Lauren Davis, an American player making her way on the women's tour who cracked the top 100 at the end of 2012.

Bill Davis has written a best-selling book about weaning yourself off wheat. The voice in the foreword is very similar to the voice in the narrative, which leads one to wonder whether Davis wrote the book and put it into the first person for Djokovic to approve, with a few of Djokovic's childhood and tennis details thrown in to personalise it. You could hardly blame him – if you're battling for your theory to be recognised and are up against the multi-million-dollar multi-national food industry (and especially the multi-million-dollar agribusiness that produces modern wheat in large quantities), you would seize on a top-level high-profile sportsman who exemplifies your message. If Djokovic was happy to put his name to the book, well, why not? He will, no doubt, have profited financially and felt good about spreading the word about his good fortune. Or the real author may be Stephen Perrine, who's listed in the acknowledgements section as the 'editor and collaborator' and who did a number of interviews with Djokovic while the book was being prepared. Whoever really wrote it, the book has some useful information about why gluten *might* be bad for you (no two people are alike, so some people may be fine with it) and how you can avoid eating it if you need to. It just feels a little dishonest because the guy whose name is on the cover clearly didn't write it.

Perhaps another reason why the tone doesn't feel right is not just its inconsistency with Djokovic but that it makes out that the gluten intolerance was the silver bullet that took him from a failure to a world-beater. It wasn't quite like that. He was world No. 3 even with the gluten, he had been Australian Open champion in 2008 and there may have been other elements that helped him move from Federer and Nadal's shadow to the undisputed world No. 1. The fact that he finished the match against Tsonga was also of significance – he learned not to give up, even if he felt like dead meat for his opponent. His coach Marian Vajda has said Djokovic started to hit his forehand harder around this time. And it was surely no coincidence that his all-conquering year of 2011 came immediately after Serbia had won the Davis Cup – as the standard-bearer of a proud nation, that team triumph was also a key to unlocking his potential (see page 209).

There's no doubt that identifying the gluten intolerance was a massive boost for Djokovic the tennis player, and it could well have implications for the restaurant culture in Serbia. The 'Novak' restaurants now offer gluten-free menu options, something of a rarity in Serbia but probably something that will be copied by other eating establishments. Yet it seems wiser to view the diet as a significant piece in a jigsaw puzzle, rather than the sole key. In a puzzle, certain pieces seem highly significant but the puzzle can't be completed without all the pieces.

Such was Djokovic's feel-good factor after working with Cetojevic that the good doctor began travelling with him to tournaments. During the year he was part of the entourage, Djokovic won the Davis Cup, the Australian Open, Wimbledon and reached No. 1 in the rankings. At that point, after the Wimbledon triumph, Cetojevic stopped travelling. He says he was getting sick of the travel – 'I don't like hotels and all that rubbish, and all the waiting around' – and he'd achieved his aim, so it was a natural time to stop working with Djokovic. Vajda was quoted as saying there had been 'differences of opinion' with Cetojevic but nothing has ever been made of them, and the fact that Djokovic brought out the book that gives massive prominence to Cetojevic suggests they parted on good terms. Cetojevic still speaks incredibly highly of both Djokovic and Vajda.

The culmination in Djokovic's battle to overcome his array of health impediments came in a 48-hour period at the end of January 2012. After beating Andy Murray in four hours, 50 minutes to reach the Australian Open final as Friday night became Saturday morning, Djokovic had to return at 7.30pm on the Sunday to face Nadal in the final. That final ran for five hours, 53 minutes and

Djokovic recovered from 2-4 adrift in the final set. This was the quitter, the man who was always calling the trainer at the slightest sniff. There was always something inconsistent between his iron-will determination and his fragility in the big matches. Finally, the inconsistency was resolved. Roddick's sarcasm, though understandable, had been misplaced – Djokovic was not 'the most courageous guy of all time', he was just cautiously trying to get his health right. Perhaps Roddick can thank his lucky stars that he never faced Djokovic in full health.

CHAPTER TEN

THE CHAMPION MUST COME FROM WITHIN

From the vantage point of 28 January 2008, Djokovic looked to have launched himself on a career as a Grand Slam champion and permanent front-line favourite for every tournament he entered. Yet with the benefit of hindsight, he was not to leave that particular launch pad for another three years. During that period he was the undisputed world No. 3 – albeit under growing challenge from Andy Murray – but could never break through Federer's and Nadal's stranglehold.

Soon after that Australian Open, it transpired that Federer had been suffering from mononucleosis or glandular fever. He had even spent a night in a Sydney hospital the week before the Open and his participation was in grave doubt. The fact that he reached the semi-finals and came through a gruelling 10–8 fifth-set win against Janko Tipsarevic in the third round have led some to wonder whether he really did have mononucleosis at all. He maintains he did, but whether it was that particular virus or something milder, Djokovic was clearly helped by playing a below-best Federer. The fact that, in the subsequent 11 majors, Djokovic reached just one final and four semi-finals suggests his 2008 Australian Open title was a positive blip in a gradual upward trend but that he was still far from the finished object.

He was after all still only 20; younger than Roger Federer had been when he won his first major. Nenad Zimonjic says, 'When Novak won the Australian Open, he was still very young, he wasn't really strong physically at the time and his serve still had the habit of breaking down.' The result was a 2008 that promised more than it was ever likely to deliver – he won another five titles over the 18 months after his Australian Open triumph, plus a bronze medal at the Beijing Olympics that seemed to mean a lot to him. But it was a period of consolidation, rather than a surge forward.

One of those five titles was the inaugural Serbian Open in Belgrade in April 2009. It was a triumph for his country and his family, given that his family was behind Serbia's first tour-level tournament. The title forms a nice pair with the Futures title he won at Red Star Belgrade, his first professional tournament victory. But the Serbian Open proved a short-lived triumph, given that the tournament faded badly after that first year and disappeared from the calendar three years later.

At the start of 2009 he had switched racket companies, moving from the Wilson frame with which he had won the Australian Open to a Head frame. Switching rackets is always somewhat risky, as the racket is the single most personal tool in a tennis professional's bag and some players opt for a lucrative deal, only to find they lose their confidence on the big points – for example the Australian Pat Cash won Wimbledon in 1987 and was runner-up at the 1988 Australian Open, both with a Prince racket, but had switched to Yonex by mid-1988 and was never the same again (although some of that was down to injuries). While he was no doubt amply rewarded in financial terms, Djokovic had played with a Head racket in his junior days, so it wasn't a completely new frame-maker for him. It took him several months to be completely comfortable with his new racket, and during those months there were plenty who were happy to suggest he had gone for the money over the best interests of his tennis. For him, that time was an investment in adjusting to a weapon with which he could conquer the world.

And yet by the middle of 2009, he himself and those around him were beginning to wonder where the next surge was going to come from. In May his ranking had slipped to fourth as Andy Murray joined the big three, which meant he was seeded fourth for the French Open. He lost to Philipp Kohlschreiber in the third round of the French and to Tommy Haas in the quarter-finals of Wimbledon. Neither are embarrassing defeats against players who, on a given day, can be the equal of the world's best players, but they were hardly the results of a player on course to break the Federer-Nadal duopoly.

So in July 2009 Djokovic and Vajda brought another voice into their team. 'This is the good thing about Novak,' says Zimonjic, 'he's not afraid of trying something different, he wants to improve, he wants to be the best he can be. He could easily have said, "Listen, I'm playing in a time when there are the two best players of all time and I'm happy to be No. 3 in the world." But no, he said he wanted to get better, to beat Roger and Rafa. And he became No. 1 in the world with them around. He beat them in the big matches on the biggest stages; he won the Grand Slams with them there. That shows how good he is.'

The person he brought in was Todd Martin. The tall, studious, softly spoken American was an interesting choice – he had twice reached the final of a major, losing to Pete Sampras in Melbourne in 1994 and to Andre Agassi in New York five years later, but was perhaps better known for blowing a 5–1 advantage in the final set of his Wimbledon semi-final against MaliVai Washington in 1996. He was regarded as a likeable man who played somewhat dour tennis and with a match temperament that could be a little flaky (although that has to be taken with some relativity, as he won eight tour titles and was a mainstay for the US Davis Cup team for a decade).

'They felt they needed someone with a stronger playing background, with experience in the latter stages of Grand Slams,' says Martin. 'Someone who played aggressively and someone to provide an element of calm into the relatively emotional mix of parents, agent, coach, physio and player. It came at a time when Marian [Vajda] wanted to spend a little more time at home. They took me on as a general consultant more than anything else, but I was at some tournaments when Marian was at home. That made some people ask if I'd taken over from Marian but I was at home when he looked after Novak.'

Martin was instantly struck by Djokovic's determination and inner confidence. He tells a story from August 2009, when the two were having a chat with a player who was no longer on the tour and who hadn't had a particularly distinguished career. 'The conversation was about the amount of support that federations provide,' he says, 'and this one fellow was bemoaning the fact that he hadn't had the support he felt he needed. When we got on to the support younger players might get, Novak said, "But the champion must come from within," or words to that effect – he said it very well. I'm a huge believer of that and I used that line on him a few times because, at that point in his career, I felt he wasn't allowing himself to be the champion. He's obviously crossed that bridge since then.'

For some reason, Martin's appointment was picked up by the media as being a case of the American being brought in to help with the Djokovic serve. Martin says that's 'a complete misrepresentation', as his role was more general, but the serve did become a central feature of his working relationship with Djokovic.

He recalls, of his first meeting with Team Djokovic,

> I went to Canada to meet them and was alarmed at what I saw with the serve. If you look at video from 2006–7, he had a beautiful service motion – way better than it is now. And he serves very well now – I actually think he serves better than he did then but his serve was a very languid, fluid, beautiful motion. It sounded like he was doing it to protect his shoulder but I have a bit of video that's shocking – it shows all the different things he was doing wrong, but really, at the core of it, the most important issue needing to be resolved was the fact that his elbow stayed straight until the very last second of the forward and upward swing, so it was never consistently loaded. One thing Novak does well in every element of his game is get loaded, he's ready to pull the trigger, but with his serve he just wasn't. Because of all the nonsense, if something goes awry and you try to figure it out with all other stuff, rhythm starts to be a really significant issue.

As a new coach, as someone who was working alongside the primary coach, Martin felt he needed to bide his time before even broaching the subject with Vajda. He encouraged Vajda to address it during the off-season at the end of 2009, but for some reason there was a conscious decision not to, and in the early months of 2010 Djokovic's serve was something of a basket case. He didn't serve well at the Australian Open, where he lost in the quarter-finals to Jo-Wilfried Tsonga – Djokovic puts one horrendous double fault to concede serve in the fifth set down to the after-effects of throwing up (see page 173) but he wasn't serving well anyway – and his serving at his next-but-one tournament in Dubai was a disaster. Yet he won the title! 'The technique was pretty bad,' says Nenad Zimonjic, 'but that showed how tough he was mentally. For me, his biggest win was in winning the Dubai tournament in 2010. It's extremely fast there, the ball flies, and he was double-faulting all the time. But he was breaking guys five or six times per match because he couldn't hold his own serve, which meant his game was improving a lot except the serve. Once he got back the rhythm on the serve, once he got back better technique, he was even stronger all round. That made him better than ever. Most guys would have given up [and] said, "Oh, my serve is so bad," and not have fought, but he fought through it and became a better player because of it.'

In late February Martin asked Djokovic if he was ready to address the serve issues. 'It was an issue for him every day,' he says, 'and he said yes. So we spent the next two weeks working on it through Indian Wells and Miami. And then we stopped.'

Much as Djokovic has many admirers for his willingness to take on short-term external help, many of those admirers are wary because of the suddenness with which some of the help has been dropped. Like others before him, Martin was phoned by Djokovic's agent and told his services were no longer required. 'I suspect his dad encouraged the end of the relationship,' he says, 'but I didn't have much to do with him. I had dinner with Srdjan once or twice and we were together in London for the ATP Finals, and maybe one other time, but largely I had little or no contact with him, mainly because of the language barrier. I do think that Srdjan was part of it all but in a different way. I think that there was a transition occurring, an establishment of some autonomy in Novak's own life. I think his existence was dysfunctional at the time and I think I was collateral damage.'

That's a fair enough assessment from Martin's perspective, but from Team Djokovic's perspective, Martin simply didn't fit. When news emerged in April 2010 that Martin had left the entourage,

Djokovic's main comment to the media was that 'it just didn't work out'. In an interview with ESPN just over a year later, Vajda said, 'There was bad communication; it was really counterproductive. He went down with the serve; he couldn't serve last year. It was terrible. Everything was tough. Novak never had the impression to [avoid] work but the communication was different. Todd was a big player and also wanted to try something new. But Novak was all set up, he only [needed] small improvements.' And in a later interview with the *Daily Telegraph*, Vajda said, 'When Todd came it was counter-productive. Somehow Todd didn't recognise Novak as a holistic person.'

Despite being fired, Martin remains on very relaxed terms with Djokovic and there appears no bitterness on either side about the way it ended. He says,

I think I helped with the diagnosis [of the serve problem] but wasn't given an opportunity to see through the cure. I had a pretty clear vision for what I felt he needed to be doing and now he starts with a bent elbow and he keeps it bent throughout his motion. But while the end of our working relationship was bizarre at the time, I walked away feeling like every coach's primary objective should be to become unnecessary. I didn't become unnecessary during my time with Novak, but I'm sure I've planted a few seeds that have contributed to my being unnecessary. I don't think anyone from the outside looking in would have come in and said much different to what I said. They'd have said, 'Eventually, you'll have to play with some force.' The first time I hit with Novak I was blown away by how heavy his ball was and then I'd watch him compete and he'd hit the ball 10 per cent slower than whoever he was playing. These days he goes out and lets the guys have it. That's effectively made him significantly more offensive than anything to do with volleying better. You don't have to volley better to be able to come to the net with more authority.

Looking at the three years between Djokovic winning the Australian Open and his *annus mirabilis* of 2011, it's tempting to look for a turning point. The match with Tsonga in January 2010 is an obvious one, as is Serbia's Davis Cup triumph in December 2010. But Djokovic himself says that, if there was a distinct point after which things really moved forward for him, it was the French Open and Wimbledon in 2010. 'There were a few particular moments that I would say were turning points,' he said in 2013, 'but probably Wimbledon 2010. Since that tournament, I started playing much better, more confident. The first six months of 2010 I was going through a lot of health issues, I wasn't able to [get] so many great results, I lost a lot of confidence but managed to come back.'

It's a point made by Nenad Zimonjic. 'After he made the semis at Wimbledon, that was the point when he got the confidence back. Then he started to play better. We noticed it at the Davis Cup quarter-final against Croatia a week later. He was under a lot of pressure, his serve still wasn't working well but he came through it. It was like a final couple of struggles that made him where he is now – everything from struggling for funding in his teenage years to his serve breaking down, it all made him stronger.'

The shock to the system that galvanised him into an extra level of determination came when he lost to Juergen Melzer in the French Open quarter-finals. He led the 29-year-old Austrian by two sets to love, then had a break midway through the final set before losing it 6–4 in four and a quarter hours. Again there were signs of breathlessness, described on the day as 'hayfever-like symptoms', and there was one controversial line-call in the final game that went against Djokovic after the umpire inspected a mark in the clay. But the sense was that he was a round ahead of himself, preparing to face Rafael Nadal in the semis before dealing with the obstinate Melzer.

Djokovic should, perhaps, have reached the Wimbledon final four weeks later. After coming back from two-sets-to-one down to beat the diminutive Olivier Rochus in the first round, he had dropped just one set en route to the semi-finals, that against the former champion Lleyton Hewitt, who was still a top-30 player. He then faced Tomas Berdych, the man who had put out the defending champion Roger Federer in the previous round. Djokovic thought his steadier groundstrokes would win the match for him but he was too conservative and the big-hitting Czech took advantage. Still Djokovic may well have won if he'd converted one of the two set points he had in the second set tie-break – he had come back from 2–6 down, saving four set points five times (at 5–6, they replayed a point Djokovic had clearly won with a lob). Once he lost the tie-break 11–9, the game was up and Berdych won in straight sets.

Had he won that match, it's hard to see Djokovic having beaten Rafael Nadal in the final. The Spaniard was in his raging best form and doused the power of Berdych's powerful groundstrokes in an emphatic display to claim his second Wimbledon title. But Djokovic had done enough to make himself feel good about where his game was going.

His victories over Croatia – over the weekend he was introduced to Igor Cetojevic for the first time (see pages 174–5) – were less important in tennis terms than in socio-political terms. This was a local derby, and while the two sets of supporters were very different in character from football fans attending a Croatia-Serbia international or a Dinamo Zagreb v Red Star Belgrade club match, it was still a highly charged atmosphere in Split's Spaladium. His straight-sets wins were over two friends: Ivan Ljubicic, by then well past his best and only turning out because of an injury crisis in the Croatian team, and the world No. 13 Marin Cilic. Cilic's win over Janko Tipsarevic meant his match with Djokovic was live on the final day, but Djokovic played an outstanding match, dropping just eight games.

The real premium from his Wimbledon confidence boost came at the US Open, when he reached the final by beating Roger Federer in the semis, saving two match points in the process. This time Federer was the conservative one while Djokovic went for his shots on the big points – including one breathtaking forehand to end a long rally and save a match point – and was rewarded with a 7–5 win in the fifth set. He was beaten in the final by the all-conquering Nadal, the Spaniard being deprived of a calendar-year Grand Slam only by the knee injury he suffered in the first set of his Australian Open quarter-final – without that, Nadal would probably have won all four majors that year. But the big story for Djokovic for the rest of 2010 involved Serbia's quest to win tennis's premier team prize, the Davis Cup. And that US Open final, which took place on the Monday evening because of rain, very nearly thwarted the Serbs.

Djokovic arrived back in Belgrade feeling worse for wear. The secret was kept from Serbia's Davis Cup semi-final opponents, the Czech Republic. Indeed, Djokovic was nominated on the Thursday to play in Friday's singles. But on Friday morning, using a rule that has to exist for pragmatic reasons but undermines other Davis Cup rules, Serbia replaced Djokovic for medical reasons, saying the player had gastroenteritis. His place was taken by Viktor Troicki, who promptly lost to Radek Stepanek. Serbia's cause was saved by Janko Tipsarevic's superb win over a tiring Tomas Berdych, whose stellar year was beginning to catch up with him.

Mirroring what Serbia had done two years earlier when Djokovic was ill for the tie against Russia, Serbia's captain Bogdan Obradovic opted to throw Djokovic in for the doubles alongside his old mentor Nenad Zimonjic (officially it was the captain's decision, but most people assume Djokovic calls the shots in the Serbian team and Obradovic has the diplomatic skills to present decisions as his own – this happens in a lot of Davis Cup teams with one dominant player). Djokovic and Zimonjic had won their two previous Davis Cup doubles but this time they were up against quality opposition in Berdych and Stepanek, and the Czechs won in four sets, ending the match with an emphatic 6–1 in the fourth. On that Saturday night, the Serbian dream of a first Davis Cup success, which had looked so favourable given their home draws, looked to be evaporating.

At least Djokovic had had some court time, which was supposed to help him against Berdych in the first reverse singles. Yet with the Czech leading by a set, and a break up in the second, it was all going wrong for the Serbs. That was when Djokovic summoned up his acting skills. By then (September 2010) he had effectively given up on his impersonations of other players' strokes, but his ability to act was needed to outpsyche Berdych and turn the tide of a match Serbia had to win.

In the sixth game of the second set, Djokovic was playing some desperate defence. He threw up a lob, Berdych smashed it into the ground and, as the ball bounced up high, the Serb lunged to try and retrieve it. It was a hopeless cause, and as he came down, he fell and ended up motionless on the surface behind the baseline. As the applause died down, Djokovic continued to lie motionless. A nervous hush descended over the Beogradska Arena. The umpire got off his chair and ran over to the player to see if he was all right. Obradovic left his bench to see if his man was all right. Only with a crowd of people around him did Djokovic start to move. He was eventually helped back to his chair on the shoulders of Obradovic and the Serbian team physio.

For a few moments, the 17,000-strong crowd thought their

dreams were over. Their hero was wounded, already struggling against a fired-up Berdych and now unable to fight back with full fitness. But Djokovic wasn't really injured. Although he wasn't going to admit this for fear of bringing the game into disrepute, he knew Berdych was vulnerable to having his rhythm disrupted, so he had to find a way to disrupt it. The Czech is one of the best ball-strikers of his era, and when he's on song he can beat the very best, but there is a slightly formulaic nature to his play, and Djokovic had figured he just needed to knock the Czech off his stride. So a thin, almost pathetic bandage was put under Djokovic's left knee, he came back out to continue the match, promptly broke back, broke again to level the match at one-set-all and duly won in four sets. Was it gamesmanship? – probably, but his country came calling, and he did what he needed to. And it was all within the rules, albeit rules written to keep tennis going when a player is injured. The more interesting interview after the match came from Berdych, who clearly felt Djokovic had exploited the rules but refused to make a big thing of it, no doubt because he felt a bit sheepish at having fallen into the trap.

With Janko Tipsarevic playing one of his best-ever Davis Cup matches to beat Stepanek in the fifth, Serbia's Davis Cup dream moved on in dramatic style. The nation was in the final, and that final would be at home against one of the giants of Davis Cup history, France.

The final was clearly Djokovic's priority at the end of the year. He played five tour events, winning Beijing and losing in the final of Basel to Roger Federer. He reached the semi-finals of the ATP Finals in London but was almost a little lacklustre in going down 6–1, 6–4 to Federer – everyone recognised that his mind was not on winning a second year-ending singles title but on the national challenge a fortnight later. Yet that defeat to Federer on 19 November 2010 should not go unnoticed. Although no one knew it at the time, it was to be Djokovic's last defeat for six and a half months – or 195 days.

The Davis Cup final followed a similar pattern to the semi-final – in fact, a similar pattern to many of Serbia's matches. There is an implicit assumption when Djokovic plays that his two singles are largely counted as bankers, with the Serbs needing one win from the three other matches. With a team of three top-50 singles players and an experienced doubles specialist, that gave the Serbs three realistic bites of the cherry, yet when Tipsarevic offered very little resistance against France's top player Gael Monfils on the opening day, and with Troicki and Zimonjic squandering a two-set lead to lose the doubles to Arnaud Clement and Michael Llodra, Serbia's dream rested on the hosts winning both the final day's singles.

Djokovic was majestic in beating Monfils for the loss of just eight games. He was feted as a conquering hero as he walked into the Belgrade Arena in his red Serbian shirt, and he crushed Monfils like a man on a mission. But the loss of the doubles meant that win only teed up a decisive fifth rubber – Djokovic couldn't hit the cup-winning shot himself. Whether it was his decision or Obradovic's, the responsibility of winning the Davis Cup was given to Victor Troicki and not Janko Tipsarevic, largely because Troicki emerged from his doubles with more confidence than Tipsarevic had emerged from his singles on the Friday. It proved an inspired decision, although the luckless Michael Llodra freezing on the other side of the net also assisted Serbia's cause. Troicki, an only child who viewed his Davis Cup team-mates as his brothers, played the match of his life and saw Serbia to the most ecstatic of victories.

It was Troicki who, during the quarter-final against Croatia five months earlier, had suggested that if Serbia won the Davis Cup, the players and team officials would all have their heads shaved. Such private bets or challenges often happen, but few expected this one to happen so publicly. A hairdresser had been hired for the day, and once Troicki had done his post-match on-court interviews, all four players, plus the captain Bogdan Obradovic, the Serbian Tennis Federation president Slobodan Zivojinovic and even the septuagenarian team supremo Nikki Pilic, all came under the electric razor. It was a nightmare for the International Tennis Federation staff, who were trying to prepare the presentation ceremony of the biggest jewel in the ITF's crown – respected marketing and organisational executives, power-dressed to give the impression of professional slickness, found themselves with brooms, sweeping away shaved tufts of hair from the presentation stage. What the players will think when they show their grandchildren the photos of the team holding the trophy is open to question – they'll probably just have to explain that they were so happy they weren't responsible for their appearance. Asked about his new look an hour later, Djokovic said in an interview, 'I'm wearing a hat – that tells you all you need to know.' Despite never having let his thick hair grow anywhere near what could be described as long, or even medium length, Djokovic was delighted that he had a few weeks for it to grow back before his next public appearance in January in Australia.

There was something touching about the chaos with which Serbia's Davis Cup triumph was celebrated. There is always an official dinner a couple of hours after the final finishes, in which it is customary for the losing team to turn up smartly dressed in a show of sportsman-ship. Such dinners are carefully organised and choreographed, but on this occasion more people turned up than had invitations, and even some of the Davis Cup's stalwart officials found their promised seat had been occupied because it was just the place to be for everyone who thought they were anyone in Belgrade society.

Later, in the small hours, there was a party in a club just off Republic Square in the centre of Belgrade. A Serbian brass band played traditional Serbian music as the players celebrated their success. None of the four would want that night to be seen as typical of their approach to the discipline required of top-level athletes – as well as having several glasses of champagne, they all smoked Cuban cigars, a sign of the opulence they must have felt (although smoking is much more a part of national culture in Serbia than in western Europe or America). The Serbian sports journalist Zoran Milosavljevic, who was present, said, 'The raw emotions Djokovic and the other players let out at that party showed just how deep the patriotism runs in him. You could see why he would do it, why some people say he would prop up Serbia with one hand if necessary.'

The players were heroes. They had put Serbia on the map and all four were given diplomatic passports in April 2011. On the night of Sunday 5 December 2010, it seemed that this was the height of their careers – what could possibly compare with this? Maybe when they all finish playing some will quote that night as the pinnacle, but for all of them, the Serbs' Davis Cup success was to prove the springboard to dramatic rises in personal fortunes over the next couple of years, none more so than for Djokovic himself.

CHAPTER ELEVEN

THE ROLE OF
SPORT IN SERBIA

To say sport is an integral part of Serbian life and culture would be accurate, but it doesn't take us very far. For a start, one needs to distinguish football from the rest of sport – football is so engrained that it has for decades been an extension of wider battles, whether inter-nation struggles and self-determination, or nationalist versus federalist systems of government. And the other sports that feature prominently in Serbian life are generally team sports, so while Novak Djokovic may come from a country with sport in its blood, you won't find many tennis balls in the arteries.

Having said that, when comparing Djokovic's standing in Serbia with, say, Roger Federer's in Switzerland, the sporting backdrop is much more in Djokovic's favour. The Swiss are a landlocked people with no raw materials – their affluence has been achieved through hard work in a variety of labour-intensive industries: watch and clock making, cheese, chocolate and tourism. As such, the Swiss are happy to admire the exploits of a top-level sportsman but respect for entertainers and athletes doesn't run to celebrity complexes. Federer has often remarked how he can still walk through the streets of his home city of Basel without too many people stopping him, and a childhood tennis-playing friend of his who went on to become an adviser in Swiss politics said, 'You couldn't imagine the Swiss having a David Beckham culture.' By contrast, sport stands on a sufficiently high pedestal in Serbian life that Djokovic can become a national hero, even if few fully understand his sport.

Football is clearly streets ahead as Serbia's top sport. Then basketball comes a clear second. Next would come volleyball and handball, and water polo is also very popular. So the top five sports in Serbia are all team sports, with tennis not really scoring. Until the Ivanovic/Djokovic golden age, tennis was thought of very much as a minority elite sport, played by the old royal family and their cohorts but not really by the people. But then all individual sports struggle for recognition in Serbia – a few boxers, wrestlers and shooters have become short-term heroes and Serbia won gold in taekwondo at the London Olympics. But it's mainly a team-sport nation, which explains the importance to Djokovic and Serbia of winning the Davis Cup in 2010. In the eyes of his compatriots, that was the ultimate achievement in his sport, especially as he was able to do it on home soil.

The magnitude of football's role in Serbian consciousness is probably best understood by the part it played in the Yugoslav wars of the 1990s, in particular the Serbo-Croat war. A full description of just how closely football and Serbian nationalism were linked in the 1990s appears in Jonathan Wilson's book *Behind the Curtain*, and these pages can only offer a brief summary.

A number of people are willing to say – quite seriously – that the opening salvo in the Serbo-Croat war was fired when Dinamo Zagreb played Red Star Belgrade in 1990. Indeed, there is a statue outside Zagreb's Maksimir Stadium that depicts a group of soldiers and underneath is the dedication, 'To the fans of this club, who started the war with Serbia at this ground on 13 May 1990.' The match came shortly after the election of Franjo Tudjman as president of Croatia on a nationalist platform, and Dinamo Zagreb's most loyal fans had pledged allegiance to Tudjman's HDZ party. Rocks had been stockpiled in advance; Red Star fans had brought bogus Belgrade number plates with them, which they put on Zagreb cars to con Dinamo fans into pelting rocks at their own nationals. Hundreds were arrested and well over 100 injured, including 79 police officers.

But if Dinamo v Red Star was a massive grudge match within the old Yugoslavia, the Belgrade city derby between Crvena Zvezda (Red Star) and Partizan is even more intense. Known as 'the eternal derby', the two teams were forever associated with rival political ideologies. Red Star was thought of as the Serbian nationalist club, while Partizan was the club of Tito's Partisans, the multi-nation force that repelled the Croatian Ustase and the Serbian Cetniks to help unify Yugoslavia after 1945. Indeed, in the late 1950s, Franjo Tudjman, a fervent Croatian nationalist, was president of Partizan and is believed to be responsible for the club's now familiar black-and-white playing strip. Partizan still exists, but the break-up of Yugoslavia means the political element has been severely weakened, even if the rivalry with Red Star is as strong as ever.

The political lines were never quite as firm as they were talked up to be. Red Star was founded in 1945, presumably by communists, as the red star is a communist emblem – it would certainly have been a smart move, given the way the political wind was blowing at the time. As the club has always been associated with the poor and oppressed, it's easy to see how it could have been founded by the communists but at the same time be anti-communist, given that Tito's post-1945 regime was a communist one (albeit without the same degree of economic collectivism prevalent in the Soviet bloc). In the 1970s, rival clubs taunted the Red Star fans with the term 'gipsies', an insult the Red Star faithful happily took on. It meant that, whenever Red Star's fans came across fans from another club, violence was almost inevitable, though in fairness, the same could be said for many leading clubs in English football in the late 1970s (the English happily forget that punch-ups were very much part of what many football fans were looking for at that time, despite the mealy-mouthed attempts by football administrators to claim it was 'only a small minority'). And if that other club was Partizan, the antipathy was at its most fierce. Support for the Yugoslav national team was always somewhat fragmented, as citizens of one constituent republic never quite knew how much to cheer for players from another nation, and that even extended to intra-city rivalry. Some Partizan players representing Yugoslavia were booed by their own crowd if there was a strong Red Star element in the stands.

The two sets of supporters of Red Star and Partizan amply illustrate the integration of sport, or at least football, into Serbian society.

Partizan's supporters are known as the 'Grobari', which means gravediggers or undertakers. Formed after Partizan reached the 1966 European Cup final, their home is in the South Stand of the club's home ground, the Partizan Stadium (formerly the JNA Stadium; JNA was the Yugoslav National Army), and the name comes from the cemetery of a church just by the stadium. They had a fearsome reputation in the 1970s and 1980s, and hooliganism accompanied them across Europe. Officially, the Grobari were shut down as an official entity in the 1990s after a rocket fired from the South Stand killed an eight-year-old Red Star fan during an eternal derby, but the name lives on in local parlance and occasional banners.

Red Star's supporters are known as the 'Delije', a word that loosely translates as 'hard men' or 'strong ones'. The Delije are broken down into several sub-groups, some with belligerent names such as Red Devils, Zulu Warriors and Ultras, and they come together at their spiritual home in the North Stand of the Red Star Stadium in central Belgrade (also known as the Marakana – see below). But this is more than just a fan club. The Delije have become known as something of a self-help society for Red Star fans. If that sounds all very nice, it's got a real edge to it, almost like something out of gangland culture. Many people in difficulties are helped but in a rather sinister, Masonic way. And when the battle for Serbian independence from Yugoslavia got underway, it's hardly surprising that the links between the Delije and the unofficial militias supporting the Serbian military should be so pronounced.

The biggest link came in the form of a mythical figure known as Arkan. His life story is pure gangster film script, and if no one has made a film about him, a chance has been missed, certainly in Serbia where – despite or because of his brutality – he is something of a folk hero.

Born Zeljko Raznatovic in 1952, Arkan was forever in trouble with the law, and imprisoned several times, including in Belgium, the Netherlands and West Germany. But he always seemed able to escape from jail, perhaps because of contacts he made with the Yugoslav state security service in his teens. He returned to Yugoslavia in 1983 and was one of the fans arrested at the notorious Dinamo Zagreb v Red Star Belgrade match in May 1990. In fact, Arkan was credited with cementing the name 'Delije' in an official inauguration in January 1989. At this time he was assembling a paramilitary force to play a key part in the forthcoming civil wars, and his force, known as the Tigers, was recruited largely from the Delije. The Tigers were involved in some of the most horrific battles of the Yugoslav wars, notably Vukovar

(Croatia) in 1991 and Bikjeljina (Bosnia) in 1992, often singing the songs they sang on the terraces at football matches. Arkan himself was indicted for war crimes during those battles but died before he could be brought to trial.

Some of those songs of the Delije and the Tigers were sung on the terraces of the flower-shaped San Nicola stadium in Bari, when Yugoslavia celebrated arguably its greatest sporting moment. That was when Red Star Belgrade won the European Cup (the forerunner of today's Champions League). The history of Yugoslav football was a tale of the nearly men. Three times they had reached the Olympic football final but come away with silver. Twice they had been World Cup semi-finalists but failed to reach the final. Partizan lost the 1966 European Cup final and Red Star lost the 1979 UEFA Cup final. No wonder many were happy to tag Yugoslavia 'chokers'.

But in 1991 Yugoslavia had a champion football team, albeit just at the moment when the country was unravelling in a sea of blood. The final in Bari was a horribly dour match, in which Red Star and Olympique Marseille – the French club that was about to be embroiled in a massive scandal surrounding its controversial owner, the French entrepreneur Bernard Tapie – played out a goalless draw over 120 minutes of normal and extra time. Red Star then won on penalties. Or perhaps it would be better to say Marseille lost on penalties, as the French club had a team full of players who had blown vital penalties in past shoot-outs and were haunted once more. Europe's most prestigious club-football title – if not the world's – was therefore a fillip for the club and, to a lesser extent, for the city of Belgrade, but not for Yugoslavia. Within a few months, the nations of some of the Red Star players were at war with each other, and within a year the club was banned from playing home games on Serbian soil.

In the mid-1990s Arkan tried to take over Red Star but failed. So in 1996 he bought a traditional but faded Belgrade club, Obilic, and within three years they were Yugoslav champions (what was left of Yugoslavia – in effect, Serbia and Montenegro). But the methods used in Obilic's seemingly amazing rise to the top of the national tree were not always conventional, with stories abounding of referees being intimidated, opposition stars developing last-minute injuries that prevented them from playing, and in one case even a delayed kick-off on the last day of the season when both the title and relegation depended on two matches, the delayed one involving Obilic.

Arkan met his end in January 2000, when someone fired 38 shots through him in a Belgrade café. His killer has never been found, which raises questions about whether the assassination was somehow sanctioned. What is clear is that 2000 was the year football died for Slobodan Milosevic.

Despite the damage to his standing caused by the loss of the Serbs' gains in the Croatian and Bosnian wars, and the Nato bombing of 1999, the fear created by Milosevic's communist regime was still very much intact in the summer of 2000. But then something happened at a Red Star game. Red Star were playing Torpedo Kutaisi from Georgia in a Champions League qualifying match. Whipped up by a 4–0 lead, the home fans started a chant that can best be translated as: 'Do Serbia a favour, Slobodan, and kill yourself.' The police stepped in as tensions were ramped up, and at one stage, a Red Star flag was seized by two police officers and trampled under foot. At that point, Red Star's coach, Slavoljub Muslin, spoke to the officers, got the flag off them and gave it back to the fans. Although a tiny gesture, it was seized upon as a sign that Red Star were willing to stand up to the Milosevic regime. After that, virtually every top-flight football match on Serbian territory became an anti-Milosovic rally, and with presidential elections due within two months, the effect was profound. Sixty days after the Red Star v Torpedo Kutaisi match, Milosevic lost the election and his attempts to cling to power were thwarted. Thus does the Delije claim to have orchestrated the downfall of Milosevic and communism.

If that's not enough of a role for sport in the political fortunes of a nation, the football writer Jonathan Wilson believes it runs even deeper than that. He says Serbia has always had the Brazilian flair, the Serbs have always thought of themselves as 'European Brazilians', and even nicknamed their main stadium in Belgrade the Marakana, copying the main football stadium in Rio de Janeiro. But he says it's more than just copying a style of football:

> I suspect it comes from a slave mentality. A lot of Brazilians come from the former enslaved peoples and survival as a slave meant adopting a mentality of cunning and trickery. It even finds its way into certain dances, and at times in Brazil it's more important to trick your opponent with a bit of clever footwork than it is to win the game. The southern Slavs have had a similar feeling of enslavement – for six centuries they were under the Ottoman Turks, and most of the history of Yugoslavia was a fight for existence in the face of the threat from Moscow. So I think the adopting of a lot of Brazilian habits in football, even if it may be largely subconscious, tells us something about how the Serbs and other former Yugoslav peoples see themselves.

An additional factor that might explain the feeling of enslavement is a theory among some ethnologists and linguists that the words 'Slav' and 'slave' have the same route. According to this theory, Slavs became slaves around the beginning of the ninth century, and the word 'slave' can be traced back through old English, old French and medieval Latin to the same word used by the early Slav peoples to define themselves. Even if there's no truth to this idea, the presence of the theory is enough to create an inferiority complex in those looking for one!

Wilson extends his hypothesis to the extent of calling Yugoslavia, and particularly the Serbs, 'Europe's most consistent chokers' in football. He cites the fact that the Yugoslav national team and its leading club teams always seemed to fall at the last hurdle. But in one case it didn't. Yugoslavia did in fact win the Under-18 football World Cup in 1988, leading some to wonder whether the country broke up just as its golden age of football was about to begin. But would Yugoslavia have done any better than Croatia did by coming third behind France and Brazil in the 1998 World Cup? No one will know, but past experience suggests probably not.

Extrapolating experience from Serbian football and transposing it on to tennis is a dangerous game because the two cultures are so different. Two of the leading tennis clubs are the tennis sections of Partizan and Red Star, and when they play each other at tennis, that too is known as 'the eternal derby', but there is vastly less sting in the tail than the football derby. The tennis fan base is an altogether more genteel crowd than the football community.

But in some ways, Djokovic has been a pacemaker for Serbian sport in the sense that he has broken the cycle that the Serbs are the perennial glorious losers. It's easy to forget that, until about 2008, possibly even as late as 2010, there was a feeling on the tennis tour that the Serbs were quitters. Ivanovic and Jankovic had reached the top but had fallen rapidly from it, Djokovic had won the Australian Open but not pushed on, and the men in general had a habit of often not allowing their opponents the achievement of winning – they often seemed to prefer to retire hurt from a match, rather than lose the final point (not just Djokovic – the very cerebral Janko Tipsarevic has retired from 25 matches in his career, tour-level and Challenger). Djokovic has turned that round by cutting out most of the retirements and demonstrating an ability to dig deep in some incredibly punishing matches. If there is a 'victim trait' in Serbian sport and society, he has shown that it can be overcome. And it was interesting to see that Sinisa Mihajlovic, the passionately pro-Serb coach of the Serbian national football team, attended all three days of the 2013 Davis Cup final to cheer on the Serbian national tennis team.

If the top five sports in Serbia are football, basketball, volleyball, handball and water polo, it's fair to ask where tennis comes now that four Serbs have topped the rankings and Ivanovic and Djokovic have become attractive icons for girls and boys. The answer is hard to gauge. Being able to fill a 17,000-seater indoor stadium for Davis Cup ties is a phenomenal achievement, but one-off events where people can tell their grandchildren that they saw the great Djokovic at the peak of his career are not a fair measurement of the general health of a sport. The Serbian Tennis Federation reported a 40 per cent increase in demand for court space in the six months after Djokovic reached the 2007 French Open quarter-finals, but will the current wave of interest last? We will probably only be able to judge 10 years after the Djokovic generation retires, when it becomes clear how many adults of working age want to play tennis having been inspired to take it up as kids because of the Djokovic boom.

One thing that needs correcting is the assumption that tennis in Serbia – even in the old Yugoslavia – began with Monica Seles, and that she and Djokovic are the first two big names. This is grossly unfair: indeed, the first national tennis association was founded in 1922 when the country was the Kingdom of Serbs, Croats and Slovenes. The royal family were keen tennis players, especially King Alexander I, who was assassinated in 1932. And a leading player in the 1920s and 1930s was Mladen Stojamovic, who had been Gavrilo Princip's principal accomplice in the assassination of

Archduke Franz Ferdinand in 1914, the act that triggered the outbreak of the First World War.

There were a number of big names in the early years, such as Dora Alavantic, and the 1970s – the growth decade of professional tennis after the end of the split amateur and professional circuits – had a number of prominent Yugoslavs. Nikki Pilic was at the centre of the 1973 Wimbledon boycott, Mima Jausovec was the French Open champion in 1977 and Zoran Petkovic (the father of the German player Andrea Petkovic) was a national champion and played Davis Cup for Yugoslavia. Then in the 1980s Yugoslavia twice reached the Davis Cup semi-finals, led by Slobodan Zivojinovic, and they did so for a third time in 1991 as Yugoslavia crumbled around them, the team of Zivojinovic (a Serb), Goran Ivanisevic and Goran Prpic (both Croats) breaking up after Yugoslavia's quarter-final victory over Czechoslovakia, as the Serbo-Croat war gathered pace.

By then, Monica Seles was world No. 1 in women's tennis. An ethnic Hungarian from Novi Sad in the north of Serbia, she won Yugoslavia's second Grand Slam singles title (after Mima Jausovec) when she became the youngest French Open champion in 1990 at the age of 16. What is interesting is that she was at the top of the world's sporting headlines in 1992, the year the five-year-old Novak Djokovic really caught the tennis bug, yet it was Pete Sampras's Wimbledon triumph in July 1993 that Djokovic always cites as more of an inspiration, rather than his compatriot's dominance of women's tennis. Seles was the runaway world No. 1 when she was stabbed on court in Hamburg on 30 April 1993. Despite her lead in the rankings, she lost the No. 1 spot within five and a half weeks to Steffi Graf, over whom Seles seemed to have a hold in big matches, certainly on hard and clay courts.

After being coached by her father Karolij and also Jelena Gencic, the Seles family moved to Florida when Monica was 12, so she could be near the Bollettieri Tennis Academy in Bradenton. The family eventually applied for US citizenship and Seles got hers in 1994, midway through the 27 months she missed of her playing career following the stabbing. It means eight of her nine major singles titles were won as a Yugoslav and only one as an American, but all nine were won with Sarasota, Florida very much her home and base.

So while tennis was recognised in Serbia before the era of Zimonjic, Tipsarevic, Jankovic, Troicki, Ivanovic and Djokovic, and had a long-standing basis in Serbia's sporting culture, it was by no means a prominent sport. It's therefore legitimate to view Serbia's golden generation a little like the emergence of soccer in America in the 1970s, or the emergence of rugby in Argentina or cycling in Great Britain – home-grown success in those sports raised the profile and participation level significantly but couldn't topple the existing established sports from their places in the national sporting psyche. As such, the future of tennis in Serbia may well depend on the post-Djokovic generation, as only the ability of the next lot to keep the fire burning will guarantee that tennis stays in the Serbian sporting limelight when there's no Djokovic to cheer and little chance of winning the Davis Cup.

CHAPTER TWELVE

'THIS IS WHAT I'M BORN FOR'

In the press conference that followed his Wimbledon victory in July 2011, Djokovic was asked to comment on a statement his mother had made: that winning the Davis Cup for Serbia seven months earlier taught him to play without fear. Djokovic replied, 'Well, if my mother says that, then it's like that. There is nothing else I can say. My mother knows me better than I know myself.'

It's easy to make the case that winning the Davis Cup freed up Djokovic and formed the missing piece in the jigsaw that allowed him to utterly dominate world tennis in 2011. Djokovic half-makes that argument himself. 'The Davis Cup title came in the right moment,' he says. 'I believe that title, that feeling of sharing one of the biggest titles in our sport with my team for our country, in our country, was one of the best feelings I experienced as a tennis player on the court. That was a great confidence boost and helped me to believe in myself, to believe more in my abilities on the court.'

But that would be too simple an explanation for his *annus*

mirabilis of 2011. There were several 'last pieces of the jigsaw', of which the gluten-free diet he discovered in mid-2010 was certainly one (whether actual or only in the mind – the health professionals are divided but his belief in the gluten-free diet was clearly of huge significance to his well-being), and rediscovering the rhythm on his serve was another. To that can be added a whole range of little things, from the orthotics in his shoes to the calm but authoritative backroom team presided over by Marian Vajda. And at the age of 23, he had a greater wealth of experience, including a more mature relationship with his father that gave him the sense of being in control of his own life, rather than having it run for him.

Yet it's important to remember that there were people at the start of 2011 who felt Djokovic may have peaked. He had won the Australian Open at 20, but since then he had spent three years clearly behind Federer and Nadal at the top of the game. Coming from a country where team sports were valued more importantly than individual sports, his biggest priority – so the hypothesis went – may well have been the Davis Cup. And with Andy Murray establishing himself as a member of the elite, there was no guarantee that Djokovic had a natural right to ascend to the world No. 1's throne when the fortunes of the great duo began to wane. So while it may look, with the benefit of hindsight, like the most natural progression, Djokovic's wonderful 2011 was by no means a given at the start of it.

He was, perhaps, a shade lucky in not having to face Nadal at Melbourne Park. Nadal went to Australia looking to hold all four major titles concurrently but he was undone by his left hamstring in the quarter-finals. Facing his compatriot David Ferrer, who has always seemed to lack belief against Nadal in Grand Slam matches, Nadal called for the trainer after three games and he left the court for treatment. Although he finished the match, it was clear he couldn't move at anything like his normal level, and Ferrer's straight-sets win took place in a somewhat bemused atmosphere, where no one at Melbourne Park could quite take what they were seeing at face value. In his post-match press conference, Nadal refused to talk about any injury, except for one hint that he couldn't move that well. It was an approach that divided the tennis community into those who felt it was all rather a fake and those who respected the dignity with which he refused to blame an injury for fear of undermining one of the best results of a fellow professional's career.

Perhaps Djokovic's biggest victory at that tournament was in beating Federer in the semi-finals. Thought of very much as a 50:50 beforehand, Djokovic outplayed Federer with his superb footwork. Federer was starting to put into practice the coaching of Paul Annacone, notably Annacone's suggestion that he play closer to the baseline to rob his opponent of vital split seconds. But every time Federer drove Djokovic wide, the Serb was there with blistering groundstrokes that would be anatomically impossible for players with lesser ankles, and the Serb won in three tight but clear sets. Interestingly, Djokovic favours his left foot when kicking a football, so it could be that he has an unusually strong left foot which allows him a firmer base than other players have for hitting big backhands when at full stretch.

He lost just nine games against Murray in the final. It's possible the real story of that final has never been fully told. Just before the walk on court, a tournament official wished Murray well, to which Murray muttered misanthropically, 'Hopefully, I can get through it.' The Scot had been suffering from back problems throughout that fortnight, and while it's hard to know what exactly to read into his rather pained body language when he's losing (until recently, Murray seldom lost a match without looking as if he was suffering greatly), he certainly didn't seem to be at full fitness. And there was almost a sense of relief for Murray that he hadn't lost embarrassingly. Invited on a couple of subsequent occasions to say whether there was anything hindering him that day, Murray has always denied it, but Nadal may have established a convention among the top players: not to blame an injury for a defeat to an opponent they respect.

And maybe Murray was beaten, at least in part, by the growing realisation that Djokovic was something of a born-again player. Six months later, Djokovic was to say, 'After the Davis Cup win I was full of life, full of energy, eager to come back to the tennis court, eager to play some more, win some other tournaments. In a sentence, I lost my fear. I believed in my abilities more than ever. Australia was one of the best tournaments I played in my life.'

Yet the biggest obstacle to Djokovic dominating tennis was the fact that he lacked self-belief against Federer and Nadal. 'I had too much respect for them,' he has since admitted. He had no difficulty believing he could beat everyone else, but there was a psychological block against the top two – certainly against Nadal.

Given that admission, perhaps the real work in the *annus mirabilis* was done in the finals of the four ATP Masters-1000 tournaments leading up to the French Open. Over more than a decade, the ATP has done its best to market its top nine tour-level tournaments as a special series, a bit like the European Champions League in football, and they do stand out from the rest of the 60-odd tour-level events that make up the men's professional circuit. But they have always struggled to get close to the four majors, and in terms of financial turnover the gap is getting bigger, not smaller. Yet for Djokovic in 2011, they were more than just warm-up events. In the finals of Indian Wells, Miami, Madrid and Rome, he prepared the ground for his final climb to the top.

In the first half of 2011 there was a strange triangle at the top of the men's game. Nadal clearly had the edge over Federer; in fact, Federer, for all his dominance, has not beaten Nadal at a major since the 2007 Wimbledon final. Federer still felt he could beat Djokovic, though Djokovic's emphatic win at the Australian Open had made their rivalry very much even. So being able to beat Nadal was the key to Djokovic's assault on the summit.

His victory in the final of Indian Wells was a boost, but it's hard to read too much into results at Indian Wells. Although the tennis facility built by the former player Charlie Pasarell is quite superb, the setting is a slightly rarefied one, in that it's part of a retirement community, making the average age of the spectators higher than elsewhere on the tour. In addition, the ball can sometimes fly in the Californian desert, so freak results can never be ruled out. In retrospect, there was nothing freakish about Djokovic beating Federer in the semis (his third victory in three tournaments over the Swiss, having beaten him in the final of Dubai a fortnight after Melbourne), but at the time, Djokovic just looked like a player in form.

When he beat Nadal in Miami on a final set tie-break, the tennis world sat up a little more. Beating the clear world No. 1 twice in successive finals was becoming a statement, but Nadal's best surface was still to come.

Djokovic skipped Monte Carlo, but after picking up a second title at his own tournament in Belgrade, he played the back-to-back Masters events in Madrid and Rome, the home straight of the run-up to the French Open. By now people were talking about his amazing unbeaten streak. Going into Madrid it was 28 matches in the year and 30 since his last defeat (to Federer at the ATP Finals). When he beat Nadal 7–5, 6–4 in the final, the tennis world was sitting bolt upright – it was his first ever victory against the Spaniard on clay and Nadal had been beaten in a clay-court final for only the third time. But again there were slightly mitigating circumstances. Nadal has never been totally comfortable in Madrid, where the altitude makes the ball fly more quickly through the air, and the Caja Magica tennis stadium often seems to help those players who play best on hard courts. That's why the real damage Djokovic did to the Nadal psyche took place in Rome. This had been something of a stronghold for Nadal – he had won back-to-back five-set finals in the days when the final was played over the full distance, and the conditions were much more similar to Roland Garros than Madrid had been. So when Djokovic beat Nadal 6–4, 6–4 in the final, he suddenly became a joint favourite for Paris.

What was Djokovic doing? He and his team had identified that Nadal's incredibly heavy topspin allowed him to play relatively safe, in the sense that he didn't need to hit into the last half-metre of the court – a three-quarter-length shot with heavy topspin that made the ball almost explode off the surface could often do the same damage. So Djokovic stepped in to make use of the shorter ball. He had always been a player to play largely on his baseline but now he stepped even further into the court to take the ball early and rob Nadal of vital seconds. It was a high-risk strategy, as it made him vulnerable to having to play balls off his shoelaces when they were hit deep, but with Nadal's game built around phenomenal speed and retrieving ability, it was worth the chance to rush the Spaniard. And once the strategy began to work, the psychological dividend kicked in, as Nadal felt the need to hit deeper when he got a softer ball, and frequently overhit.

By the time the Roland Garros semi-finals came round, Djokovic's unbeaten streak was up to 45 matches. But on a glorious if gusty spring day in Paris, the streak came to an end on one of the best days of tennis played in the history of the sport.

After Nadal had celebrated his 25th birthday by beating Andy Murray in the first semi-final, everyone was expecting the Nadal-Djokovic final that would crown the series of their four Masters finals. Djokovic took to the court against Federer knowing that victory would take him to the world No. 1 ranking. But it was to be the day Federer breathed life into his faltering career in the match of the tennis year. He not only served well but he had a game plan that he carried out with great intelligence. When Federer won Wimbledon 13 months later in July 2012, he traced his revival back to the win over Djokovic in Paris, the one that gave him belief that he could still hold his own with the best.

Although the record books have it as a four-sets win for Federer, that doesn't show how close Djokovic came. Having dropped the first two sets, he rallied back to take the third, and when he served for the fourth at 5–4, the daylight was disappearing to such an extent that they looked dead set to come back on the Saturday morning to play a one-set shootout. In that, Djokovic would surely have been a clear favourite, but it didn't get that far. Federer played a superb game to break back, and as the level of tennis rose in tandem with the rapidly fading light, he held his nerve to take the tie-break 7–5 on his third match point.

Djokovic was gracious in defeat. He recognised that his great run would have to end somewhere and that he had been part of a great sporting spectacle, but it still hurt for him to lose his winning run in such a high-stakes match. The run was over but a feature of the Serb's career has been his ability to accept that a defeat has gone, regroup and come back stronger. He wisely realised that he needed a break after Paris, so reneged on his commitment to play at London's Queen's Club and was next in action at Wimbledon.

His Wimbledon draw was not without pitfalls. Kevin Anderson, Marcos Baghdatis and Michael Llodra all had the potential to hurt him, but he reached the quarter-finals for the loss of a single set. A four-sets win over the 18-year-old Australian Bernard Tomic should have set up a repeat of the Paris semi-final against Federer but the Swiss was beaten from two sets up by Jo-Wilfried Tsonga. For the second successive major, Djokovic went into his semi-final knowing that victory would give him the No. 1 ranking. This time he didn't falter – he beat the Frenchman in a highly entertaining four-setter to set up a final against Nadal, who recovered from a poor start to beat Andy Murray in the other semi-final. The top spot Djokovic had dreamed about as a child was his, but the question was whether he would celebrate it with the biggest individual title of his career or as a consolation for having to make do with the Wimbledon runner-up prize.

This was the match where the four Masters-1000 finals really paid their dividend. It helped that Djokovic played some of his best tennis in the first two sets; in fact, some of the points in the second set were breathtaking. At times he seemed to be toying with Nadal, and when the score stood at 6–4, 6–1 for the Serb, it was almost like a dream sequence. But could it last? Djokovic's level visibly went down at the start of the third set. It was no disgrace – few players could have kept up the level he'd shown in the first hour – but Nadal capitalised and broke. When he broke again and took the third set 6–1, he was back on track to repeat his remarkable Paris-Wimbledon double from 2008 and 2010.

Djokovic was perhaps a little lucky to break early in the fourth, but it was what happened after that that was most remarkable. Nadal is human, he makes mistakes, but he hardly ever makes them on big points – record the first four games of any Nadal set and you'll find some errors, but record the last two of any set and there are very few. But as the fourth set wore on, he made more and more errors. Djokovic wasn't playing badly but nor had he rediscovered his level from the first two sets. It was as if the work done in those four Masters-1000 finals was eating away at Nadal, and the seemingly indestructible competitor almost self-destructed.

'I was trying to take myself back to the four matches where I'd beaten him,' Djokovic explained later. 'I had that in the back of my mind. I was trying to perform the same way: aggressive, taking my chances, not giving him opportunity to take over the control.' Easily said but much harder to do. The fourth set was a feast of scrambling, with the noise level from both players' grunting rising with the tension of the match. But what Djokovic did on several occasions was to throw in a soft ball after a succession of big baseline shots, and on most of them Nadal went for too much and overhit. That was the psychological damage Djokovic had inflicted from the four victorious finals. Nadal even got the break back and served at 3–4 to get back on level terms, but Djokovic broke him again and thus served for the Wimbledon title.

At 5–3, 30–30, after a long baseline rally that had gone to Nadal, Djokovic threw in a change of tactic. He served out wide and volleyed the return into the open court at full pace on the backhand. If the strategy had misfired and he'd been broken and lost the match, people might well have pinpointed that move and said that was where he blew it. It could have happened, but at that point, Djokovic knew he had his man on the ropes and it was worth the risk to try and ram home his advantage. On the next point he again came to the net, though not behind the serve, but he didn't have to play the volley as Nadal's backhand sailed out.

Djokovic fell to the turf and moments later even ate a mouthful of grass, saying he 'felt like an animal'.

Was this what he imagined when, as a seven-year-old, he found a plastic vase and pretended it was the Wimbledon trophy? He's not the only kid to dream of winning Wimbledon but one of the few who has the drive and the determination to go on to realise that dream, so did he think of his childhood dreams at the point of victory? 'I did,' he said. 'When I finished the match, when I ate the piece of grass, I had a flashback of my whole childhood, what I've been through, memories, first tennis courts that I grew up on, days spent in Belgrade. It was beautiful.'

An hour later when he faced the assembled tennis media in his post-final press conference, he was more considered but still effusive.

This is what I'm born for, to be a tennis champion. I was just chatting with my brothers and my family and my team in the locker room, just kind of remembering those days of the hard work that we put in in Germany and back in Serbia when I was eight, nine, ten, eleven years old, the dreams I had. It's really beautiful. I mean, this success kind of makes you rewind the old days, makes you come back to your childhood and remember what you've been through to get to this stage. It wasn't an easy way but I guess that's necessary in order for you to fight for what you want to achieve. We all know the situation in our country, how it was with the wars and things like that. It was definitely really difficult to become a tennis professional, with tennis being not one of the most popular sports in our country. It didn't have any history. But then [at] the end of the day, now when you think about it, that's something that we needed. Not just myself but Ana Ivanovic, Jankovic, Tipsarevic, Zimonjic – all these players who have been successful these last couple of years in men's and women's tennis, we had a tough way to go through. That made us mentally strong.

Djokovic also made the statement, 'I'm going to celebrate like a Serb', which went down well with the British who liked the sound of it, even if they didn't really know what it meant (could a well-oiled Brit really imagine Djokovic singing Serbian folk songs as a way of celebrating?). Back home in Belgrade, an estimated 100,000 fans turned out to greet him in a pop-concert-like reception in Republic Square. He rode in an open-topped bus from Nikola Tesla Airport to the city centre with his replica of the Wimbledon trophy, waving to fans who lined the route.

In the days after his Wimbledon title, there were instances of kids fixing up ropes between two posts and finding two bits of wood and a rubber ball with which they would pretend to play tennis. It would be wrong to read into this the birth of a popular sport in Serbia, but it was a reflection of a national hero and children traditionally like to ape their idols – this particular idol played a sport that was largely unknown in Serbia but he was no less an idol for it.

Whatever he had achieved back home, in tennis terms he had shaken up the establishment. Given how the decade starting around 2004–5 has become the Federer/Nadal/Djokovic era, it's easy to forget what a massive sea change Djokovic's win at Wimbledon represented. Since Gaston Gaudio's almost freakish win at the French Open in 2004, just three men (Marat Safin, Juan Martin del Potro and Djokovic) had stopped Federer and Nadal duopolising the 28 major singles titles up for grabs. Djokovic was not just world No. 1, he had beaten Federer and Nadal eight times in nine matches in the previous six months. He had broken the Federer-Nadal bank.

By the time Djokovic left Wimbledon, he'd played 49 matches in 2011 and won 48 of them. Having achieved two of his biggest goals in the last three days of Wimbledon (the No. 1 ranking and the Wimbledon title) and three in the previous seven months if you count the Davis Cup, he could have been forgiven for losing some of his bite in the remainder of the year. But he said after Wimbledon, 'I want to win more Grand Slams, I will definitely not stop here,' and he strolled through his first tournament back, the Canadian Masters in Montreal, and was only prevented from winning the Cincinnati Masters when a shoulder injury caused him to retire at 0-3 down in the second set to Andy Murray.

That created a couple of days of speculation about whether the man of the year would be able to play in the US Open, but the withdrawal in Cincinnati was largely precautionary, and Djokovic was fully fit by the time the US Open began just over a week later. More than that, he was trying out a new health gizmo. As the US Open got under way, the *Wall Street Journal* reported that Djokovic was spending three lots of 20 minutes a week in 'an egg-shape, bobsled-sized pressure chamber'. Many players spend time in hyperbaric environments, which put more oxygen in the blood to allow them to recover from punishing matches, but this was supposed to be vastly superior to your bog-standard hyperbaric chamber. It was made by a Californian company, CVAC Systems, who claimed its $75,000 contraption could enhance athletic performance 'by improving circulation, boosting oxygen-rich red-blood cells, removing lactic acid and possibly even stimulating mitochondrial biogenesis and stem-cell production'. It made for a good story and Djokovic was happy to say he was using it, but when asked 16 months later whether he had one with him in Australia, he said he had only made 'limited use' of the chamber in the USA.

He certainly looked fully fit at Flushing Meadows, dropping just 12 games in his first three matches. Things got steadily tougher after that, with a 16–14 tie-break against Alexandr Dolgopolov, a gruelling four-setter against his Davis Cup team-mate Janko Tipsarevic in the quarter-finals and another bruising five-setter against Roger Federer in the semis.

For the second year running, Djokovic saved two match points, but this victory was almost a steal. Federer had dominated for the first two sets as Djokovic had struggled to find his rhythm. Federer broke to lead 5–3 in the final set, and at 5–4, 40–15, he had two match points. On the first of them, Djokovic went for a gamble with a big forehand return of serve and made it with a spectacular clean winner. It was clear from the post-match press conferences that this winner had outpsyched Federer. Perhaps it was Djokovic raising both arms to the crowd to milk some support after most of the fans had been shamelessly pro-Federer from the start, perhaps it was the fact that the gamble had paid off, perhaps it was the cheeky smile Djokovic delivered as he prepared to return serve on the second match point. Whatever it was, Federer netted a forehand on the second match point and was a broken man after that. In his post-match news conference Federer seemed almost to imply that going for such a gamble on match point was disrespectful. His comments probably shouldn't be taken too literally, as the disappointment must have been overwhelming, but it made the point that Djokovic had not just outpsyched Nadal but could outpsyche Federer too. 'I didn't want to have him do to me here what he did at the French Open,' Djokovic said.

That set up another clash with Nadal, their second successive final both at the US Open and in the majors. Fortunately for Djokovic, this ill-fated US Open, which had had to deal with earthquakes, hurricanes and water seeping through cracks in court surfaces, had to go to a third Monday, giving him more time to recover from his five-setter against Federer, and in another physical match the extra time was probably crucial. Nadal had sounded an ominous warning at Wimbledon. 'When one player beats me five times, it is because my game doesn't bother him a lot,' he'd said after the final. 'I have to try to find solutions and that's what I'm going to try.' Nadal was to find those solutions (a word he uses a lot in English) but it was to take him until the following year. In fact, the US Open final followed a remarkably similar pattern to the Wimbledon final.

History records that Djokovic beat Nadal 6–2, 6–4, 6–7, 6–1, but the numbers don't reflect the brutal physicality of the spectacle and the breathtaking nature of some of the rallies. This was tennis at its closest to boxing, and while the two men played a longer final in

Melbourne four months later, this was at least as physical, if not more so, even if it did last 'only' just over four hours.

The big similarity with Wimbledon was in Nadal falling away in the fourth set when he had every reason to be mounting a comeback. Djokovic had served for the title at 6-5 in the third set, but Nadal had broken back with some of the best tennis of the match and had then never been behind in the tie-break. Djokovic then took a medical timeout at the end of the third set to have some tightening muscles in his back loosened. Yet with everything lined up for Nadal to muscle his way physically and psychologically back into the match, he fell away. There weren't the errors that had characterised his fourth-set collapse at Wimbledon, but he did allow Djokovic to play and the Serb took full advantage. When he hit an in-to-out forehand to win the match and fall to his back on the concrete, he had reaffirmed the message he had confirmed at Wimbledon – that he was the world's best and had not only joined but eclipsed the Federer-Nadal duopoly.

In the remaining two-and-a-half months of the year, nothing of note was added to the body of work that makes up Djokovic's *annus mirabilis* of 2011.

He wasn't helped by a scheduling conflict that is understandable but counterproductive. Several years ago, the International Tennis Federation asked the players which weeks they would prefer for Davis Cup ties. The popular response was the week after the majors, which makes sense for most of them, as even a good run at a major means they will be out of the tournament by the second Tuesday, which gives them 10 days to prepare for representing their country. Mindful of its need to keep the players on-side, the ITF acquiesced and has two of its four Davis Cup weekends a year in the week after Slams.

But that is a terrible week for the marquee names, who find

themselves in Grand Slam semi-finals and finals on Friday/Saturday and Sunday (or sometimes Monday) and then have to play a vital singles just a few days later, often on a different surface, often on a different continent. So having just won his first US Open in a brutal four-hour final on Monday night, Djokovic was due on court barely three days later in Belgrade as Serbia took on Argentina in the Davis Cup semi-final. Rumours abounded that he had an injury, but you didn't have to be a conspiracy theorist to accept the wisdom of throwing Janko Tipsarevic and Viktor Troicki into singles action on the opening day, to give Djokovic two more days to recover.

The problem for Serbia was that Troicki was ranked higher than Tipsarevic, so played at No. 1, but his form was on a downward trend. And when David Nalbandian beat him in four sets, it put Serbia on the back foot, especially as Juan Martin del Potro beat Tipsarevic as expected. Troicki and Zimonjic's win in the doubles kept the tie alive and paved the way for Djokovic to have the hero's welcome that his exploits during the year warranted.

On Sunday afternoon he walked out into the Beogradska Arena to the kind of welcome very few people experience. Wearing his red Serbia shirt proudly, almost defiantly, he marched through the dry ice into the arena, highlighted by a spotlight amid dimmed lights, accompanied by the strains of *Carmina Burana* as 17,000 fans screamed wildly. It was the kind of reception normally reserved for pop stars and prize-fight boxers. If anyone could turn the semi-final round for Serbia, Djokovic could.

All went well for a set, but Djokovic couldn't break free from the tall Argentinean. To beat del Potro you have to return well, and Djokovic's blistering returns were absent without leave. Normally he can run for an hour or two and get himself into the groove, but how much gas did he have in the tank? The set went into the tie-break, and although Djokovic got a mini-break back to level at 4–4, he lost the tie-break 7–5.

So what happens now? Here was the hero of Serbia, clearly not fully fit, understandably very tired, having played for an hour and still in need of three sets. Something in Djokovic's subconscious must have given way at that point. He lost his serve lamely to go 0–2 down and, as del Potro drove Djokovic wide to his forehand side on the point for 3–0, Djokovic went down with a scream of anguish and lay motionless on the ground. The exact same thing had happened a year earlier, but if that was partly tactical to get into Tomas Berdych's head, this was tactical only in the sense that he knew he couldn't go another three sets to give Serbia a chance of victory in the fifth rubber.

Such phrasing makes it sound as if the injury was a fake. It wasn't. It emerged that he did have a tear in a back muscle that he'd picked up at the US Open. He knew he had a chance of aggravating it if he played against del Potro but he calculated he would have a better chance of beating the former US Open champion than Troicki had. In that he was almost certainly right, but in retrospect he had to win the first set. Once that was gone, the game was up and something in the deeper reaches of his being rescued him by sparing him the remainder of a lost cause. As many people are happy to admit, he was willing to try, whereas most players in his position would have considered the risk of aggravating the injury wasn't worth it. He had a 4–0 record against del Potro going into the match and surely no one could begrudge him the hero's walk on court at the start. 'It was my decision but the gamble backfired,' he said, which is a fair assessment. It was Serbia's first defeat in the Beogradska Arena and was to remain the only one until a weakened team lost the 2013 final.

After that, his stellar year fizzled out somewhat. He suffered some defeats that were more the result of anti-climax and fatigue than an opponent playing better tennis, and he had the sense of fun to walk on court for a match in Basel on 31 October dressed in a

Hallowe'en mask, complete with a shock of black hair. His willingness to do that – to dispense with the 'game face' at a phase of the match where he would normally have been so focused and serious – suggests he felt his year's work was done, which it effectively was.

He finished the year as the runaway No. 1. He had broken the Federer-Nadal duopoly and he received a raft of awards. The most prestigious was the Laureus World Sportsman of the Year. This is an award that ought to be the pinnacle of global sporting recognition, and it probably is, although it does seem to have a bias towards tennis that takes a little of its credibility away. Maybe it is just that tennis is enjoying an extraordinary era with Federer, Nadal, Djokovic and Serena Williams, but there is always a sense that the best in a year in tennis is always going to feature in the Laureus Awards.

Nonetheless, Djokovic was a worthy winner when he stepped up to receive his award the week after his endurance marathon at the 2012 Australian Open. 'It's really difficult to describe in words how much this means to me,' he said, before adding significantly, 'not just me but my family, my team, my country, all the people who've been supporting me throughout my whole career.' It is common practice at trophy-presentation ceremonies for players to thank their team, and many thank their family. But few thank their country. Novak Djokovic had conquered the world in 2011 – he had done what he said he would when his age was still in single digits. And he had done it as much for his country as for himself.

How was he ever going to follow his achievements of 2011 in 2012? It's easy to look back and say 2011 was as good as it was going to get, and that may well prove the case in the course of Djokovic's whole career. But although he lost the No. 1 ranking mid-way through 2012, he ended the year as the world's top player, reached three of the four Grand Slam finals and added to his legend with a remarkable third Australian Open title. He also spent most of 2013 at the top of the rankings, and while he was pipped by Nadal in October, he ended the year playing the best tennis, including two drubbings of Nadal in October and November. It would therefore be wrong to put 2012 and 2013 too far behind 2011 – fairer would be to say that from the start of 2011 Djokovic was the world's most consistent tennis player for the subsequent three-plus years.

His Australian Open title in January 2012 may well go down as his single biggest achievement. He played four hours, 50 minutes in his semi-final on the second Friday night of the tournament, beating Andy Murray 7–5 in the fifth set. Many thought Murray had done enough to set Nadal up for an easy win in the final by draining Djokovic's resources of energy, especially after Nadal had beaten Roger Federer on Thursday evening in more than an hour less. But that weekend Djokovic proved that draining his reserves is well-nigh impossible.

The first week of a Grand Slam often seems a formality for the big names. They can't win the title in the first week, they can only lose it, but the first week of this one was remarkably important for Djokovic's chances. He expended the minimum of energy, dropping just 14 games in his first 11 sets of the tournament and reaching the semis having conceded just one set, which was to Lleyton Hewitt in the fourth round. So while he played two punishing matches in the space of 48 hours at the end, his larder was well stocked going into the sharp end of the tournament.

It was again a case of the big four reaching the semis. Federer took Nadal to five sets but never seriously looked like winning, while the Djokovic-Murray encounter was a genuine 50:50. Towards the end of the final set, Murray often looked the likelier winner, but Djokovic had the confidence of his stellar 2011 and edged the victory.

Then came the match that was certainly the longest final in Grand Slam history, probably the most physical and, at least towards the end, one of the best in terms of quality. Djokovic was slow to get going, as he often is against Nadal, and found himself a set down after just over an hour. But he bounced back in the second, and throughout the third and most of the fourth he looked distinctly the stronger player. But Nadal came back at the end of the fourth set after a short rain delay and snatched the set on the tie-break. With the tournament now into its third week and the final going past midnight, Nadal looked the stronger. He broke for 4–2 but Djokovic got the break straight back. That signalled another momentum swing, and when Djokovic broke for 6–5, he was serving for the match. If Nadal had seized the break point he had to get back to 6–6, the momentum might easily have swung again, but Djokovic saved it with a boldly angled backhand and then sealed victory with a serve that left Nadal stranded, allowing the Serb to hit an in-to-out forehand to end the match.

The match time was five hours, 53 minutes, and after embracing Nadal and shaking hands with the umpire, Pascal Maria, Djokovic ripped off his shirt, his inner animal finally released from captivity. His celebration was almost frightening – he walked bare-chested across the court to his entourage, clenched both fists with a primeval scream, and after shaking a few hands, thumped an advertising hoarding several times before retreating back to his chair. You wouldn't have wanted to meet him in a bad mood when he tapped into that energy.

Tennis relies on its sponsors, but the farce of having the chief executive of Kia Motors, the principal sponsor of the Australian Open, giving a three-minute speech at almost 2am after the two players had provided nearly six hours of scintillating tennis was painful to watch. It was only when the second of the speeches, given by the president of Tennis Australia, began that someone twigged that Nadal and Djokovic were suffering physically as they waited for their trophies. Eventually, the tournament director, Craig Tiley, signalled to some court staff to get the players chairs, a gesture that elicited the biggest applause of the awards ceremony before the players were allowed to take centre stage again. Within the hour, the two players were sitting in ambulances in the dock of the Rod Laver Arena, both of them on intravenous drips and being monitored, while the 'bump out' operation to dismantle the arena as a tennis stadium took place around them.

Inevitably, Djokovic was asked after the match whether it was the greatest win of his career. 'I think it comes out on top,' he said, 'because just the fact that we played almost six hours is incredible. I'm very proud just to be part of this history, part of the elite players that have won this tournament several times. I was very flattered to be playing in front of Rod Laver, in front of the all-time greats, and in front of 15,000 people that stayed until one-thirty [in the morning].' Given the dictates of the media and the journalist's quest to write the first draft of history, it was understandable that he should be asked to assess his victory, but a more considered assessment will have to wait until the end of his career. What is certain is that, even if he never wins another major title, Djokovic's heroics that night in Melbourne guarantee him his place among the great athletes in world sport.

Any assessment of Djokovic's achievements in 2012 and 2013 risks falling into the trap of not having enough elapsed time to assess the true magnitude of them. Despite the blistering start in Australia, he was never going to repeat what he achieved in 2011 – true, Roger Federer won three majors out of four in three years out of four (2004, 2006, 2007) but he had an almost effortless style of playing that took much less out of him than Djokovic and Nadal. The fact that Djokovic ended 2012 as world No. 1, having lost the top ranking in mid-year and ended 2013 playing clearly the best tennis, even if he was pipped in the rankings by the returning Nadal, will probably mean history judges him the world's best player over the period 2011–13, and possibly longer, but we just can't tell at this stage as we're still too close.

There was a marked difference between the Djokovic of the European springtime in 2012 and the one from 2011. In April he played Monte Carlo, a tournament he'd missed the previous year, and reached the final, where he played Nadal. That Nadal won 6–3, 6–1 to turn the tables on the pattern of the previous year was not the story. Djokovic's grandfather, Vlada (Vladimir Djokovic), died midweek after a long illness. Djokovic received the news as he warmed up on the morning of his match against Alexandr Dolgopolov and was clearly very upset. He was all over the place in the first set against the mercurial Ukrainian and was perhaps lucky to be playing an opponent who has yet to show he has as much steel as he has talent. Djokovic bounced back to win in straight sets, and then beat Robin Haase and Tomas Berdych before losing to Nadal.

'I definitely don't want to take away anything from Rafa's win,' said Djokovic in his post-match news conference, 'but it's a fact that I didn't have any emotional energy left in me. I just wasn't there. I've never been caught up in this kind of emotional situation before. It's been a very difficult week for me to go through mentally. I won three matches since the news. I mean, I think I did pretty well.' Given that this was the grandfather who acted at times as a third parent, whose flat served as a shelter for the entire family during the Belgrade bombing of 1999 and who is reported to have funded some of the tennis facilities the Djokovics set up after it became clear they had a prodigy on their hands, it was generally thought to be a legitimate excuse for winning just four games in a Masters Series final. Yet, regardless of the circumstances, Nadal had the psychological win he needed, and when he also beat Djokovic 7–5,

6–3 in the Rome final four weeks later, he had the form in Masters finals going into the peak Grand Slam season that Djokovic had enjoyed the previous year.

Djokovic's US Open triumph meant the French Open was the last of the four majors he had yet to win. With Federer having completed his set in 2009, and Nadal in 2010, it's easy for modern-day fans to think achieving a 'career Grand Slam' is just a milestone that all top players go through. But it's an extremely difficult accomplishment to pull off. Prior to Federer, only two players had done it with all players eligible to complete: Rod Laver and Andre Agassi. While Laver's pure Grand Slam in 1969 is a phenomenal achievement that has yet to be matched, three of the four majors were on grass in those days, so only Agassi had won all four since they encompassed the four different surfaces they have today.

Arriving in Paris for the 2012 French Open, Djokovic was not just going for the career set but also to be only the third man in history to hold all four major titles at the same time. He sailed close to the wind with a five-sets win over Jo-Wilfried Tsonga in the fourth round that required him to save four match points, but he came through, and when he set up a final against Nadal, it was the climax everyone wanted to see. Except, perhaps, the weather gods, whose intervention heavily influenced the course of the match.

Nadal won the first set and, as the drizzle started midway through the second set, Djokovic earned a warning after dropping serve at 3–3 for hitting his courtside bench so hard a bit of it splintered on to the court and had to be cleaned up by a ball-kid. With Nadal leading by two sets and a break up early in the third, Djokovic seemed out of it but used his seemingly hopeless position as a springboard to go for more risks. The tactic worked, and the Serb reeled off eight straight games. At 2–0 in the fourth set, a dramatic turnround was on the cards, but at that point the rain got so heavy it was simply not possible to continue and they came off for the night.

The following day, Nadal broke Djokovic in the first game of the resumption, taking away the fourth-set advantage Djokovic still carried over from the night before. From then on Nadal was always ahead and Djokovic had to wait for five minutes while rain and thunder graced Roland Garros with Nadal just a game from victory at 5–4. Djokovic held for 5–5 but conceded his next service game on a double fault, as Nadal claimed his seventh French Open title and broke the streak of three major finals in which he'd lost to Djokovic.

So did the rain rob Djokovic on Sunday? It's hard to make a convincing case that it did. Yes, the momentum was truly with him and the overnight break came at a good time for Nadal. But the rain had helped Djokovic get back in the match early in the third set. By making the balls heavier, it had blunted some of the merciless topspin that's a feature of Nadal's game and made it a more even contest. The ideal for Djokovic would have been for the drizzle to remain very light, or to be intermittent with some dry spells still under heavy cloud – such weather is possible, but is it right to say that only such a very precise combination of conditions would have levelled the match? In addition, who's to say Nadal would not have come back if the match had continued to a conclusion on Sunday? Although the Spaniard is known for his phenomenal fitness, he is not just a physical player but a superb match player – he is remarkably immune to succumbing to his opponent's momentum, frequently bouncing back when his opponent is having a purple patch. It's quite likely he would have done the same if the weather gods had allowed a Sunday finish.

Djokovic recognised as much when he spoke after Monday's conclusion. He acknowledged that the rain break had come at a bad time for him but also that the rain had helped him get back into the match. And he recognised that Nadal was the better player over the two days. He had put up a credible challenge, but no one could claim it was an unfair result.

The full story of how Djokovic surrendered his Wimbledon title in the 2012 semi-finals to Roger Federer has yet to be told. It's possible there isn't much of a story to tell – after all, while Djokovic went into the match as a slight favourite, he had never beaten Federer on grass, and losing a four-setter to the great Roger Federer at his most successful tournament is hardly a disgrace. And yet...

Djokovic said he had too many ups and downs and that a poor spell towards the end of the third set cost him a match that, until then, had been very even. It's a plausible explanation. He also said he failed to make the most of his second shot of many rallies, in particular when he was serving. That prompted a question in his post-match press conference: 'Was there any particular reason why you didn't feel as sharp as you were on that second ball? Did you feel good coming into today?' Djokovic replied, 'Not so great really. I had [a] bad last couple [of] days. Last five, six days I wasn't feeling great. But I don't want to talk about it now.' Whatever the story was, he will tell it when he's ready, but it was a strangely subdued Djokovic that day, and it would not be a shock to learn he had some illness or minor injury. In some ways, it's almost a relief to know that the guy whose body can carry him through two punishing five-setters in 48 hours the way it did in Australia six months earlier can also rebel and deliver him only 80 per cent of his normal energy, even in a tournament as big as Wimbledon. It makes this remarkable sporting specimen human.

His final comment at Wimbledon was, 'You know, life goes on. This is sport, I have to move on.'

By the time he'd moved on to his next tournament, he should have been in cinemas across the entire world. Never one to shun the limelight, Djokovic had accepted a tiny cameo role in a follow-up movie to the 2010 gangster hit *The Expendables*. In *Expendables 2*, a remarkably plot-free film 'written' by Sylvester Stallone and starring Stallone, Bruce Willis and Arnold Schwarzenegger, Djokovic was filmed in a 10-second appearance in which he single-handedly wipes out three (or is it four?) machine-gun-wielding terrorists, all with his tennis racket. For a man who gave up the single-handed aggressive backhand when he was about seven, he takes out one of the terrorists with a superb one-hander that Federer would have been proud of. A bit like the Indian tennis star Vijay Amritraj, who wielded his racket as a mean weapon in the 1983 James Bond film *Octopussy*, Djokovic looks like he's having great fun. Yet the scene never made it to the final version and his 10 seconds of heroism was left on the cutting-room floor, although it did make it on to YouTube. As long as it remains visible, he no doubt has scope for a corny peace message along the lines that you don't need guns, only tennis rackets.

A small detail from his appearance is that he was wearing his Sergio Tacchini zip-up top. That was part of the contract he signed in 2009 that saw him switch from Adidas, the German clothing company whose sportswear he had worn since he was a junior, to the company set up by a former Italian tennis player, Sergio Tacchini. His deal with Tacchini was nominally for five years, but after just half of it, Djokovic parted company with the Italians in May 2012 to sign up with the Japanese clothing giant Uniqlo. Tacchini was reported to be in financial difficulties and Djokovic would have been costing the firm a fair bit; whether it was in difficulties or not, the split was amicable. The result was that, with filming having taken place in Bulgaria in 2011 when Djokovic was still under contract to Tacchini, the *Expendables* clip shows him wearing the Tacchini label several months after switching to the Japanese company Uniqlo.

The switch to Uniqlo is interesting for what it says about the changing economics of tenniswear. For several years, youngsters have tended to play tennis in cotton T-shirts and only used specific tennis shirts for matches (which is what the top players do). At the same time, tennis shirts have become appropriate clothing for casual and smart-casual social occasions. In 2005 the French company Lacoste, set up by the legendary French player from the 1920s, René Lacoste, signed up Andy Roddick because it specifically wanted to target the US leisure market. While the world's two market leaders in tenniswear, Nike and Adidas, have concentrated on sports clothing, Djokovic was signed up by a Japanese company looking to enhance its standing as a leisurewear retailer in high streets, shopping malls and on the Internet. At the same time as Djokovic was becoming Uniqlo's global brand ambassador (players don't just wear the clothing, they're termed 'brand ambassadors' these days), another 'high street' brand, the Swedish chain Hennes & Mauritz (H&M), was signing up another top-10 tennis player, Tomas Berdych. It prompts the question of whether Next, Marks & Spencer or other familiar fashion names will soon start sponsoring tennis players.

By losing to Roger Federer at Wimbledon, Djokovic lost his No. 1 ranking. However, with Nadal off the tour after a mysterious second-round defeat at Wimbledon to Lukas Rosol, the Serb was still thought of as the man to beat. Yet he looked strangely off-colour when he went back to Wimbledon for the Olympics (then again, the All England Club was also off-colour, adorned as it was with bright Olympic-pink drapes incongruously set against the Virginia creeper that grows around Centre Court). After losing his semi-final to Andy Murray 7–5, 7–5, Djokovic seemed strangely unmotivated in the bronze-medal playoff against Juan Martin del Potro. Perhaps he just wasn't up for a second bronze medal after the one he won in Beijing in 2008, or maybe del Potro was fired up after coming so close to beating Federer in a four-hour semi-final. Whatever the reason, del Potro won 7–5, 6–4.

The following week Djokovic won another Masters title but a somewhat diminished title, as the Canada Masters in Toronto in 2012 didn't feature all of the top players (many were still in London enjoying the Olympics). He reached the final in Cincinnati where Federer beat him in two sets, the first of them a 6–0 drubbing that lasted just 20 minutes and in which Djokovic won a mere 10 points. But Djokovic looked all set to retain his US Open title when he eased into the final having dropped just one set.

Facing him was Andy Murray, who had had a much tougher route to the final, as well as all the pressure of seeking to become the first British man to win a major title since 1936. It was a fluctuating match. Murray won the 87-minute first set on a 12–10 tie-break and led 5–1 in the second. Djokovic bounced back to 5–5 but lost the set 7–5. Djokovic then played superb tennis in the third and fourth sets, picking up his level after being given a time violation, and as the players took bathroom breaks before the start of the fifth set, Djokovic looked the likelier winner. But Murray bounced back to break twice at the start of the decider, and not even Djokovic calling for the trainer at 2–5 to have a groin strain massaged could knock Murray off course. There were those who wondered if it was a tactical move, but whether it was or not, Murray was so in the zone that he barely seemed to notice the delay before he served for the championship. And when Djokovic overhit a forehand return of serve on championship point, the title was Murray's.

Given the closeness of the two in their progression through the junior ranks, it should be no surprise that Djokovic and Murray should play out 50:50 contests when they face each other at full tour level. But this was psychologically very important for Murray.

They had played each other a lot on the tour but it had taken Murray until their fifth match to win one. And in their Grand Slam matches Djokovic always came out on top, so this win was massive for Murray. Djokovic was magnanimous in defeat at the end, respecting the enormity of Murray's first Grand Slam title, but there was no sense of him feeling he'd lost to the better player the way there was in the French Open final. To Djokovic, this was probably one that got away.

But then the tables were turned four months later when Djokovic beat Murray in the Australian Open final after seeming to be heading for defeat. Djokovic had come through the match of the tournament, if not of 2013, in beating Stanislas Wawrinka 12–10 in the fifth set in five hours and two minutes. That was in the fourth round and he had a lapse in the quarter-finals against Tomas Berdych that cost him a set. But by the time he reached the final, he had recovered and was raring to take on his British rival. Murray had beaten Roger Federer in the semi-finals in a match that was odd for being a five-set crushing. That ought not to be possible – a five-setter is by definition close, but Murray won all his sets comfortably while Federer won both of his on tie-breaks.

After Murray took the first set of the final, he had Djokovic on the ropes at 0–40 in the second game of the second set. It looked to all those in the Rod Laver Arena as if Murray would triumph. But then two things happened. Firstly, Djokovic played three of his best points of the match to come back to deuce and ultimately save his serve. Secondly, in the second set tie-break, a feather floated down from a passing bird as Murray prepared to deliver his second serve at 2–2. He stepped forward to remove it, went back to his baseline and promptly double-faulted. Given that there had been no breaks of serve until that point, it was a crucial lapse which Djokovic seized on. He won the tie-break to level the match, after which Murray needed renewed strapping to protect blisters on his foot. Djokovic broke in the eighth game of the third set to emphasise the momentum shift and broke twice in the fourth as he snuffed out Murray's challenge.

It made Djokovic the first man in the 'open' era of tennis to win three consecutive Australian Opens and emphasised that he was the world No. 1 for a reason. The question was now whether he could complete his set of majors.

At the end of January 2013 it was easy to see Djokovic and Murray as the new top two in the game. Federer was still around but showing signs of fading, while Nadal had been off the tour for seven months. There was much talk of his comeback, originally scheduled for the Australian Open but then delayed until the lower-ranking clay-court events in South America beginning the day after the Australian. But while many felt Nadal would still be a factor on clay, few expected him to put up a sustained challenge on all surfaces. How wrong they would prove to be.

Nadal's comeback was impressive. He reached the final in his first tournament in Chile, won the second and third in Brazil and Mexico, and then served notice that he was likely to be a factor by winning on the hard courts of Indian Wells, beating Federer, Berdych and del Potro en route to the title. It meant the first meeting of the year between Djokovic and Nadal was eagerly awaited, especially as it came in the final in Monte Carlo, the clay-court tournament where Nadal had never lost. The score of Djokovic's 6–2, 7–6 win doesn't adequately illustrate just how dominant Djokovic was that day. In the first set he ate Nadal for breakfast, and while the Spaniard battled back in the second, Djokovic always seemed to have the upper hand. With rumours circulating that Nadal's knees were playing up again, the Monte Carlo final looked to be both psychologically and physically significant.

Yet Djokovic had a poor run-in to the French Open, losing in the first round in Madrid to the maddeningly erratic Grigor Dimitrov, and in the Rome quarter-finals to Berdych. Meanwhile Nadal won both titles, so went to Paris with real form.

Because of the months he had spent off the tour, Nadal's ranking had dropped and was still only back to four going into the French. It meant the top two players on form were not guaranteed to be in separate halves of the draw, and indeed the names came out of the hat in a top-heavy formation that left Djokovic and Nadal set to meet in the semi-finals, with Federer and David Ferrer set for the bottom half. And so it came to pass that the most eagerly awaited match of the tennis year took place not in the final but the semis of the French.

Midway through the second set, it looked a mismatch. Nadal had won the first set convincingly and Djokovic was fighting to keep in touch in the second. Nadal broke to lead 3–2 while Djokovic was hesitant and had slipped a couple of times on the increasingly dry clay that was being baked by strong sun. But then Nadal played a poor game; Djokovic seized his chance and broke twice to level the match. But Nadal regained the momentum at the start of the third and had two set points for a 6–0 set before Djokovic finally won a game. In the fourth set, Nadal broke for 4–3, only to be broken straight back. He served for the match at 6–5 after another break but still Djokovic came back. The set went into the tie-break, Djokovic was never behind and won it 7–3. That wave of confidence swept Djokovic to a 4–1 lead in the decider with a double break. Nadal got one back and, at 4–3, he again put pressure on the Djokovic serve. That was when the incident happened that this match is remembered for.

Djokovic had recovered from 0–30 and then saved two break points. On the third deuce he opened up the court and had a simple putaway smash at the net. But in playing it, he stumbled and touched the net before the ball had bounced a second time (or in this case, landed in the crowd). As it was right under the umpire's chair and he had hit the ball well within the umpire's range of vision, Pascal Maria had a good view and called the point for Nadal. Djokovic argued with him for a couple of minutes but must have known deep down that, if the ball hadn't bounced a second time before he touched the net, the umpire had no choice but to call the point for the Spaniard. Djokovic said afterwards he 'should have won' the point and thought it might have gone to him as the ball had 'left the dimensions of the court' before he touched the net. But he didn't sound convincing; he could scarcely have proved it had left the dimensions of the court, so he wisely stopped himself from saying it was an outright mistake.

Did that incident cost Djokovic the match? Looking at the flow of points, no. It cost him the point, which gave Nadal a third break point, but Djokovic saved it. So they were back at deuce. It was then that Nadal won the next two points to level at 4–4 and was never behind after that. But in a finely balanced match, such incidents can change the momentum. One could also point to Djokovic complaining about the dryness of the court as he walked out to serve at 7–8 – whether he was right or wrong, he lost the next four points, including one horrendous error on a smash, as Nadal ran out a 9–7 winner in four hours, 38 minutes.

That fact was that, while Djokovic could well have won, Nadal's victory was not unfair based on the course of the match. It was only Djokovic's indefatigable refusal to accept he was beaten in the second and fourth sets that allowed him to be in a winning position in the fifth. And this is where Nadal is a match for Djokovic as a competitor – the Mallorcan seldom seems to suffer for long from his opponent having the momentum; his ability to turn the tables is always a clear and present danger to the guy on the other side of the net. That is why their matches are normally such brutal and bruising affairs and why this French Open semi-final was no different.

By contrast, Nadal's next match, the final against David Ferrer, was a walk in the park. This was the high watermark of Ferrer's career. He had beaten Federer's conqueror Jo-Wilfried Tsonga to reach his first (and so far only) Grand Slam final, a reward for unfailing, ever courteous, low-profile striving to maximise his potential in the shadow of the great Nadal. But while Ferrer deserves to be regarded as the best of the rest, he was always a class below the big four in the matches that mattered, and Nadal made mincemeat of him in a colourless final.

If Djokovic-Nadal was the new (or revived) rivalry at the top of the game, it wasn't a consistent one. In his next match after winning the French, Nadal was beaten by Steve Darcis in the first round at Wimbledon. With Federer losing in the second round and other big names going out, Djokovic and Murray resumed their rivalry, which could not have continued in Paris, as Murray missed Roland Garros due to a back injury that necessitated surgery later in the year. Following the carnage of the first three days, a Djokovic-Murray final was on the cards from the evening of the first Wednesday. Ten days later it finally came round, despite Djokovic having had to go four and three quarter hours to beat Juan Martin del Potro in the semi-finals in the best match of the tournament. The number seven played a big part in the build-up to the final – it was 77 years since a Briton had last won the men's singles at Wimbledon, Murray had beaten Djokovic seven times but never at Wimbledon and the match took place on seventh day of the seventh month.

Because of the intensity of the build-up surrounding Murray, Djokovic was almost relegated to a bit-part player until the match finally began. And yet he seemed to be affected by the hype and even by the heat, which was negligible by the standards of many cities on the tennis tour but was sweltering by British standards. He was never sure whether to wear his cap or not and he was making uncharacteristic errors. He lost his serve twice in the first set and used up his three challenges too early in the second set, so he had nothing left on a questionable line call at 5–5. He ended up losing that set having been 4–1 up and again let a 4–2 lead slip (after being 0–2 down) in the third set to leave Murray serving for the title at 5–4.

At that point he seemed to succumb to his oft-stated belief in destiny – perhaps somewhere deep down he believed it was Murray's destiny to win Wimbledon, so he was just going to make sure the home favourite had to win it, rather than get it handed on a plate. If that was in his mind, he played some canny tennis with Murray on the point of victory. Djokovic saved three championship points and had three break points of his own for 5–5. There are many in the tennis world who believe that, if Murray had dropped serve then, the whole match would have turned, and subsequent admissions by Murray that his arm was feeling very heavy with the pressure of the moment suggest that could easily have happened. But it's one of those 'what if' moments of history that serve only to enliven a conversation in the bar. The factual account records that Djokovic netted a backhand on Murray's fourth championship point, for Wimbledon to explode in the kind of ecstasy many of the 15,000 crowd (and another 15,000 watching on Henman Hill) never dreamed they would witness.

Djokovic was sensitive and smart enough to recognise that this was a moment in which he was, by now, the invited guest at someone else's wedding, and his on-court post-match interview was a model of diplomacy. 'Congratultions to Andy, you absolutely deserved this win, you played incredible tennis. Congratulations to his team, I know how much it means to them and how much it means to all you guys and to the whole country – so, well done! I'm aware of the pressure he gets – there is a lot of expectation on him – and that makes his success even bigger. On my side, I gave it all, it was an absolute pleasure and honour again to be part of this final. Thank you.'

From the brevity of his interview and the speed with which he came into his post-match press conference and then disappeared, Djokovic just wanted to get out. A great champion who has given everything but still lost may have the awareness to recognise another man's big moment, but it's not an environment in which many champions are comfortable and he didn't want to hang around.

Another thing great champions don't like is being struck by a rival. At the Montreal Masters four weeks later, Nadal and Djokovic met in the semi-finals in a three-setter that Nadal won on a deciding tie-break. In the fifth game of the final set, Djokovic played a drop shot and followed it into the net; Nadal played a backhand down the middle of the court, Djokovic was slow to see it coming and the ball struck him on the nose. Nadal instantly put his hand up to apologise; Djokovic saw it but turned away without apparently acknowledging Nadal's apology. The umpire tried to defuse the situation by announcing 'Nadal has apologised' as the crowd began to whistle. After the match, Nadal apologised verbally, even though the play had been entirely legitimate. Djokovic declined to escalate the incident and said it was 'all fine'. A look at the match video suggests Djokovic was more stunned than hurt (Nadal's backhand was not particularly fiercely struck), but in his moment of intense competitiveness he wasn't going to acknowledge the apology. It all happened so quickly that there was no time for premeditated action, but by the time they came off court, Djokovic was able to say the right thing for the issue to pass by as uncontroversial.

That night, Djokovic and a male friend from Serbia went out for a night on the town. They went to a Montreal night club, bought several bottles of champagne and spent the time in the company of a number of young women who will have dined out on their good fortune ever since. But once again, Djokovic had the ability to temper his own intake of alcohol and remain a dignified reveller. He didn't drink more than the odd glass and he was at all times respectful to the women who fawned over him. He clearly enjoys himself but has limits he sticks to, both for himself and for those he socialises with.

And he knew he had to be in optimum condition for the next battle against Nadal, who had clearly bounced back after his shock first-round defeat at Wimbledon. They went to New York each having won one major in 2013 and, when they met in the final of the US Open, it clearly meant a lot to the Serb. At the end of the year he described his defeat to Nadal at the French as 'my toughest loss', but he seemed more emotionally devastated by his four-sets defeat to Nadal in the US Open final. It was effectively the match that allowed Nadal to finish the year at the top of the rankings, although that might have happened even if Djokovic had won at Flushing Meadows.

The match followed a similar pattern to the Paris one. Nadal got off to the better start and took the first set. Djokovic broke back to take the second and have the better chances in the third, before Nadal reasserted himself to take a 2–1 lead. There the scripts departed from each other, Djokovic failing to rally in the fourth as Nadal won in four. But the real damage was done in the second and third sets. Djokovic hadn't broken the Spaniard until the sixth game of the second set but finally did so at the end of a 54-stroke rally. There had been one of 54 strokes in the Djokovic-Murray final a year before but this one was more punishing, both players delivering the kind of strokes that would have been clean winners against most other players but having to see the ball come back with interest. To think Nike built a TV commercial around a 24-

stroke rally played by Pete Sampras and Andre Agassi in the first set of the 1995 US Open final – that was club afternoon tennis compared with this!

Yet, far from being the rally that changed the course of the match, it almost undid Djokovic. He had finally broken serve but that rally had taken so much out of him that he lost the subsequent service game to love as Nadal looked fresh as a daisy. The psychological advantage Nadal took from that proved crucial as the match wore on. Djokovic was able to get his break back and serve out the set, and when he led 2–0 at the start of the third, he had won six of the previous seven games. Nadal bounced back but Djokovic had three break points at 4–4. Had he taken one of them, the outcome might have been different (or might not), but Nadal saved all three, broke Djokovic in the next game to take the set, and then raced through the final set for the loss of just one game.

Again Djokovic said the right thing at the end – 'He was too good, he definitely deserved to win this match and the trophy' – but this time it was said with the energy of someone who was genuinely devastated to have lost a hard-court final to Nadal. He was to beat Nadal twice more before the end of the year; in fact, it was to be his last defeat of 2013. But it seemed to hit him hard, however quickly he was able to bounce back from it.

After leaving the Beogradska Arena with a torn back muscle on the final day of the 2011 Davis Cup semi-final, Djokovic announced he would sit out the 2012 Davis Cup year. For an athlete for whom playing for one's country is a massive part of the sport, this was a slightly risky move, even if it made total sense in practical terms. But unlike Roger Federer, whose relegation of Davis Cup in 2005 to lower-priority status in his schedule led to a lengthy downgrading of how he viewed the team competition, Djokovic promised he would be back in 2013 and was as good as his word.

His loyalty to his country was sorely tested in the first round when Serbia was drawn away to Belgium. Belgium may be an unfashionable country in tourism terms but it has some beautiful places. Unfortunately Charleroi isn't one of them, yet the Belgian tennis authorities have a habit of choosing Charleroi for Davis and Fed Cup ties (it even played a Fed Cup final there at the height of Justine Henin's and Kim Clijsters' fame). So having just beaten Andy Murray in a four-set Australian Open final, Djokovic had to fly to Brussels to be on duty five days later against Olivier Rochus. At least it was only the world No. 127, and Rochus's best days were behind him, but it was still a major effort. Less well known is that the Serbian team had five hours to kill at one stage in the Charleroi trip, and Djokovic led players and backroom officials in several hours of the game of charades, frequently revelling in the role of acting out the clues. One of the members of the Serbian team said it 'showed he was a real leader, not just on court but in the way he dealt with everyone involved'.

His loyalty was tested still further in the quarter-finals, when he went from the Miami Masters to the sleepy Mid-West town of Boise in Idaho to lead the Serbian team against the USA. After beating John Isner on the opening day, Serbia lost what was thought to be the vital second singles, when Sam Querrey beat Viktor Troicki in five sets. With the Bryan brothers expected to beat Serbia's makeshift team of Nenad Zimonjic and Ilija Bozoljac, it looked set to go to a nervy fifth match. But the Serbian pair posted a remarkable win, 15–13 in the final set, to leave Djokovic with the chance to put Serbia into the semis. In the third game of his reverse singles against Querrey, Djokovic twisted his ankle, fell to the ground and writhed in agony. He continued to grimace as the Serbian team trainer strapped the ankle, and he continued playing, gingerly at first but then with more conviction. He was clearly worried about it and said afterwards, 'If I wasn't playing for

Serbia, I don't know if I'd have gone all the way.' Although Djokovic took the first set, Querrey took the second on the tie-break, which put wind into the sails of the Americans, especially as Djokovic's ankle might have become more painful as the match wore on. But from the start of the third set Djokovic played outstanding tennis and blew Querrey away. He dropped just one more game after that, and the ankle proved to be mildly bruised rather than a more serious injury.

September's semi-final allowed him to use the hero's welcome he always gets in the Beogradska Arena to help overcome the disappointment of defeat to Nadal in the US Open final four days earlier. On a clay court laid to blunt the big serve of Canada's Milos Raonic, Djokovic found himself playing to keep Serbia in the tie after Zimonjic and Bozoljac had played another marathon doubles, this time losing to Daniel Nestor and Vasek Pospisil. But his straight-sets win showed how much ground Raonic still had to make up against the players at the very top, and he then cheered his team-mate Janko Tipsarevic as he beat Pospisil, the strains of Saturday's doubles certainly giving the Canadian a much harder task than if he'd had a day off.

In his on-court interview after beating Pospisil, Tipsarevic said, 'Hopefully, we'll have Viktor [Troicki] back for the final.' Not only did Serbia not have Troicki for the final (see pages 250–1) but it didn't have Tipsarevic either. At the tournament in Valencia in mid-October, Tipsarevic picked up a heel injury that proved agonisingly slow to heal. He turned up for the final, and even on the Wednesday night he was saying he hoped to be able to play. But he was playing in pain, and on Thursday morning he bowed to the inevitable and withdrew from the Davis Cup final. Djokovic clearly had a say in the decision to pick Dusan Lajovic as Tipsarevic's replacement for the final against the Czech Republic, but the bigger decision was whether Djokovic would play doubles. He had said throughout the year he was up for two singles but Serbia had to find the third point from somewhere else – now with both Tipsarevic and Troicki unavailable, would he step in for Saturday duty in the hope of seeing Serbia through? The answer was no. He told his team-mates on the Friday night he would give everything in the singles but couldn't add the doubles at the end of a punishing year that had seen him finish with 23 matches unbeaten. He made it 24 by taking apart Tomas Berdych, leaving him with seven singles wins out of seven for the year in Davis Cup and just one set dropped. But Lajovic, at 117 in the rankings, was no match for the wily Radek Stepanek, who was playing some of the best tennis of his career, and the Czechs retained their trophy with an anti-climactic win in the fifth match of the final weekend.

Would Serbia have won if Djokovic had played doubles? It's impossible to say with any conviction. Berdych and Stepanek have a phenomenal record together and they played with such confidence that they would have been hard to beat by any pair. But Bozoljac had a nightmare and Djokovic would certainly have got more returns in. At the end of the day he stuck to his deal, but when a team of – essentially – three singles players finds it's down to one, it's very hard to win a Davis Cup final.

With Tipsarevic still absent (though by now more though paternity leave than injury) and Troicki still suspended, Djokovic decided not to play in the Davis Cup first round in February 2014. The decision was a late one, and who knows what went through his mind when he found that Roger Federer was on the plane to Novi Sad to join his compatriot, the newly crowned Australian Open champion Stanislas Wawrinka, in a full-strength Swiss team? Maybe Wawrinka's win over Djokovic in Melbourne made Djokovic reluctant to face him so soon after such a painful defeat? Or maybe the presence of both Swiss meant Djokovic couldn't have helped Serbia to win unless he'd played on all three days. Either way, it meant 2014 was not to be a Davis Cup year for Djokovic and the Serbs.

In the second half of 2013, Djokovic's role as a statesman intensified markedly. In August he became one of the very few athletes to address the United Nations General Assembly. The UN had called a press conference to announce 6 April 2014 as the International Day of Sport for Development and Peace. The announcement was made by Vuk Jeremic, the Serbian foreign minister who was at the time president of the General Assembly and who the Djokovic family had installed as president of the Serbian Tennis Federation after the 'coup' they instigated in early 2011. Jeremic had asked Djokovic and the outgoing International Olympic Committee president Jacques Rogge to accompany him.

Djokovic addressed the assembly on behalf of the global sporting community. He said he hoped the international day would motivate people to do more to cultivate intrinsic sporting values such as fair play, teamwork and respect for opponents. 'These ideals are universal,' he said. 'Every successful society is built on them and the more we instil respect for these ideals in ourselves, the better the world will be that we leave to our successors.'

Asked about the experience afterwards, he said,

I think the invitation was the coolest part. Just having this privilege of speaking in the name of the global family of athletes on such a historical day. Historical because it's in the United Nations and we all know how the United Nations is important as an organisation. You have over 120 member states deciding about the biggest issues in the world. So there was definitely a special feeling that I didn't experience before. You had this kind of sensation that you are part of something that is very big – just that experience, you know, brought me chills. Being in a position to speak was quite an honour. The president of the General Assembly is a Serbian, so to have two Serbian people speaking on such a historical day is even bigger for our country. It's something I will definitely never forget.

If his speech was a safe, set-piece appearance, a few days later he ventured more of a controversial opinion. After trouncing Joao Sousa in the third round of the US Open, Djokovic was asked in his post-match press conference what he thought of the prospect of air strikes against Syria. The Middle Eastern country was at the time in the midst of a brutal civil war, and evidence was emerging of the use of chemical weapons by the governing regime against its own citizens, news that had prompted the US president Barack Obama to seek a majority in Congress for intervention in Syria.

Few tennis players venture opinions on international political issues, but Djokovic showed no reticence. 'I'm totally against any kind of weapon, any kind of air strike or missile attack,' he said. 'I'm totally against anything that is destructive. Because I had this personal experience, I know it cannot bring any good to anybody.' And in another answer in the same conference, he said, 'Those particular times that me and my fellow countrymen and colleagues from Serbia have been through is definitely, you know, a period of life that we don't wish anybody to experience. War is the worst thing in life for humanity. Nobody really wins.' An interesting footnote is that he checked the transcript of his press conference with the transcribers before he left the interview room, just to ensure they had down what he intended to say (if that sounds like censorship or rewriting the record, there are occasional discrepancies between the typed record of a press conference and what was actually said).

And after the US Open when he was back in Serbia for the Davis

Cup semi-final, he appeared alongside the British former royal Sarah Ferguson at the opening of a primary school in central Serbia. The school in Kadina Luka had been renovated with funds from the Novak Djokovic Foundation. The school is entitled 'Skolica Zivota', which doesn't translate exactly but is probably best as 'small school for life' (see page 286).

And in the fortnight between the Davis Cup semi-final and the China Open in Beijing he got engaged to his girlfriend of eight years' standing, Jelena Ristic. She had been taking on an increasingly large administrative role managing his international sponsorship and PR work, not dissimilar to the role Mirka Vavrinec took on before she married Roger Federer. The engagement certainly did nothing to harm his tennis, as he won his next 26 matches.

His friend Dusan Vemic says of Djokovic, 'He's very happy in the limelight.' It's not said with any inherent criticism, merely as a statement that Djokovic is a performer, so when the China Open asked him to recreate the infamous 'Battle of the Sexes' tennis match from 1973 by playing China's top tennis icon Li Na in Beijing, he was happy to oblige, though more in a spirit of fun than fighting for gender equality. Throughout 2013 there had been many 40th anniversary tributes to the founding of the Women's Tennis Association and Billie Jean King's victory over the chauvinistic American Bobby Riggs at the Houston Astrodome in 1973. Li's victory over Djokovic was somewhat more low-key – like King and Riggs, they played a best-of-five match but it was best of five games, not sets, and Djokovic began all five games 0-30 down. Li emulated King's achievement by winning for the women by three games to two, after which they were treated to an enormous cake to celebrate the tournament's 10th anniversary. It's not known whether it was a gluten-free cake. What is known is that Djokovic beat Nadal in the final a week later.

Even if Djokovic is very much a sporting statesman, it's easy to forget that, for all his worldly wisdom, he's still only midway through the third decade of his life. And sometimes a lack of experience in broader issues catches up with him. One such instance came at the end of 2013, when he launched a scathing attack on tennis's governing bodies in defence of his friend and Davis Cup team-mate Viktor Troicki. Djokovic showed himself to be very eloquent, but at times his emotions got in the way of clear thinking.

Troicki had been suspended earlier in the year for 18 months for failing to provide a blood sample at the Monte Carlo Masters in April. He claimed he had a life-long fear of needles, which was exacerbated when he was unwell. As he said he was unwell in Monte Carlo and said he had suffered the effects of strong sun, he asked the Doping Control Officer responsible for his blood and urine tests whether he could forego his blood test, as he feared he would faint. He claims she said yes but changed her story later. She said she never gave him any such assurance and warned him he could face sanctions if he didn't do his blood test that day. On examining the case, tennis's anti-doping authorities said missing a test was a serious breach of the regulations, and they banned him for just six months less than if he had taken the blood test and been found positive for a banned substance. Troicki appealed to the Court for Arbitration in Sport (CAS), which delivered its ruling during the ATP World Tour Finals in London.

The CAS judged that Troicki was at fault, but found that the Doping Control Officer in Monte Carlo could have sought the assistance of an ATP official to help persuade Troicki to provide the sample. It therefore concluded the sentence was a little too harsh and reduced it from 18 months to 12. But that was of little consolation to Djokovic. Not only was his friend deprived of a full year of his professional career but Serbia was deprived of one of its Davis Cup players for the following week's final at home to the

Czech Republic. The Serbs could have won without Troicki as long as Janko Tipsarevic was fit, but Djokovic knew Tipsarevic was in a race against time to recover from his heel injury and was in serious danger of missing the final. Troicki's ban was therefore a serious setback for Serbia.

The CAS judgement was delivered on the day Djokovic played Roger Federer in London, and the former's post-match press conference was rife with anticipation about how he would respond to the confirmation of Troicki's ban. Normally in post-match press conferences, the player walks in, sits down, takes questions and walks out at the end. This one was different. After the usual questions about Djokovic's victory against Federer, he was asked whether he had any comments to make about the judgement. Djokovic reached for his pocket, took out some notes and proceeded to speak for seven minutes uninterrupted. It was highly impressive, but the eloquence gradually gave way to emotion and he left himself open to attack on several fronts.

Djokovic outlined his grievance as follows:

It's very bad news that we got for him [Troicki], and for me, for all of us who are close to him. But I think it's just not bad news for him, it proves again that this system of Wada [World Anti-Doping Agency] does not work. Why am I saying that? Because, first of all, as a tennis pro, our job is to play tennis and respect all the rules and know all the rules of our sport. But when you are randomly selected to go and provide the test – blood test or urine test – the representatives of Wada who are there at the tournament are supposed to give you the clear indications and explain [to] you the rules and regulations and what the severe consequences or penalties [are] that you might undertake or you might have if you fail to provide the test. The representative didn't do that in his case. So first, he's not positive on any banned substance. I'm not saying that it's completely not his fault, but ... she did not clearly present him [with] all the severe consequences that he will have if he avoids that. She told him that he needs to write a report and that he will be just fine. And because of her negligence and because of her unprofessionalism, he is now off the tour for one year. And now it makes me nervous as a player to do any kind of test.

Djokovic was effectively seizing on one element of the judgement to make it sound as if the whole process was a lottery. The CAS's judgement did indeed say that the Doping Control Officer might have misled Troicki by suggesting he write to the ITF setting out his reason for not wanting to take the blood test – the CAS said this 'led him erroneously to believe that she was confident that the outcome would be positive' – and that she failed in her duty to 'always ensure that there is no possible misunderstanding involved' and that she should 'always encourage the athlete to proceed with the doping control' by making him understand 'perhaps with some persuasion [...] the importance of following the procedures'. But it also said there was no objective justification for Troicki failing to provide a blood test and added that Troicki's memory was 'coloured by his subsequent reconstruction of events'. So Djokovic was judging the whole case on Troicki's version of his conversation with the Doping Control Officer, a version that had been thrown into doubt by the judicial body looking at every detail of the case. Accusing a professional of 'negligence' and 'unprofessionalism' on that evidence is skating on thin ice.

He also said Troicki's decision to take a blood test the following day – a test that was found to be clear – showed that Troicki had not committed any offence. But that doesn't hold water, as there is the potential for substances to show up in a blood test one day that would not show up the next day, so giving the blood sample at the time it's requested is a crucial part of the integrity of the anti-doping process.

Djokovic was honest enough to admit that Troicki was 'a very good friend of mine', someone he had known since the age of eight, and that this meant he was 'emotionally connected' to the case. Perhaps for that reason the tennis world appeared happy to accept that Djokovic had gone into bat for a friend, and that, if his defence of Troicki was passionate to the point of not being rock-solid, well, that's what sometimes happens when you see your first loyalty as being to your friend and team-mate. But he was probably more than a little shocked when, later the same week, both Roger Federer and Andy Murray totally rejected Troicki's defence – Federer said that, when a player is asked for a sample, he or she has to give it, and Murray said Troicki had been 'unprofessional' not to undergo the blood test and while he had some sympathy for the player's position he had no sympathy for his argument.

No one should have too much of a dig at Djokovic for taking one element of the CAS's judgement and trying to maximise its impact. That is the staple of politicians and lawyers fighting their corner in the face of inconvenient evidence to the contrary. But he has to be careful about fighting for a friend so hard that he risks undermining the credibility of tennis's anti-doping measures. He himself is a man who has taken fitness, endurance and recovery at the top of the game to new levels, but he will only receive credit and respect for that if his sport is seen to be clean. He will be aware of athletes, cyclists and performers from other sports whose achievements have never quite received the recognition they deserve because of the drug-induced exploits of their predecessors, so as one of the leading proponents of tennis Djokovic has a duty to make sure the image of a clean sport is not undermined.

Where the emotions really took over was in his subsequent attack on the ATP. He said, 'The ATP, who is supposed to be an association of players, of tennis professionals, who is supposed to be the governing body, the association that stands behind the players, is not going to answer on this announcement, is not going to do anything for Viktor.' He went on, 'The system [in the ATP's governance] is so complicated, and it's not working for players because the ATP is 50 per cent players, 50 per cent tournaments. So every time you want to vote for something, you need a majority, which is impossible because you're going against tournaments. Players have no energy or time to spend on these things. We don't have time for politics. The structure right now doesn't go in favour of players.'

This is seriously flawed argumentation on many fronts. For a start, it seems to assume the players are more important than the tournaments – true, the tournaments can't function without players, but then players can't function without tournaments, so the two have to work together. Secondly, if he says he has no time for politics, he has to trust those who do – that is a law of life, not just of tennis. Oddly, he has been involved in tennis politics. He is a former member of the ATP Player Council and is very close to Ivan Ljubicic, a former president of the council who tried to tackle the alphabet soup of tennis's governing bodies. It means that any attack on the ATP is an attack on himself as a member of the ATP. And it was a little tacky to issue a stinging attack on the ATP at the ATP's flagship tournament of the year – it's not quite like insulting the host who has invited you to dinner, but he might have chosen another moment, especially as his beef was with the Doping Control Officer and the Court for Arbitration in Sport, not primarily with any of tennis's governing bodies.

Despite the holes that can be shot through his argument, Djokovic came away from his outburst on behalf of Troicki with his reputation for eloquence enhanced. He had made the point very clearly that, whatever the rights and wrongs of tennis's anti-doping regime, he and other players felt vulnerable to being caught out by the system while trying to play strictly by its rules. And he had made the point that if a player doesn't play strictly by the rules he (or she) can lose a year of their career, whereas when a Doping Control Officer doesn't play strictly by the rules there appears to be no sanction against them. There were many who felt this was a tennis administrator of the future in the making. At the time he made his comments, the ATP had still not replaced the late Brad Drewett as its chairman and chief executive, which heightened the sense that Djokovic might one day be appropriate for the role. At 26, he could be forgiven for being politically wet behind the ears, or for putting the interests of a childhood friend ahead of a coherent argument. In the long term, however, a greater appreciation for the complexities of governance will be needed.

Interestingly, he didn't mention the International Tennis Federation in his monologue about Troicki, despite being known to harbour resentments about certain decisions taken by the ITF. Perhaps this was a bit of *Realpolitik*, based on the fact that the ITF owns and runs the Davis Cup and the following week he was to be the star act in the Davis Cup final in his home city of Belgrade. Ultimately, Serbia lost a strange final in which all five matches were decided in straight sets and Serbia's inability to parade Troicki and Tipsarevic cost the hosts dear. At the trophy-presentation ceremony, Djokovic shook the hand of the ITF president Francesco Ricci Bitti and smiled at him, but he and Tipsarevic were the only members of the Serbian team not to show up at the official Davis Cup dinner later that night. It would be too strong to say they boycotted the dinner, but it was certainly a silent protest.

Health problems in the family of Marian Vajda caused a rethink in the Djokovic team in the latter part of 2013. Vajda made it clear he didn't want to be on the road as much, so he and Djokovic discussed who might come in as a new principal coach, albeit with Vajda still heavily involved. The choice they made took the tennis world by surprise: Boris Becker.

Becker had spent most of his time since retiring in the late 1990s as a television pundit. The complexities of his private life, which included fathering a child from a one-night stand in the broom cupboard of a London restaurant, had made him into a celebrity figure of constant discussion and speculation but hardly one of the world's movers and shakers. A man of great charm and immense charisma, he attracted attention wherever he went, especially in his native Germany where he is something of a deity, but also in Great Britain, partly because he had a home in Wimbledon. But his comments on tennis were not widely viewed as profound, and a feature of many of his pronouncements was the constant presence of his ego. As he had never coached a touring professional before, the tennis world wondered what Becker would be able to say to Djokovic.

The official line from Djokovic was that Becker would be helping with the mental aspect of Djokovic's game, specifically how to handle the big points in the big matches. In some ways, this made sense – Djokovic had lost a number of big matches he arguably should have won, such as the 2012 French Open final, the 2012 Wimbledon semi-final, the 2013 French semi, the 2013 Wimbledon final and the 2012 and 2013 US Open finals. Becker is one of the few people who knows how to turn a match round that is slipping away and how to win the big titles. But can he impart this knowledge? That was the unknown quantity and was still unknown as this book went to press.

It was easy to make fun of the arrangement when it was announced. Becker had had an awful 2013, with various personal problems and ballooning weight following an ankle problem that required surgery. And with Andy Murray having hired Ivan Lendl in 2012 and Roger Federer hiring Stefan Edberg, Marin Cilic hiring Goran Ivanisevic and Kei Nishikori hiring Michael Chang, all in late 2013, it seemed like a draft of the big names of the 1980s and 1990s that Djokovic didn't want to miss out on.

Their first outing together didn't bode well. Djokovic lost his Australian Open winning streak in the quarter-finals, his 25-match unbeaten run at Melbourne Park ending with a 9–7 final-set defeat to Stanislas Wawrinka. The defeat looked a little better five days later when Wawrinka lifted the trophy – his first Grand Slam title was assisted by a back injury to Rafael Nadal in the final, but Wawrinka was playing well enough to have won the trophy even without the help of Nadal's back. And by the end of the fortnight in Melbourne, the relationship seemed to have sent out the message that it was serious and not some kind of publicity stunt.

So why did Djokovic hire Becker? The reason given has some credibility, although much will depend on whether Becker can pass on his experience and on-court presence to someone else. Djokovic greeted Becker with a request to speak German with him so he could freshen up his command of the language; with Djokovic living for much of the year in Monaco where he speaks French (he has a dog called Pierre, so one assumes he speaks French to the dog), and speaking Italian with his manager Edoardo Artaldi, it's easy to joke that he picks his team on the basis of which languages he can add to his collection. But there may be two deeper-lying reasons for his choice of Becker.

What was clear in Melbourne at their first tournament together was that the appointment of Becker had created a buzz around Djokovic that wasn't there before. His practice sessions were suddenly sought-after events, even though Becker was doing little more than feeding tennis balls to a hitting partner because he was still recovering from his ankle surgery (he had lost a few kilos and had worked out a training programme, so the German was clearly taking the arrangement seriously and benefiting from it personally). Questions abounded in Djokovic's press conferences about Becker and he even acceded to a request from Jim Courier in an on-court interview to perform his impersonation of Becker after a victory on the Rod Laver Arena – the rocking service motion performed under Becker's eyes brought the house down. If the leading three figures in world tennis all need an image to sustain their profile, Federer is the stylish traditionalist, Nadal the physical bull, while Djokovic is something of the amiable professor. But Djokovic's image doesn't translate as easily as the other two, and the world doesn't always get his blend of the heart-pumping warrior and the Tolstoyesque philosopher. Having Becker in his camp certainly gave him a popular standing that he didn't have with Vajda.

Whether that is enough reason on its own to hire the German is doubtful, but the Serbian tennis journalist Vojin Velickovic offers another possible reason. 'People think Igor Cetojevic gave Novak only the gluten-free diet,' he says, 'but I talked to him and he believed he gave Novak two things: the diet and a form of conversation that is very important to Novak. He likes to work things out, to think them through, and I think Cetojevic was able to have conversations with him that gave him a very clear mind going into matches. Maybe he has missed that and the relationship with Boris is a chance to have these conversations and prepare his mindset before matches?'

Becker may also be able to help with things like tournament planning. At the end of a punishing 2013, Djokovic played several exhibition matches in South America with Nadal and then played no official warm-up tournaments for the Australian Open. Much as it would have helped his bank balance and his profile in Latin America, it may have left him short of match practice for the Grand Slam at which he has been most successful. Becker is likely to be stricter on tournament planning at the end of 2014. It's clear the future of the Djokovic-Becker partnership hangs on several factors, including perhaps Vajda's willingness to travel if his family situation becomes more conducive.

CHAPTER THIRTEEN

A 'GIVING' PERSON

In October 2013 Serbia's national airline JAT (Yugoslav Air Transport) signed a deal with the Abu Dhabi airline Etihad for Etihad to buy a 49 per cent stake in JAT and run the Serbian carrier. Part of the deal was that JAT would be rebranded as Air Serbia. It included a new logo to grace all the tail fins, a variation of the Serbian double-headed eagle. That symbol from Serbian heraldry had become associated with Serbia's reputation as an aggressor in the 1990s wars, so the fact that it was the basis of the new Air Serbia logo showed perhaps that the Serbs were becoming less coy about using some traditional symbols from their country's cultural heritage.

Another part of the deal was that 14 planes would be named after iconic Serbian figures. And it should surprise no one that the first plane was named Novak Djokovic. The simple fact is that Djokovic is Serbia's best ambassador by a country mile, and the nation's leading lights are falling over themselves to make the most of him while he's around.

Boris Tadic was Serbia's president from 2004 to 12. He was frequently courtside when Djokovic and Serbia's other top players played for the biggest titles and for their country in the Davis and Fed Cups. 'Serbians feel very proud because of Novak,' Tadic said after Djokovic's Wimbledon triumph in 2011. 'The people have been suffering very much in the last few decades and that kind of victory is very helpful, it makes people very proud. For sure, he's helping to change Serbia's reputation. The first association people have of Serbia is Novak Djokovic, not the Serbian president, and that's very good. We had a first association with Serbia through the former president [Slobodan Milosevic] and that was very bad. Now the situation is totally different and I'm very proud about Novak.'

Dragan Djilas, the leader of Serbia's Democratic Party and mayor of Belgrade until October 2013, told a group of international journalists, 'I think it would be very useful if one day the world's media would start to speak about Serbia not in terms of the wars, not about Milosevic – I know this is interesting and every few months it comes up – but it's important they speak of Serbia through someone like Novak Djokovic or some other successful guys from Serbia, scientists, professors, young people, people from culture. Djokovic is great – we need more like him to promote a different image of Serbia.'

What's interesting is that Djilas was clearly trying to find a list of Serbian role models but could think only of Djokovic. For the record, the second person to have a plane named after them in the Air Serbia fleet was Emir Kusturica, the film director, who is playing a similar role to Djokovic in the arts world.

The need for an ambassador may seem a little strange to citizens of countries like the USA or Great Britain; nations which are largely blissfully unaware of the way some parts of the world view them with contempt. The Serbs are in no doubt that their international reputation needs some repair. Two of Serbia's top tennis players of the pre-Djokovic era, Nenad Zimonjic and Dusan Vemic, had to make their way on the circuit during and immediately after the wars of the 1990s, with sanctions and visa restrictions widespread. 'There were stories going round in the nineties when they blamed us for things we didn't do,' says Zimonjic. 'There was often proof that we weren't to blame, but no one talks about that and the bad reputation hangs on. So it's nice when we have someone who can present a positive image. Hopefully, what Novak is doing will give a chance for the world to look at us objectively and maybe can create the conditions for upcoming generations to question some of the things that were misrepresented.'

Vemic says the problem with Serbia's reputation went further than just the Yugoslav wars. 'We were always represented in the late 1990s and early 2000s as criminals and terrorists, not just in the news but in many movies,' he says. 'We were always the bad guys. I'm sure he's helped change that, at least a little bit. He's given us some recognition in the world in a positive light. He has always represented our country in a really positive and proud way. For the country, he was the best ambassador.' Vemic is not the only Serb to note that the Serbian terrorist or criminal is a stereotype among film directors, and it throws an interesting light on Djokovic's cameo performance for *Expendables 2* as a racket-wielding killer, even if the sequence ended up on the cutting-room floor. It's worth noting that there has been a Hollywood convention for many years that when a villain is needed an English accent is normally used, yet by and large the English don't seem to notice.

It's possible therefore to make the case that the Serbs have an inferiority complex, but even if they do it's still real, especially to those who travel abroad and have to deal with the world's reaction to the name of the country. When an American, a Briton, a Frenchman, a German, an Australian, or indeed a citizen of any one of the four dozen most prominent countries of the world says where they come from, there is normally instant recognition of the country. But until recently, a Serb travelling abroad would encounter either hostility or puzzlement. It's something Djokovic himself was very aware of when he started travelling. 'Not many people knew where Serbia is,' he says, 'and some of them even thought I was saying Siberia. It was an adventure explaining to them where Serbia is, but I enjoyed it. I felt that I was on a mission to bring as much good as I can to stand next to my country's name, because the media wasn't bringing out the best news about my country at that time.'

The Serbian television commentator Nebojsa Viskovic tells the story of the first Grand Slam tournament he covered. 'It was the 2001 US Open, just before 9/11,' he says. 'When I said where I came from, people would say, "Where?" I would whisper it. Since the tennis euphoria it's such a different story. When I do interviews, people from other television stations sometimes ask me where I come from, and when I say "Serbia" they give me the thumbs-up. Because something nice happened, something nice came from Serbia – not only Novak but the women as well, Ana and Jelena. Now I say I'm from Serbia with pride.'

Ana Ivanovic herself says, 'Many times I've been asked, "Oh, is it safe to go to Serbia?" When you meet people at tournaments around the world and people ask where you're from and you say Serbia, they often ask, "Is it safe there?" and I say, "Yes, it's very safe there." At the movies all the gangsters and criminals, all the bad guys, are either Serbians or Russians, so it's not really fair. I really hope people can have a better image of Serbia.'

This illustrates the importance to Serbia of having an international role model, and indeed some people interviewed for this book say they now find the instinctive reaction to the word 'Serbia' is, 'Ah, Novak Djokovic.'

Responding to all the big names who say he is the best

ambassador Serbia could have, Djokovic says, 'That's a lot of responsibility. I feel the pressure. It's because we have a harder way to succeed in life, we Serbs, because of the past we've had, because of the history. We have to dig deeper and we have to do much more in order to be seen and to be spotted.'

Not that Djokovic has any difficulty being spotted; in fact, he seems to be a born performer. He has been invited on to many of the big US television shows and has been happy to oblige with all sorts of publicity stunts that many players would have run away from. He sang a song at the 2008 Eurovision Song Contest which was hosted by Serbia in Belgrade. Asked to take part in a fashion show in Montreal in 2009, he ripped off a silk bathrobe to reveal the briefest pair of briefs. And at the end of 2010 he allowed himself to be strapped to the wing of a bi-plane, wing-walking and volleying tennis balls in a commercial for his racket company Head ('My mother asked me, "Why did you do that?" – it was crazy, one of the craziest things I've done in my life for sure.'). But there's a valuable dividend for his country in his showmanship. Writing in August 2011 about Djokovic's appearance on Jay Leno's talk show *Tonight*, the Serbian-American writer Ana Mitric said, 'Before Djokovic, the three most "famous" Serbs were dictator Slobodan Milosevic and military "leaders" Radovan Karadzic and Ratko Mladic [all three of whom have ended up in the UN's war-crimes tribunal in The Hague] – not exactly the type of guys who get invited on to the *Tonight* show.'

Although he's streets ahead of anyone else in Serbia in terms of his international profile, Djokovic is not alone. Four months after his first Grand Slam title at the 2008 Australian Open, Ana Ivanovic won the French Open title and made it to the top of the world rankings, so she and Jelena Jankovic were also ambassadors for their country. Ivanovic says,

It was one of the great honours we had as sports people to represent Serbia. I think sport brings people together and no one judges where you come from; they judge what you achieve. In a way I, and I think everyone else, felt like it was a chance to bring a better name to our country. The few times we had a chance to meet our president [Boris Tadic], he always showed appreciation and gratitude for that. He used to say, 'You guys are the best ambassadors we can have.' What Novak is doing now is amazing and it helps our country so much. He's told me it was a great honour and the chance to show a different face, and to show that we have funny people.

It's not just that Djokovic is a good role model – how he goes about his nationality is part of what the world finds appealing. He is patriotic and never misses a chance to promote Serbia but there's nothing messianic about it. Given that his mother is Croatian, it should be no surprise that some of his best friends are Croats (in particular, Ivan Ljubicic and Marin Cilic), but given how Serbia and Croatia fought each other in the early 1990s, it's a fact that's not without significance. And there was the trophy presentation in Montreal in 2007 when Djokovic was introduced by the master of ceremonies as being from Croatia. He laughed it off, saying, 'I don't mind you calling me Croat. Serbs and Croats, it's almost the same. We're all people.' In an interview with a Croatian newspaper, Djokovic said, 'I would put myself above all the nationalist *conferva*. For someone abroad, it is very difficult to distinguish between our people, our borders, who we are, what we are. That is why I am not offended. I know how much effort I need to explain where I come from and where these mountainous Balkans are.'

Although Djokovic would always have been an internationalist in some way, he has perhaps been helped more than is obvious by his friendship with Ivan Ljubicic. A Croatian born in Bosnia of mixed

Bosniak-Catholic parentage, Ljubicic could have had one of at least three nationalities but ended up a national hero for Croatia. 'I feel part of the world,' he says. 'I was never nationalistic – people mix up nationalism with patriotism, which are two different things. I love playing for the country and support the country but it doesn't mean I hate others. I respect everybody. Once you circle the world with other people, you can't just enclose yourself with such a small environment.'

Ljubicic wonders whether Djokovic's strong Serbian consciousness has detracted from him being a truly global star. 'I think he did a tremendous job – I'm not sure how much people in Serbia are giving him credit for this, but Serbia really had a negative reputation in the past and I know he's done a lot and he's trying hard. Maybe some people don't see him as a global star because he's really proud of being a Serbian and he's putting Serbia at the front all the time. He's trying to promote the country harder than anyone else before him, probably because he feels the reputation the country has is not right and he wants to change that.'

The American Todd Martin, who was a member of Djokovic's coaching team in 2009–10, tells an interesting story about Djokovic the diplomat:

Novak has a pretty good understanding certainly of his own country's history and some of the relationship stuff with other countries. He's also a bit of a people person, so he hasn't wasted this opportunity of travelling the world and experiencing different cultures, and he's generally pretty aware. That meant there were times when I was the one American with lots of people from the Balkan or Slavic regions. One time in particular it was pretty difficult to be that guy without a great knowledge of Serbia – Serbian-American relations were never a huge part of my course of study, whereas America is the big fish for the Serbians and for a lot of other countries. One fellow we encountered – I forget whether he was Serbian, Croatian, Slovenian or what – thought the American government was to blame for some of the issues his country had experienced over the years. He may be right, I needed some better understanding of the background which I didn't have, so I did my best to play dumb, which isn't really too difficult for me. But this guy was particularly aggressive with his opinion, and I felt Novak did a tremendous job of explaining the perspective without necessarily taking a side and without upsetting his friend, so it wasn't confrontational. I was impressed.

Given the battering Serbia's reputation in the world took in the 1990s, the question arises as to whether Djokovic could in some way atone for his country's atrocities. A straw poll of a number of Serbs illicits a near universal answer: 'That would be treachery', 'He'd be a traitor to his country' and such like. These responses highlight the dual role Djokovic plays as a Serb and an international citizen. As an international citizen, he recognises the need for reconciliation and the part that the acknowledgement of transgressions against human decency plays in that reconciliation, yet as a Serb he has to be loyal to his country. This is why he sometimes seems more of a warrior when playing in Serbia and more of an athlete when playing in the world's greatest tennis stadiums. And why he has to tread carefully at times. For example, as a noted supporter of the Red Star Belgrade football team, he's sometimes asked to put on the team shirt for publicity photos, but Red Star is currently sponsored by the controversial Russian energy giant Gazprom, and Djokovic will be aware of Gazprom's dubious reputation in the west so doesn't overdo the occasions when he wears the shirt.

The thoughtful Serbian sports journalist Zoran Milosavljevic observes, 'What drives him is his patriotism and desire to represent Serbia in the best possible way. There's a lot of defiance in it. His driving force is to show that Serbia is not an aggressive backwater but a modern, civilised country. He does this by his good manners, language skills and general sense of humour.'

Amid all the talk about him representing Serbia abroad, it's important not to overlook his ability to help heal the still latent divisions within the states of the former Yugoslavia. His mix of being a Serb born to a Croatian mother and an ethnic Montinegrin father from Kosovo is not dissimilar to the mixed parentage of Tito, and while there are plenty of people in the former Yugoslav lands who have mixed ethnic heritage, the importance of such mixed parentage in a high-profile hero could be significant. Dejan Petrovic says of Djokovic's standing in Serbia, 'Nole can be like Tito, doing the job of uniting people, definitely within Serbia if not for other countries that were formerly Yugoslavia.'

Djokovic himself says, 'I actually love all the ex-Yugoslav countries, and that includes Croatia too, regardless of the horrible war. I am not a person who holds a grudge over something for too long, I have a forgiving nature. Maybe it's because I haven't experienced the worst from the war, because I didn't lose my family or my home, like other people who have a much harder time forgiving and forgetting. But I honestly don't think that we as countries have any more reasons to fight. The media tend to stir the pot way too often. The moment we start forgetting, they keep reminding us and pulling us back into the past, which is not very helpful.'

Through all this talk of Djokovic as a statesman and a diplomat, it's important not to create the impression that the animal in him has somehow gone away. It is still very much there, and while he knows how to keep it behind bars, it does make occasional appearances.

The most striking of these was at the end of his marathon Australian Open final in January 2012, when, after shaking hands with the umpire and embracing Rafael Nadal, Djokovic ripped off his shirt, roared from the bottom of his gut, and as he went over to his entourage showed the body language less of the goalscorer who wants to hug his team-mates and more of the warrior who wants to show he's the leader of the pack. There was something of the Maori 'Haka' about it.

But there is also the occasional sense that the animal is never far away when things go wrong. In the 2013 Wimbledon final, when Djokovic started getting the sense that everything was against him, he lost a bit of his cool towards the end of the second set, screaming at the umpire Mohamed Layani after running out of challenges. That was nothing compared with the tongue-lashing he gave another umpire, Ali Nili, in the semi-finals of the Shanghai Masters in October 2013 against Jo-Wilfried Tsonga, after Nili judged – correctly – that Djokovic had let a ball go, so his opponent's successful challenge to the electronic review system meant Tsonga won the point. And there was a marked transition during Djokovic's seven-minute monologue in defence of Viktor Troicki at the 2013 ATP Finals – while Djokovic started off calmly and rationally, the emotions gradually took over and he ended up almost ranting.

The task therefore is to keep everything in balance. His former assistant coach Dusan Vemic says,

When he gets the balance of his emotions right, he's as close to perfection as he could be. If he's too mellow: not good. If he's too wild: not good. But when it's just the right amount, he's a remarkable tennis player. Tennis is a sport where nowadays most players are very square in the sense of being just another tennis player on the court, but when he's in the right place he's amazing to watch. When he plays for himself, you can see he's sometimes a little more stressed, but when he plays for his country he's very determined, very focused, a lot of good energy, especially when he plays in front of our crowd – he really draws all that energy from them and always performs extremely well. Sport is a great thing, it can take people of a young age away from a potentially wrong path, but sometimes he needs the aggression to keep the balance right.

He appears always to have been like this. Jelena Gencic talked about the piercing eyes that went with his immense focus and ability to learn. And the Serbian tennis commentator Nebojsa Viskovic, who had a long-running feud with Srdjan Djokovic, remembers meeting the 12-year-old Novak for the first time.

He was very polite, with such nice manners, and respect for my age. But very confident and very serious – he looked like he was going to be a scientist. He's very clever. He almost has a split personality – one we see, the other is seen only by people in specific situations. And even as a boy he knew how to manage the relationship with me. I can't say we were friends but we were close. Our relationship was very good all the time. After the difficulties with his father, the relationship stayed strictly professional, but at the highest level. He never told me anything [about the issues Viskovic had with Srdjan], I never told him anything, neither of us brought up what had happened. People around him were protecting him from many of the hassles that Srdjan causes. Like his father Novak has his dark side, but unlike his father he knows how to shut it down and when to bring it out. He's a great tactician.

Maybe that is an underestimated characteristic of greatness – the ability to keep one's dark side shut down, or at least to detonate it in a safe environment? Roger Federer has done the same, overcoming a hot-headed, sometimes petulant side to his character that threatened to hold him back, and finding ways of releasing it off-court so he can be totally efficient about the management of his emotions when on court. Maybe that is why playing Davis Cup is so important to Djokovic – he's known to be unhappy about the cup's scheduling and has left officials of the International Tennis Federation in no doubt about his feelings, but he very seldom skips Davis Cup weekends. He seems to feed off donning his red Serbia shirt and playing for his country, almost as if it allows him to be a soldier for his country in a way that playing as an individual doesn't. He can certainly let his inner animal have greater expression when playing a home Davis Cup tie than he can in most of his tour matches.

Another attribute that his friends speak about is his memory. Some say he will always remember a conversation, prompting many of his friends to be careful what they promise.

The role of humour is also important for him. Those who have worked with him say he has a great sense of humour and a great need to play it out, but he keeps his fun time and his work time strictly demarcated. 'He's a lot less funny than people think,' says Todd Martin, who worked with Djokovic for several months in 2009–10, 'and he's a lot smarter than people think. If you sit down with him, he's not cutting jokes the whole time, he's a pretty serious guy and very smart.' That's why his decision to don a Hallowe'en mask for his walk on to court for a match in Basel in October 2011 was such a break from the strict demarcation between work and fun, and was pretty much a signal from him that he felt his year's work was effectively complete.

At the 2014 Australian Open he was asked what the best part of being Novak Djokovic was. He was clearly captured by the question and gave it a few moments' thought before answering. 'Usually, I don't like to talk too much about myself,' he said, 'I leave that to other people, but for me it's important to always know where I come from, be grateful for the life I have, of course cherish and nurture every moment spent on the court. I don't take any situation for granted. Being aware of all these things is the best of being Novak Djokovic.'

An element of Djokovic's life that is hard to assess in the more secular west is the role the Serbian Orthodox Church plays. It would be wrong to suggest that he is devoutly religious, but the ritualistic role the church plays in the life of Serbia is sufficiently strong that it is very much part of his life. He always wears a cross as a medallion on his neck chain, and he frequently crosses himself and looks to the heavens after winning matches.

He has also contributed to church funds and in April 2011 was awarded the Order of St Sava, first degree, by the church's patriarch, the highest order presented by the Serbian Orthodox Church. Such is the link between the award and financial contributions that there is almost a tariff for it, generally held to be around €100,000. Djokovic has certainly given well over that amount, largely to help Serbian people and the sanctuaries of the Holy Church, particularly in Kosovo and Metohija. 'This award is certainly the most important I've ever been given,' he said on receiving it. 'As an athlete and a religious person, it is hard for me to find appropriate words to describe my feelings of gratitude for the confidence I gain from this. It can be earned only with hard work and self-belief, belief in your loved ones and in God.' (He has also been awarded the Order of the Star of Karadjordje, the highest civilian award that can be given by the Republic of Serbia.)

There have been several born-again tennis players over the years, many of whom wear their religion very openly. The Williams sisters often credit 'Jehovah' in interviews and trophy ceremonies, and Michael Chang never missed the chance to thank 'the Lord' whenever he spoke at trophy presentations and sponsor events. Djokovic is not in this category and will seldom volunteer information about his faith unprompted. But the presence of a faith – even if it is more ritualistic than deeply thoughtful – is no doubt a factor that helps him keep his inner animal behind bars and keeps his job of hitting a bit of fluffy rubber backwards and forwards over a net in perspective.

Djokovic has put tennis on the map in Serbia and the country has a window of, possibly, another four or five years to make the most of what is likely to be a once-in-a-lifetime player.

In the ructions that engulfed the Serbian Tennis Federation following the 2010 Davis Cup success, there seems little doubt the Djokovic family – particularly Srdjan – thought about founding a rival national association. But out of that carnage arose a new structure in the existing association that may have left the development of Serbian tennis in the Djokovic and post-Djokovic era in better hands. While much media coverage centred on the ousting of 'Bobo' Zivojinovic and his replacement by the politician and UN diplomat Vuk Jeremic, the real change was in splitting Zivojinovic's job into president of the federation and chair of the board. Jeremic is president of the federation, which in reality means he chairs the annual meeting, while the chair of the board is now Toplica Spasojevic.

A former basketball player, Spasojevic is one of the most successful businessmen in Serbia, having built up his company, ITM, from nothing into a workforce of 1,400 employees in seven countries. It was the distributor for Nike in Russia after the communist system was disbanded and has had other very big contracts in the sporting world. But he has a sense of *noblesse oblige* (or perhaps that should be *richesse oblige*) – a belief that his success in business requires him to put something back – and he is president of various associations and initiatives, including the Serbian chamber of commerce and several promotional societies. He was, for a while, president of Red Star Belgrade and in 2011 took over as chair of the tennis federation's board.

Through his broad experience in sport, Spasojevic has observed what works and what doesn't. He is generally impressed with how basketball built on the boom it had in Yugoslavia in the 1970s and 1980s, and how the Serbian volleyball fraternity has built on its successes in the last decade. Out of that, he has evolved a four-point plan to make the most of the Djokovic years. Firstly, he wants to improve Serbia's tennis infrastructure so that there are more courts and tennis facilities. There are putative plans for a national training centre and out of that should emerge a national tennis school or academy. Secondly, he wants to increase the number of tournaments in Serbia, not tournaments that top players should be attracted to (that was the mistake Germany made in the Becker-Stich-Graf era – when those three retired, most of the tournaments on German soil became economically unviable) but for lower-ranking players to provide them with a rising scale of competition, so they can get further up the ladder before they have to travel internationally. In 2010 Serbia had 10 Futures tournaments (the level below Challengers, so generally attracting players between 1000 and 250 in the rankings). By 2013 it was 22 and the number is rising, and it now has 400 local ratings tournaments. Thirdly, there are plans to provide grants for the most talented youngsters to help them with the expenses needed to make the transition from being good juniors to tour players. The federation is budgeting for 30 kids to receive between €15,000 and €30,000 a year, and occasionally more – Serbia's top-ranked junior Nikola Milojevic received €120,000 from the federation in 2012 to help him travel to tournaments in more exotic places than he could have afforded on his own. And fourthly, there is a programme to train up more coaches and umpires. When all that is in place, the theory is that any Serbian child who has talent and wants to play tennis can find the facilities, support and competitive opportunities they need without having to go abroad.

What will count as success? 'We'd like another Novak,' Spasojevic says, knowing full well that players like Djokovic are rarities that no national association can legislate for. Certainly the chances for one of Djokovic's brothers look increasingly slim – Marko made it into the world's top 600 in 2012 but has slipped back badly, while at 18 Djordje still has time but most 18-year-olds who are headed for the top 100 have done more than Djordje has (his highest ranking at the time this book went to press was 1463, which makes him about 30th in Serbia). His role model should be Patrick McEnroe – seven years younger than his illustrious brother John, Patrick had a fraction of the talent but still carved out a career as a reasonable singles player and a top-level doubles player, and went on to be a vastly more successful Davis Cup captain than John.

Spasojevic may well find that the legacy of the Djokovic era is that Serbia has half a dozen players in the world's top 100 a couple of decades from now, even if more of them are ranked between 50 and 100 than in the top 50. The immediate outlook for the country is not bad, with Niko Milojevic and Laslo Djere both shining on the junior circuit; in fact Serbia even enjoyed the glow of having two boys in the world's top three for a short period in 2013.

Milojevic spent a period working with Dejan Petrovic, who was Djokovic's first touring coach. Petrovic is well aware of how much easier it is for Milojevic having had Djokovic at the top of tennis. 'Without a doubt, Novak has played a huge role in the whole of Serbia for the expansion of tennis,' Petrovic says. 'It's now just a matter of how the clubs organise themselves to make the most of the boom, but a lot of small kids want to be like Nole, so they look for the best tennis clubs where they live. A lot of kids choose team sports for financial reasons because the outlay isn't as great. Novak's legacy will probably be a stream of players between 30 and a 100.'

Note too that, while it would help to have Djokovic coming back home to do clinics and hit balls with youngsters, the federation's four-point strategy is not dependent on him. 'We recognise that he needs to switch off when he's here,' Spasojevic says. 'We'd like him to do as much with us as possible, but his real value to us is as a role model, and we'd like him to stay at the top for as long as possible.'

The reason Spasojevic may succeed where others have – or might have – failed is not his experience, although that clearly helps. It's his belief that his work should be invisible, so he's not looking to capture the limelight. One of the first diplomatic things he did on taking over from Zivojinovic was to find 'Bobo' a role as honorary president-for-life of the federation. That allows Zivojinovic to be an ambassador for Serbian tennis, to carry out the glad-handing side of the role, which his laid-back personality makes him good at, to be on the ITF's Davis Cup committee and other bodies, and leave the nitty-gritty work to harder-headed and more organised people. Spasojevic, a tall, handsome man with a calming presence, has also overseen a quiet, behind-the-scenes *rapprochement* with Srdjan Djokovic. Gone are the threats from Srdjan to set up a rival national association, and Spasojevic talks of having a 'stable long-term relationship' with both Srdjan and Goran. So peace may be gradually breaking out in the ranks of Serbian tennis. If it is, the chances of the country profiting in the longer term from Djokovic's legacy are good.

But the mountain it needs to climb is still a massive one. 'We have just a thousand kids playing tennis,' bemoans Bogdan Obradovic, Serbia's Davis Cup captain and the owner of an academy in central

Belgrade. 'In China you have 50 million kids playing, in America 10 million, even a country like Australia has one million, but we just have a thousand. There are probably around a hundred thousand kids in Serbia who want to play tennis, but it's such an expensive sport that they don't even try it because they have no money.'

The truth is that, despite Djokovic, Serbia will not be relying on tennis for securing its place in the world's consciousness. Serbia is a relatively small country in a part of the globe where the number of 'new' states has exploded over the past two decades, so if it is to stand out, it will have to do so for other reasons.

Economically, it has signalled its intention to be part of the European Union. Assuming it becomes a member in the next five years or so, it will gain the weight of the EU's combined negotiating power in world affairs, although some argue it will become just another small member state and therefore lose something of its identity. Harmonised minimum standards, which Serbia would be obliged to sign up to in a whole range of industrial and social areas (everything from limits on working hours to the amount of sulphur allowed in diesel), exist to guarantee roughly equal conditions for trading across all states of the Union and do not have to mean the dilution of a country's culture. But some EU citizens feel that acquiescing with EU rules has indeed diluted their national and regional culture, and a defiant people like the Serbs might find that difficult.

Smoking is an interesting social barometer in this regard. The fact that some tennis coaches in Serbia don't show even a flicker of embarrassment by lighting up in a café, when their work is supposed to be promoting a high level of fitness and healthy living, testifies to how much smoking is very much part of the culture. A meal in a traditional Serbian restaurant resembles a trip down Memory Lane for those from many western European nations,

America and Australia, with clothing impregnated with stale smoke the morning after. The EU does not ban smoking but it does require its member states to offer non-smoking areas in restaurants and certain other public places, and to some this is the thin end of the wedge towards a ban. The 'Novak' restaurants and cafés have been pioneers in Serbia in offering non-smoking areas (as well as options such as gluten-free food), so Djokovic has helped his people along the road to healthier living. But the Serbs can be trenchant in defending their right to smoke, almost as if they are proud of being different from those in the west.

Despite its traditional diplomatic, religious and linguistic connections to Russia, Serbia is unlikely to have the same difficulty putting its faith in Europe as Ukraine has had. Moscow is likely to be less worried about Serbia leaning towards the west than it has been with Ukraine – after all, Serbia's eastern neighbours, Romania and Bulgaria, have both been members of the EU since 2007, Serbia is not as important an economic partner to Russia as Ukraine is, and Ukraine shares a border with Russia while Serbia doesn't. Serbia was important to Russia in the latter decades of the 19th century but it is too small to be of major significance to Moscow now, whereas Ukraine is a much larger land mass and has (or at least still had at time of writing) a lot of the former USSR's Black Sea coastline, in particular the Crimea peninsula with its strategically significant port cities of Sevastopol and Yalta. (The big parallel between Serbia and Ukraine is the risk that Ukraine's mix of Orthodox and Catholic communities could ignite in a civil war similar to that between the Serbs and Croats in the early 1990s, a concern that was very much alive as this book went to press.)

It's hard to see an industry in which Serbia could shine transnationally, the way Brazil and Kenya do for their coffee, Argentina does for the tango, and countless cities and states do for their tourist appeal. If Emir Kusturica's film of Andric's novel *The*

Bridge over the Drina becomes a hit, the Balkans could become a cultural attraction, a bit like Vienna enjoyed the glow of Carol Reed's *The Third Man* for several decades after it was released in 1948, but while Serbia might benefit from much of the ensuing tourism, Visegrad and Andricgrad are not actually in Serbia but just across the border in Bosnia.

It looks like Serbia's best chance of achieving international recognition is through another sporting success. The most fertile ground is football, and if either Red Star Belgrade or the Serbian national team could discover a golden generation of players, Serbia could yet find itself much more in the international consciousness than it is at the moment. But then again, Croatia had the massive boost of coming third in the 1998 football World Cup – yet how high is Croatia's profile in international consciousness today? In a crowded global market place that sees more than 200 countries take part in the opening ceremony of the summer Olympics, it's very hard to make your mark if you're not one of the traditional big nations. To that extent, having a global name carrying the flag, as Djokovic did at the 2012 London Olympics, is probably as much of a magnet for the world's attention as a country like Serbia is ever going to get.

Djokovic will of course still be Serbian even after he stops playing tennis, but the question of Serbia's standing in the world leads on to the question of what Djokovic will do when he finally hangs up his rackets. There are certain jobs he could walk into, like television commentator, entertaining performer on the oldies' tennis tour (especially with his impersonations), and he can be Serbia's Davis Cup captain pretty much at the time of his own choosing.

'He can do whatever he wants,' says his friend Ivan Ljubicic. 'I can do whatever I want and I'm only two per cent of what he is. I can tell you he's not going to sit and relax, that's for sure.

Davis Cup captain or TV commentator? He's bigger than that. I think he has to have an important role where he feels he can make a big difference.'

That reflects the general consensus of those interviewed for this book – he will want something demanding, something in which he can make a difference. The question is: what? There are three obvious areas in which he could end up: some administrative position in tennis or sport in general, something ambassadorial/diplomatic, or politics.

When Jelena Gencic died, Djokovic talked about continuing or following up on her legacy. The word 'legacy', when applied to Gencic, could be taken to mean any number of things but the obvious area would be in tennis development. Even now, his passion for both the game and his country means he's always willing for the Serbian juniors to practise with him. The fact that, as world No. 1, he had a number of negotiations with leading figures in tennis's governing bodies means he has had an apprenticeship in how the game is run, with the chance to develop his own thoughts and ideas as to how it might be better run.

The television commentator Nebojsa Viskovic says, 'He's a man with such a big field of interest, I just can't imagine what could fill him in the future. When I look at Vlade Divac, he was the greatest basketball player in Yugoslavia, now he's president of the Serbian Olympic Committee – I could never see him doing that during his playing days. So who knows what Novak could do?' Djokovic himself has spoken admiringly about the responsibility Divac has taken on, which doesn't of itself mean he will look to do something similar, but it's not a massive leap of the imagination to see him as president of the Serbian Tennis Federation, the Serbian Olympic Committee, or something of that ilk.

His popularity in Serbia and the respect his compatriots have for him means a political career is always a possibility. 'If he's going to participate in politics, I'm going to help him,' says the former president Boris Tadic (conveniently overlooking the possibility that Djokovic might not want his help – Tadic isn't held in the highest regard among Serbia's chattering classes). Tadic adds, 'If he ran for president, he would win.' He would now, but politics is a much more complicated business than just milking your own popularity. Alliances have to be formed, sometimes with unlikely allies; programmes have to be formulated that are distinctive enough to catch the public imagination but appeal to a wide enough section of the electorate that they can be carried through; events can overtake the best-laid plans; and the media has to be managed. In an era of 24-hour news coverage and the rumour mill that is social media and the broader Internet, managing information is crucial. Many an honest politician sets out with the aim of saying things straight and giving honest answers, and then realises that this approach risks conceding the political agenda to whomever is asking the questions; so they clam up, become careful with their utterances, and are soon as colourless as all their political colleagues. Is Djokovic capable of playing that particular game? Does he even want to? He says no, though that could change.

Dusan Vemic, who has spent a lot of time with Djokovic on the road in recent years, believes Djokovic is aware of the pitfalls of politics. 'I don't think he will get into politics,' Vemic says, 'I don't think he's interested, but if he did go into politics, it would probably be with a big idea with which he wants to make a difference.'

And when Dejan Petrovic says, 'Nole can be like Tito, doing the job of uniting people,' he may well be right, but how? He would need a role and it's hard to see – at the moment – what that role could be.

Viskovic appears to be on a similar wavelength to Petrovic and Vemic. 'He's doing for Serbia what nobody could do,' he says. 'If he ran for president, he'd win it 100 per cent. But his family is down in the public's estimations because they represent Serbia in a very different way. I think it helped him that he had to tell them to calm down; their behaviour in the crowd was a disgrace. The people of Serbia have had enough of ugly things, they just want something nice to happen – Novak is nice but his family is not nice. So yes, he could be president, but it would be much smarter to be an ambassador.'

So what of an ambassadorial or diplomatic role? It's important to stress that the terms are used loosely here because the role of a country's ambassador to a foreign capital, or of a diplomat representing a government in transnational negotiations, is a very precise and constrained one. Djokovic is already an ambassador for his clothing and racket companies, and there are doubtless hundreds of Serbian (and non-Serbian) firms that would be delighted to send him on the road to represent them and put in a good word for them. But would that really satisfy someone of boundless energy and an active but focused mind? It's hard to think it would.

In 1980 the then US president Jimmy Carter appointed the former world heavyweight boxing champion Muhammad Ali as a special US envoy to Africa. Ali was to go to a number of African countries and encourage them to join the US boycott of the 1980 Moscow Olympics in protest at the USSR's invasion of Afghanistan in December 1979. It would be easy to see Djokovic taking on such a task, especially if there was a children element involved that would dovetail with his foundation's work, or a peace element that would allow him to say – as he did at the 2013 US Open – that he's 'totally against any kind of weapon, any kind of air strike or missile attack'. But anything like that would be a short-term assignment. It's easier to see him taking on an international charitable role, or possibly even a United Nations function that would be a development of his work as a Unicef ambassador.

'I think an ambassadorial function would be possible for a lot of the guys who have played tennis,' says the twice Grand Slam runner-up Todd Martin.

It's a global game. At one moment you have to fight like a dog against somebody competing for the same prize. The next moment you have to share a locker room with that same person. The next moment you have to schmooze at a cocktail party with people you don't speak the same language as, or whatever it is. These are the talents that go into being something of that ambassadorial nature. Many players can learn the stuff that's necessary to do their job, but there are a few like Roger and Novak who are plenty smart enough to learn all the wider stuff.

Asked what role he sees for himself after his top-level playing days are over, Djokovic appears to be leaving all options open when he says, 'I will be trying to give as much as I can to my country, but not in a form of a politician. I think there are many ways to help, and currently I choose to do it through my charity, the Novak Djokovic Foundation.'

Most of the world's top athletes have charitable foundations these days, prompting cynics to wonder whether these are motivated more by reasons of tax advantages than by genuine concern for the wider world. It's a difficult question to answer – if a government claims less in tax because some citizens are paying a certain amount of their income into a charitable foundation, the donors don't benefit personally; in effect, they simply decide how to spend some of the tax they would have had to pay anyway. Does that allow us to judge how strong their charitable motives really are?

With Djokovic's foundation, the motivation is somewhat closer to heart. In a 'letter' outlining the rationale behind the foundation, he writes, 'I'm coming from a war torn country, a place where many kids do not dare to dream big. I was blessed to have the support of my whole family throughout childhood. They believed in me and dreamed with me, all the way. Today, I have realised my childhood dream. It is very important for me to start building my philanthropic legacy now, while I'm young and have a lot of people's attention. I want to share the focus that is on me with the work of my foundation and help many kids to fulfil their dreams. They can learn from my example – many things are possible if we believe and work hard.'

Djokovic started the 'Novak Fund' in 2007 – essentially a pot of money that could be used for all sorts of diverse projects, such as emergency relief efforts in areas that had suffered from fighting or extreme weather, grants for kids who needed medical treatment outside Serbia, travel grants for young players to go to tennis tournaments, and even donations to fund the upkeep of historic churches and monasteries. But in February 2012 he changed it into the Novak Djokovic Foundation (NDF), with his girlfriend Jelena Ristic as chief executive and a more specific focus on children, largely in Serbia but also around the world. In September 2011 Djokovic was named a Unicef ambassador – so are plenty of other athletes, but his role was specifically to help raise the awareness of low enrolment rates in pre-school education in Serbia, given that Serbia has one of the lowest percentages of children in pre-school education (44 per cent).

Out of this has arisen a trio of projects supported by the foundation that reflect the thinking of Friedrich Froebel, the 19th-century German educationalist who developed the theory that, if you meet a child's needs in the 'early years' (which he defined as three to seven years old), they will by and large be able to deal with anything you throw at them after that. Froebel coined the term

'Kindergarten' out of his conviction that children under seven learn best by playing in the garden, and devotees of Froebel's work tend to set up schools with low numbers of under-sevens and a strong focus on outdoor learning; they tend to be known as 'small schools'. It's easy to see how Djokovic's belief in a child's right to dream and Froebel's care and attention up to age seven fit together, and one of the NDF projects is the 'Skolica Zivota', which best translates as 'small school for life'. Djokovic says on his foundation's website,

> The project has developed as an expression of our desire to encourage children to dream, and also inspire adults to do everything in their power to help kids realise those dreams. Kindergartens, parks and playgrounds are natural schools of life, where children play and learn through play, resolve situations, and make friends for life. We want those places to become something more – to become seedbeds of goodwill, the right values, activism, self-care, and caring concern for others. It is the best way to strengthen parents, professionals, local communities, and above all children; to regain their strength, self-confidence and faith in life; a belief that they can do something for themselves, their present and future. Only that way will new generations of responsible citizens emerge, of people who care about each other and the environment they live in.

The 'Skolica Zivota' project currently assists four schools but the scope for it to help more is obviously immense.

In parallel, Djokovic has recognised that a good small school in itself may not be enough to help children to dream, or to realise those dreams, if the child's home life is not nurturing. That's why the foundation is undertaking a major project jointly with Unicef and the Serbian government called 'Supporting Families at Risk'.

The aim is to prevent the separation of children from their families, by strengthening families to cope with crises so they can still provide their children with adequate care in a safe and stimulating environment. A team of 'family outreach workers' is working with 53 families encompassing 118 children. Ristic says,

> This service has been necessary in the social protection system for several reasons. First of all, our centres are overcrowded with families in need. Social workers simply do not have time for continual work to enable children to become stronger and modify their behaviour. They are working on 300 cases per year, and our staff will need two and a half years for this because attention and dedication, as well as time, are required for accomplishing the results. A child's biological family is irreplaceable, and in most cases it has no alternative. Of course there are situations when there's a threat to the life of a child and it must be removed from the family. But there are many more situations where families just need someone to direct them, to give a suggestion, to motivate them, take them to the doctor, provide documents, to enrol their child in kindergarten, to give them advice on how to overcome the situation. All those families must voluntarily agree to be included in the service. We are sure that after six months they will be much stronger.

Interestingly, the third project of the trio is a children's toy library in Kragujevac, which includes provision for Roma children, particularly vulnerable ones. The library lends out not just toys but material with inherent teaching characteristics. Given the way the Roma community has often been ostracised from Serbian society, this is not just a children's welfare project but one that has an element of breaking down barriers caused by prejudice.

'Our mission is to help children in disadvantaged communities to grow up, play and develop in stimulative and safe environments while learning to respect others and care for the environment,' Djokovic says. 'Many people around the world have recognised my foundation and joined us in our mission.'

Although he relaunched the foundation in February 2012, it really got going at a fundraising dinner in New York in September 2012, which raised $1.4 million for early-years education. A week later he visited a Unicef kindergarten in the town of Lesnica, and a month after that he launched the initiative 'Clothes for Smiles' with his clothing supplier Uniqlo, a programme that aims to help nurture the dreams of children worldwide. For all this, he was recognised by the British homelessness charity Centrepoint, which awarded him its first Premier Award at the seniors' tennis tournament at London's Royal Albert Hall in December 2012. Djokovic received the award from Prince William, the heir-but-one to the British throne and a keen tennis fan who has watched matches at Wimbledon and the Australian Open.

When Djokovic talks about his foundation, the word 'dream' is ever present in his vocabulary. 'Let's believe in their dreams together!' he writes on the foundation's website and, when he was appointed a Unicef ambassador, he said, 'Through my work with Unicef, I want to help Serbian children realise their dreams. I want to help them understand that they have rights and that those rights should be protected. I want them to believe that anything is possible.'

It's almost as if these are the emotions that he can't let out until the conclusion of a match; this is the idealism that is the counterweight to all the hard work he puts in on the practice court and in the gym. It is this side of Djokovic that makes so many people think he will end up in some way involved in a cause to change the world for the better. Dusan Vemic says, 'He's realising more and more that he's a giving person, and I believe whatever he does in the future will reflect that idea of making a difference – I think he realises that he already makes a big difference in the lives of millions of people in this country, and many athletes look up to him around the world'

Are we reading too much into Djokovic the person? Should we perhaps simply view him as a man whose passion is playing tennis, who does it so well he's one of the world's greatest, and that, as an intelligent human being, he takes an understandable interest in the rest of the world but that it's no more than that? There's a case for it, but it would almost certainly be selling him short.

There are essentially three elements to Djokovic's greatness. The first two are at play with all successful athletes, and other performers for that matter: natural abilty and dedication. Some people have all the natural ability but insufficient dedication, while others have modest ability but a blinding determination to succeed that takes them past more gifted rivals. Djokovic has both phenomenal natural talent and the drive to make the most of it. He needs both these attributes to succeed in the fiercely competitive world of today's professional tennis. You can say the same for Roger Federer, Rafael Nadal and Andy Murray, and for top players from past eras and even for those players who fall just behind them in the rankings.

But that determination – the single-mindedness needed to succeed in an environment where the slightest weakness is punished – leads to a crop of largely dull personalities. That is no criticism – if your life from the age of around six or seven is dominated by practice after school, and most weekends and summer holidays being consumed by tennis camps and tournaments, and you then have to subject yourself to a disciplined regime of fitness and tennis training for pretty much 52 weeks of the year, it's not a recipe for well-roundedness. But every now and then a person comes through this brutal regime with the natural intelligence to take such a weird existence in their stride and get a sense of the world from it. They emerge with their personality intact, and that makes them seem so normal when they are anything but. Djokovic is one of these, and this is the third element of his greatness.

He is not alone in this. His closest match is Roger Federer, who also combines natural ability, a serious work ethic and a charming personality that manages to see the big picture. The relationship between Federer and Djokovic hasn't always been smooth, but they have tremendous mutual respect for each other and any tension may stem from the fact that they are both remarkable sporting states-men, both of them once-in-a-lifetime figures who happen to be around at the same time. Compliments for Federer and Djokovic imply no criticism of the other members of the phenomenal 'big four' of the current tennis era, Rafael Nadal and Andy Murray. Nadal's inherent good nature and Murray's quiet down-to-earthness make them equally admirable as people as well as athletes, and it's possible that Murray may mature into someone of Federer's and Djokvic's intellectual stature. But for the moment, Federer and Djokovic are the seriously smart cookies who are more than just great sportsmen but international icons who transcend the boundaries of their sport and their respective countries.

They also bear comparison with past eras. Rod Laver was the most successful player of the first period of 'open' tennis, but he had a quiet, understated personality that meant he was never more than a great sportsman. The same goes for Bjorn Borg, albeit with much greater star appeal than Laver ever had. Jimmy Connors and John McEnroe both transcended their sport, but their brash personalities always made them controversial figures rather than players to admire beyond their sporting and competitive abilities. Boris Becker was the most charismatic player of his generation but never sought to be a leader, only a personality. And of the 1990s generation, Pete Sampras was the most successful but was never comfortable in the limelight, while Andre Agassi was too much of a troubled soul to make the most of his immense natural intelligence; of that generation, Jim Courier was the most eloquent, yet his eloquence only really developed after his playing career stopped and he wasn't at the top for long enough to make a serious mark. The only other figures from the open era of tennis who might rival Federer and Djokovic are two women: Billie Jean King and Martina Navratilova. They were both pioneers but have probably been appreciated more since their playing days than during them. What Federer and Djokovic have achieved is the mixture of greatness and admiration during their careers (Federer more than Djokovic), to the point where they both merit the term 'statesman' in a way few others do.

Ultimately, what people like Djokovic mean to those they inspire is up to the individual who's inspired by them, and it's going to be different from person to person. The Serbian player and coach Dusan Vemic says touchingly, 'I'm really happy that I have him in some way or fashion in my life, so I can reflect on him as a human being, a great role model, a great example. I'm well aware that my best is not as good as his best, but the example he sets is that I still feel motivated to make the effort to do my best. As a human being, he's got to the point where he represents his country and his comrades, all the positives. It's very pure. His motives are very straightforward and innocent, and it shows.'

The world won't stop when Novak Djokovic hangs up his tennis rackets, nor will Serbia cease to exist. In fact, Serbia will probably be a much richer country at the end of his playing career than it was at the beginning. But at that point we will start to get a sense of whether Djokovic was 'just' a tennis player, or whether he will go on to achieve great things on whatever stage he chooses to enter. He has the intellectual capacity and benevolent personality to put together his experiences of family struggles, the Belgrade bombing, Jelena Gencic's worldly wisdom, being booed in a 23,000-seater tennis stadium, fighting through the pain barrier in a near-six-hour final, and others, and emerge as someone with a major contribution to make. The coach Dejan Petrovic says, 'Whatever Novak would have touched, in any sport, he'd have succeeded. He just had that hunger for winning that was incredible. He would work immensely to achieve that; he never said, "I'm tired, I can't do that."' If Djokovic brings that same hunger to his next career, it might yet be that the sport of tennis was merely the launch pad for the career of a global statesman.

BIBLIOGRAPHY

There are no English-language biographies of Novak Djokovic. One biography did appear in 2013 in Portuguese, written by Blaza Popovic and published in Brazil. Popovic is a Belgrade-based tennis journalist who doesn't travel much. The Brazilian connection came because he became friends with Gustavo Kuerten's communications manager and it went through a Brazilian publisher. In some of the publicity for that book it was claimed Popovic had spoken to the Djokovic family, but he confirms he has never spoken to the family and that all quotes were taken from television interviews the family gave in Serbia.

The books about Serbia, sport in eastern Europe and Djokovic that have been used in researching this book are:

Andric, Ivo – *The Bridge over the Drina* [*Na Drini cuprija*], 1945 (English translation by Lovett Edwards, published by George Allen & Urwin, 1959)

Wilson, Jonathan – *Behind the Curtain*, Orion, 2006

Djokovic, Novak – *Serve to Win*, Bantam Press, 2013

Little, Allan, and Silber, Laura – *The Death of Yugoslavia*, BBC Books 1995, Penguin 1996

Plus two essays by academics who specialise in Yugoslavia which were used to provide background material:

Hayden, Robert – 'Serbian and Croatian Nationalism and the Wars in Yugoslavia', in *Cultural Survival* issue 19.2, 1995

Judah, Tim – 'Yugoslavia: 1918–2003', BBC On-Line, 2003

INDEX